STANDING
IN
THE WINGS

STANDING IN THE WINGS

THE BEATLES, BRIAN EPSTEIN AND ME

JOE FLANNERY
WITH MIKE BROCKEN

The
History
Press

I dedicate this book to my beloved city of Liverpool.

First published 2013

The History Press
The Mill, Brimscombe Port
Stroud, Gloucestershire, GL5 2QG
www.thehistorypress.co.uk

British Library Cataloguing in Publication Data.
A catalogue record for this book is available from the British Library.

ISBN 978 0 7524 9009 0

Typesetting and origination by The History Press
Printed in Great Britain

CONTENTS

FOREWORD BY PHILIP NORMAN

IN 1979, AS I was embarking on my Beatles biography *Shout!*, I asked Bill Harry, John Lennon's fellow art student and founder of *Mersey Beat*, to suggest interviewees who might give me a fresh perspective on a story everyone thought they knew. 'Why don't you talk to Joe Flannery,' he replied. A couple of weeks later, I knocked on the front door of a neat 1920s house in Aigburth, Liverpool, and was greeted by a tall, quietly spoken man whose name appeared in none of the Beatles reference books then available. Biographers, especially in the rock music area, depend greatly on luck: that was one of my luckiest days ever.

Joe Flannery's perspective was fresh indeed. His cabinet-maker father, Christopher, used to supply custom-built chests-of-drawers to Harry Epstein, the Liverpool furniture dealer, whose older son, Brian, would one day manage the most beloved pop band of all time. Joe had met Brian – and already fallen more than a little in love with him – when they were children. Both grew up to be gay in an era when homosexuality was outlawed in Britain and particularly anathematised in macho northern cities like Liverpool. With Joe, Brian had his only happy, stable relationship in a love life otherwise shadowed by fear, guilt, violence and disgrace.

The two lost touch for a few years, then met up again in 1962, by which time Brian was running the record department at his family's central Liverpool electrical store. As a side-line, he had decided to manage a black leather-clad 'beat group' called the Beatles who, he insisted – to general mockery – would one day be 'bigger than Elvis'. Dapper, well-spoken

Brian, however, had no idea how to talk to the tough Merseyside dance promoters who were the Beatles' main employers. So Joe volunteered to handle their bookings, and also made his house a base-camp for them after late-night gigs when it was too late to return to their respective homes. As a result, he could tell me Beatles stories that no one had ever heard before: of John (who always called him 'Flo Jannery') lying on the rug in front of his living-room fire, turning out endless drawings and poems; of Paul, asking him for guidance on social etiquette rather like Pip in Dickens' *Great Expectations*; of giving George driving lessons in his car in the dawn hours while the others were asleep.

He also proved fascinatingly authoritative about the band's mythic pre-Epstein period, with their pre-Ringo drummer Pete Best, playing drunken all-night shows among the strip-clubs and mud-wrestling pits of Hamburg's red-light district, the Reeperbahn. He'd later gone out to Hamburg himself, acting as a kind of den-mother to other Liverpool bands like Lee Curtis and the All Stars, whose vocalist was his younger brother. Under his tutelage, I spent a week on the Reeperbahn, drinking the same beer and eating the same German hotdogs that the Beatles once had, and popping the same 'uppers' to be able to stay awake all night.

Brian had died of a drink-and-drugs overdose in 1967 – prefiguring the Beatles' drawn-out, messy collapse – but to one person, at least, he'd never been forgotten. Each year on his birthday, Liverpool's Long Lane synagogue gave Catholic Joe special permission to break with Jewish custom and place flowers on his grave.

As we became friends, Joe told me about the hellishness of being gay in 1950s Liverpool, even if one didn't take the horrendous risks Brian did. He related blood-chilling stories of the 'queer-bashing' gangs that used to roam the streets; of the eminent citizens who preyed on gay young men with impunity in the backs of their Rolls-Royces; of the homophobia of police, the judicial system and, worst of all, one's own family. His father never came to terms with Joe's sexuality – though his wonderful, doughty mother, Agnes, shielded him from the worst of Christopher's brutality. At one heartbreaking moment, Joe tried to express his love for his father by buying him a record, Eddie Calvert's *O mein Papa*. 'O mein Papa', the lyric runs, 'to me he was so wonderful/O Mein papa, to me he was so good ...' Christopher took one look at the old-fashioned shellac disc, then broke it over Joe's head.

There were other, happier stories, too, from the long ages before the world had heard of John, Paul, George and Ringo: of growing up in the next street to the crooner Frankie Vaughan; of working as a waiter at Liverpool's Adelphi Hotel in its glory days, when Joe often found himself serving Queen Elizabeth the Queen Mother: of his latter long, happy relationship with a sweet man named Kenny Meek, and his artists' management partnership with Brian Epstein's younger brother, Clive, who bore just enough of a resemblance to Brian to ensure that Joe's love never died.

There was the phone conversation he had with John Lennon in New York, shortly before the fateful night of 8 December 1980, when John talked about making a triumphal return to Liverpool and asked 'Flo Jannery' to hire the QE2 to bring him up the Mersey. And there was always the Flannery humour, permeating even moments of greatest stress or sadness. After John's murder, he wrote a tribute song entitled *Much-Missed Man*, which was to be recorded in Liverpool by one of his new young protégés, Phil Boardman. On the day of the session, typically, Joe drove to the studio with a red carnation for Phil's buttonhole. As he told me at the time: 'You know how much my religion means to me – but if a Catholic nun had been thumbing a lift into town, I wouldn't have stopped because it'd have meant moving that carnation I'd arranged so carefully on the seat beside me.'

For years, I've been urging this dear, modest man to claim his rightful niche in pop music with a book 'about the Beatles but not all about the Beatles'. I'm delighted he's now done so.

INTRODUCTION
BY JOE ANDERSON,
MAYOR OF LIVERPOOL

IT ISN'T AN exaggeration to say that without Brian Epstein, the Beatles we know and love today wouldn't exist. The former Beatles' manager helped shape the musical landscape of the city, guiding the Fab Four from being a popular cellar act to global superstardom.

As a city, we want to make sure the legacy of one of Liverpool's greatest sons continues, and it was a real honour when Brian's family gave us permission to rename the Neptune Theatre to The Epstein – signalling a new chapter for the refurbished music venue which will hopefully discover the next generation of outstanding musical talent in the city.

This book by Joe Flannery sheds new light on the Epstein story, providing some previously unheard anecdotes about the man referred to as the 'Prince of Pop' – a man who changed the face of the music industry forever and, as a result, put Liverpool firmly on the map as a city overflowing with culture and creativity.

1

EARLY CHILDHOOD: 'IF YOU DON'T KICK A FOOTBALL, YOU'LL GET YOUR HEAD KICKED-IN'

THE FLANNERYS CAME to Liverpool, via Cornwall, from Ireland. They were peasants from the rural area just west of Dublin and came to England to escape the potato famine of 1845. Land was in short supply in Ireland at this time and this family, like many others, grew what they could to sustain themselves on insufficient and meagre soil. My great-grandfather was one of nine children and his parents originally had about 2 acres of farmland; however, they had decided to let 1 acre of it go because a good potato crop could sustain even a large family on only 1 acre. There would always be spuds, it seemed, and it didn't give the impression that it was worth the rent to farm 2 acres. Potatoes were the staple crop in Ireland at this time and it has been estimated that at least 4 million out of a total population of 8.5 million could, like the Flannerys, afford little else. But by the summer of 1845 potato blight had already appeared in England and by the autumn it had spread to Ireland; catastrophe ensued. Thousands starved to death, and the Flannerys gave up all they had – which was probably very little in the first place – and, along with countless others, decided to leave Ireland once and for all. The rural working classes in Ireland were faced with a very simple choice: stay and starve or leave and begin again. The Flannery family chose the latter and after initially trying their luck in the south-west of England in tin mining and fishing, they eventually ended up, along with many others of their kind, in the seaport of Liverpool.

By this time Liverpool was England's second city, unimaginably wealthy via trade and commerce (which included slavery up to the beginning of

the nineteenth century); yet, not even a mile from the commercial heart-
land of the city could be found the densely overpopulated Scotland Road
and Byrom Street districts. It was here that the vast majority of Irish
immigrants were forced to live … 'live'? Survive, more like, for dumped
as they were amid the squalor, rats and degradation of Liverpool's infamous courtyard dwelling houses, they struggled to keep their heads above
water in this city built on capital; they survived, but little else. A drab and
dreary lack of choice seemingly followed them around; Irish and Catholic
meant Scotland Road, docks and rats – it was pretty much as simple as
that in a city that, one might argue, contributed to the destruction not
creation of society. By the 1850s almost one-third of Britons lived in cities
like Liverpool. What kind of places these actually were can only be estimated by our vivid imaginations. Smoke and filth dominated paltry water
supplies and sanitation, street cleaning and open spaces, and epidemics of
cholera and typhoid (together with respiratory and internal diseases) considerably shortened people's often miserable lives.

My father, at least on the surface, appears to be a typical example of a
working-class Liverpudlian: second-generation, poverty-stricken, regional
Irish gradually making some kind of cultural space for himself. But it was
far more complicated than such class-based visages allow. By the time the
twentieth century had dawned he was actually suffering at the hands of an
immigrant-based class system that had evolved within the Liverpool-Irish
communities. In order to survive in such a city, working-class immigrants
were forced to create their own echelon systems. Pre-industrial experiences, traditions, wisdom, and to a degree moralities were no adequate
guide to living as an immigrant in an urban environment such as in
Liverpool but, as with the equally diasporic Italian communities, they
were used as marks of authenticity, thus rank. Material incentives were
often determined by one's so-called 'Irish' heritage and class while still
in the 'old country'. As a consequence the Flannerys were considered in
Liverpool to be rather low-class Irish, even by their own immigrant community's criteria. This had little to do with religion per se (that particular
war raged essentially as an inter-district conflict), but more to do with the
previous status of families back in Ireland.

So, as far as the Flannery side of my family was concerned, they
appeared to possess very little kudos because of their rather rural hin-
terland background, and this increased the fragility of their social and
economic position. Urbanity stretched to Dublin, it seemed, but not to
its bucolic surroundings. Thus, although the Scotland Exchange political

district of North Liverpool (where they were based) was fiercely Irish and regularly returned Irish Nationalist MPs for many years, this sense of Irishness and Irish nationalism was not cohesive and certainly not without its class echelons: hardly the 'united' district of Liverpool that local historians often spuriously claim it to be. How could it be? To deliberately misquote the great British industrial historian Eric Hobsbawm, if the immigrant Irishman in Liverpool earned more than the pittance he regarded as sufficient, he might indeed take it out in leisure, parties and alcohol, but he might also consider such financial extras as providing ways and means of rising through the ranks of his immigrant-based stratum. While Hobsbawm presumes that ignorance and thus poverty was all-pervading via these economic realities, he neglects how important money and influence could be. To have succeeded in the Liverpool of the early to mid-twentieth century, even as a second-generation Irish immigrant, was technically very difficult, but not impossible. If a rural or regional Irish background militated against progress, one way of jumping such hurdles lay within contacts: not necessarily exclusively from one's own community (especially if it appeared to lack cohesion), but rather from other diasporic communities, such, as in my father, Chris Flannery's, case, Jewish migrants. Rationality was required to come to the fore to understand the vagaries of trade across migrant communities; if it did and one possessed a skill (my father was a time-served joiner) progression was possible.

My mother's family, the Mottrams, were also Irish Catholics but from County Mayo. They lived on the so-called correct side of Scotland (known locally as 'Scottie') Road – the 'sophisticated' side. Before the deluge they had been well established back in Ireland and, by the early years of the twentieth century, had already commenced rising up the social ladder in Liverpool. During the First World War, they were making a reasonable living out of housing working horses (aka stable housing) and also became involved in a little light haulage or 'carting', as it was known locally. By the early 1930s my mother's brother Andy Mottram had expanded his small freight business to incorporate well-known Liverpool hauliers Cameron's. The Mottrams subsequently dropped their own moniker and traded on this well-established name for many years. Cameron's wagons could be seen regularly carrying flour along the dock road for the mills of Wilson King, south of the Albert Dock. Money was far from plentiful, however, for it was a very competitive trade and, particularly after the Wall Street Crash of 1929, the family only really spluttered along, just like everybody else.

Mother was thus imbued with a sense of business acumen which featured prominently in both my own childhood and adulthood due to the fact that she was forced to finance the family largely from her own funds. This was due to my somewhat wayward father's tendencies to spend his (albeit hard-earned) money on wine, women and song (as Eric Hobsbawm suggests). So my own interpretation of my family history is rather pro-Mottram, for I feel that I have inherited very little from the Flannery side of my genes. I have always reflected the Mottram sensibilities and these appear to me to be my real family foundations. My sense of Irishness was affected perhaps negatively by the tribal nature of the aforesaid factional echelon system. While I fully acknowledge that my blood is Irish, I have never really considered it to be part of my make-up, as such. One of the great historical myths of our time is that all Liverpudlians, including the Beatles, have been positively affected by their Irish ancestry; I have always disputed this. Liverpool has absorbed many different cultures throughout history, not only that of the Irish (think of the geographical proximity to Wales, for example). Any Irish heritage in the Mottram family featured only sporadically because I suppose that, perhaps apart from the regular intervention of the Catholic Church, it was essentially considered irrelevant. They, like many other immigrant families, were a functional lot. They tended to concentrate on the here and now and there were few if any Mottram longings for an imaginary, pre-digested and idyllic homeland, rearticulated into a Liverpool hierarchy of influence. Liverpool, England, the United Kingdom became their collective home, and for me that was enough to be going along with!

Apart from my mother, my family hero was Uncle Peter, who was a Royal Air Force pilot prior to the outbreak of the Second World War. I still have great memories of Peter in his RAF blue serge, looking so smart. Being smart was an iconic statement for my young self. I enjoyed dressing well even as a child and the attention to detail on Peter's uniform fascinated me. Peter lived up to his uniform, too, at least in my eyes. He was very suave, sophisticated, with a typical RAF glint in his eye. He served throughout the war, contracting malaria in Burma and finally ending up at the Sealand Royal Air Force camp, near Chester, conveniently close enough at hand for us all (Chester was only an hour's bus or train ride from our Liverpool home). As suggested previously, however, Chris my father was regarded by the Mottrams as a little 'low class', a ladies' man and a bit 'fly'. He was treated with a great deal of suspicion by mother's family and received a hard time from them. I suppose they were, in their own way, snobs, and father reacted very badly to snobbery aimed directly at him for he was a 'maverick', recognised himself as such, and was determined that he was seen by others as an entrepreneur. He established a joinery workshop and although teetering on the brink of failure from time to time, he was able to connect with Jewish businesses across the city, seeing himself in the process at the centre of a rags-to-riches saga – thus expanding his locus of business, social and womanising activities. But there was always something of a rift from the moment that he and my mother were married, and it never went away.

So, resentment burned very deeply in my father, I think, and this coupled with the fact that he was always a ladies' man, somebody who really did desire women, meant that personal calamity and heartbreak never seemed very far from our door. My late mother described him as very handsome when they met. He apparently had a keen eye for detail and when they were courting, his cap, silk scarf and white tennis shoes were the height of fashion on Scotland Road! Six siblings were born between 1926 and 1939, the eldest being my sister Jean and the youngest my brother Peter (later 'Lee Curtis'). Even when Jean was born in September 1926 and, despite the fact that father doted on his daughter, mother felt ill at ease. It was as if father had a restlessness that simply could not be satiated by a loving family relationship. The all-round disapproval of the Mottrams obviously added to his paranoia for, according to my mother, they were never reluctant to remind both of them that Agnes (mother) had effectively married beneath her.

Father was, and was also known to be, very quick and useful with his fists. It was a man's world, no doubt about it, and in his eyes a real man had to watch his back. But he took to using his power whenever it pleased him and his violence began to rule our lives. I was born in 1931 and as I grew I became increasingly aware of two distinct atmospheres: one created by my mother's unconditional love, and another that sprung from my father's violent presence. A child of 3 or 4 may not know a great deal in the conventional sense of the word but he or she feels a lot. Just like my old friend John Lennon, I've always been a great believer in karma. I probably instinctively detected negative karma from my father from a very early age. Funnily enough, the first kind of memory (more of an image or a scene from a play than a memory, as such) that I have is a strange one. I distinctly remember my mother falling down the stairs with my father shouting, at the top, on the landing. I latterly discussed this with mother on more than one occasion and she stated, categorically, that the only time this happened in my presence, so to speak, was when she was carrying me.

And yet I remember it as if it were yesterday. Father often moved very fast and silently when his violence came to the fore. No one else would be present (at least that's what he thought) and he would leave little trace of damage, at least physically. Those areas that were bruised and swollen were usually covered by lint, clothing and dignity.

It became increasingly apparent to my less-than-devoted father after I had reached the age of about 7 or 8 that I was never going to, metaphorically speaking, 'play football' – with all of the implications that this must have carried for him. He would almost threaten me, telling me that if I didn't start kicking a ball around then people would start to question him as a father. He frightened me. I didn't understand what he was going on about. I mean, I didn't dislike football, and would occasionally join in with a few other lads in the street, but football as a symbol came to mean so much more to him than me as the years went by. One of the few areas that a man could relate to a boy was through masculinity and he deeply resented the fact that the machismo that was part of physical contact sport was never part of my make-up. Not only had my father apparently married into a bunch of people who (he alleged) looked down on him from a higher social status, but he had also been provided with a son who was a 'wet Nellie'. I became immersed in psychological tug of war between my parents' desires for their son. I suppose that it resulted, in the long run, in my mother's everlasting love and my father's everlasting shame. It destroyed him that I was not of his mentality. He was ashamed that I could never use my fists. He was chagrined that I was a Mottram and not (by any stretch of his imagination) a Flannery. Yet I was proud of his name, and wanted him to be proud of me – but how?

As I look back upon these rather faded memories of childhood in the Liverpool of the 1930s, I can honestly say that, despite the fear that my father provoked, it was generally more than compensated by the love of my mother and her family. And, even though I cannot truthfully say that I have ever really loved my father, as such, as a consequence of the suffering that he inflicted upon my mother and myself, I feel I can at least try to understand his fatal flaw. The nexus of his crisis, I think, revolved around the status of family life, for he was forever confused about what he regarded as its shackles. I believe he viewed the family as something of a fallacy. Of course the fact that it remains at the centre of Western society's social universe, irrespective of whether it always works or not, is something of a delusion. I have known young people for whom the family has only meant misery. It is an institution that is regarded as somehow natural, but this has never fully explained itself to me. How can it be natural for somebody such as my father to be evidently so miserable after being compelled to involve himself in it? And don't tell me that he had a choice, for there was no choice at all. In the 1920s and 1930s, one didn't choose anything very much. You grew up and you got married.

My father was probably never the sort who was going to lead a conventional family existence; he was somebody who would always walk that very fine line between the safe and not so safe. Being practically driven into family life via peer pressure and convention is not a promising start to adulthood and he found it deeply disquieting, despite loving my mother. I was the living incarnation of a sort of laceration, for Gerard my brother had been born differently, and my father's hopes lay in my birth. But I proved to be my mother's son, and he found this to be seriously troublesome – in fact, my constant adherence to my mother's side proved to be part of a critical period in which important changes to his world view were made, and none were to the benefit of his family, that's for sure. For example, he was in no way, shape or form a religious man. Yet as a child I wanted to be a priest (I still do, on occasions!); he was a man's man but he thought of me as a so-called mummy's boy. He wanted to buy me a pair of football boots, whereas I had my heart set on a pair of dancing shoes. It was all too much for a masculine maverick with a heart of stone, methinks. I functioned as an embodied wish fulfilment for a person who evoked masculinity as power, which for me still leaves a nasty aftertaste – what a disappointment I must have been for him.

So, family life had become something of a sham, even before I had started school. It takes very little time for a child to see through the thin veil of artificial happiness. My father could be a brute; I was living in fear of him for most of my waking hours but, as I look back now some seventy years later, I can see that he had been deluded by society. Not everybody can be a family man. Father subsequently carried this delusion around, like a monkey on his back, for the rest of his life. We, as a family, had to suffer too, and how we suffered. In any case, his violence had apparently begun before the arrival of young Joseph, although my presence undoubtedly exasperated him. He had pulled the bed from under my mother on one occasion, only three weeks before she gave birth to my brother Gerard in 1928. Mother had injured her head on this occasion, and Gerard was subsequently born distinctly different from Jean. There was no evidence to connect one event with the other, of course, but it was generally assumed that Gerard's impediments were the result of the incident with that bed.

In re-examination, I would suggest that it was probably more likely that Gerard was born the way he was after an unhappy pregnancy, rather than one, albeit explosive, incident. My father's frustration was quite palpable even at this early stage; so too my mother's ambiguous devotion to this man. The best days of her marriage, according to mother, were the ones that she described as 'those days of three-pennorth of corned beef and a pennorth of pickles'.

She had very fond memories of the times prior to Gerard's birth. These early years were times of struggle but relative bliss. As the decade turned, father's joinery business began to expand and become quite profitable, eventually leading to his first set of wheels for 'business purposes'. In truth, he was increasingly buying freedom with this acquisition, and following this important milestone for him we seldom saw him during the week. Occasionally we might hear him return home late in the night, having dropped off a 'business friend' earlier. An argument would usually ensue, followed by my mother sporting a real shiner the following morning. Occasionally, he would return with Harry Epstein. The Epstein family (pronounced 'Epsteen' in Liverpool) were Jewish and Harry's father Isaac Epstein was from Lithuania (then part of the Russian Empire), and had arrived in England in the 1890s, at the age of 18. Harry's mother, Dinah, was the daughter of Joseph and Esther Hyman, who had emigrated from Russia to England with their eldest son, Jacob. The Hymans would have six more children.

Isaac Epstein married Dinah Hyman in Manchester in 1900. In 1901, Isaac and Dinah were living at 80 Walton Road, Liverpool, with Isaac's sister, Rachael Epstein, above the furniture dealership he had established. Dinah and Isaac's third son was Harry Epstein. Eventually the family moved to a larger home at 27 Anfield Road, Liverpool (now a Beatles-themed hotel called Epstein House). After Harry and his brother Leslie had joined the family firm, Isaac Epstein founded 'I. Epstein and Sons', and enlarged his furniture business by taking over adjoining shops at 62–72 Walton Road, to sell a range of other goods such as musical instruments and household appliances. They eventually called the expanding business NEMS (North End Music Stores), which offered lenient credit terms, and from which Paul McCartney's father once bought a piano. Harry Epstein's wife was formally named Malka (she was always known by her family and friends as Queenie, malka translating as 'queen' in Hebrew), and she was a member of the Hyman furniture family, which also owned the successful Sheffield Veneering Company.

So Harry, Leslie and my father were conducting considerable business by the mid to late thirties. My father would manufacture furniture which the Epsteins would retail; from time to time Harry Epstein and Chris Flannery would meet socially. Usually they would arrange a visit to the wrestling at the Liverpool Stadium (promoted by Johnny Best – I would later have a great deal to do with this particular Liverpool family) or the Tower Ballrooms in New Brighton. Harry never informed his wife Queenie of these outings. He knew he was slumming it a little and also realised that Queenie would have undoubtedly considered his activities far too beneath his social status, even a little treacherous and base; as such she was never put in the picture and, right up to her death many years after Harry, Brian and Clive Epstein had died, was never aware of her husband's class-based felonies. Many years later Queenie actually briefly fell out with me over this.

The birth of son Chris in 1933 followed my seemingly untimely arrival, and the final two pieces of the family jigsaw were conceived in that eerie period of unreal peace that had descended over the country prior to the outbreak of hostilities in September 1939. Peter was a 'war baby' for although he was conceived in peacetime he was born at Halloween 1939; Teddy had been born a year earlier. This birth had taken place at my Auntie Winnie's home at 15 Worsley Crescent in Norris Green. By the late 1930s Norris Green was regarded as a district of Liverpool even though it was actually in those far off days part of the county of Lancashire, on the north-eastern boundary of the city. The estate was developed in the 1920s and named after the Liverpool-based Norris family. It is thought the land on which Norris Green was built on was donated to the city by Lord Derby, but that he didn't actually own it in the first place – a typical Liverpool story concerning the provenance of land, to be sure! So after much legal wrangling it was actually purchased by the council for the sum of £65,000 from the estate of the Leylands and Naylors; it was then developed into a splendid council house estate – most of its well-built housing still stands to this very day.

Mother had temporarily moved away from the family home in Everton, 16 Walton Lane, along with her brood, because she had not wanted to run the gauntlet of my father's increasingly violent behaviour. In the latter days of her pregnancy he had again been especially violent to her, and there was no alternative but to try to protect her unborn child, which she did; she then gave birth and promptly returned to him once again, which dumbfounded even us kids. Sounds bloody daft, doesn't it, but it's not so unusual. Married life is full of contradictions, I suppose, especially when you are a Catholic family in Liverpool in the 1930s with no visible means of birth control. Under these circumstances what appears to be the most practical and desirable if short-term solution often involves a great degree of personal sacrifice for the woman. Interestingly, however, these first instances of pragmatism on behalf of my mother were productive in the long term, for she began to appreciate that a certain level of independence was vital, and thus her family business acumen began gradually to come to the fore, eventually leading to almost total financial independence from my father.

One might glibly presume that my father's ideas about the role of his wife were based around that imaginary Victorian principle of a woman's role being something of an 'Imperial production line' of cannon fodder. However, this would be far too simplistic a hypothesis for, as I described, his most violent periods manifested themselves during mother's pregnancies. As I grew older, this certainly came to suggest to me that his fears of entrapment in the family 'prison' were very pronounced indeed. As I write this I feel rather sorry for him in a way, but then again, perhaps not. Whenever I try to understand my father, images return from this confusing period of my life. Such as the day that father almost threw Teddy out of the window because of the child's incessant crying. Babies cry, don't they? Why such violence? Why such constant, continuous, catastrophic violence with never the slightest indication of contrition? So, as we all grew through the pre-war thirties, we became increasingly aware of mother's precarious position. In addition, we were also acutely aware of just how much the Mottrams as a family (and a force for good) were involving themselves in our daily welfare. The Flannery branch were usually nowhere to be seen, except on high days and holidays, and the little practical things as far as we kids were concerned such as sweets and occasional treats were invariably doled out by members of mother's family.

My cherished auntie, a woman with the wonderful Liverpudlian-cum-German name of Mary-Jane Fitson (a Mottram by birth), was a wonderful human being. Very forceful yet compassionate, she would always ensure that we kids were in safe condition. Her husband Wilhelm Fitson (Uncle Willie), perhaps originally Fitzon, was for us children a 'mysterious' German, originally a farmer from outside Hanover who became a teacher in Liverpool. Throughout the growing political tension of the mid to late thirties, we kids would frequently invent exciting stories about him working for the German government or meeting Hitler on the docks or gun-running to Ireland or other such nonsense. A little cruel, perhaps, but that's kids for you. He was a lovely man, actually, but the total antithesis to Mary-Jane. He was probably Lutheran or some such nonconformist and didn't attend church too much, whereas Mary-Jane was a totally devoted Catholic. But Mary-Jane was also amazingly nonchalant, dispensing vividly realised observations at every turn. She lived her life in a series of vignettes, each one dispensed as a lesson. Her faith allowed her to combine nuggets of truth with extraordinary moments of mirth and she was always ready to surprise and amuse without over-sentimentalising; she was, I suppose, incredibly wise – a wisdom perhaps brought about by a combination of her faith and her love for a man outside of her social milieu in possibly every sense. This for me has always been the true nature of Catholicism – discipline, yes, but liberation and wisdom also.

Spiritual matters were therefore taken care of by a combination of the Mottram-Fitson alliance together with the illustrious and ubiquitous Roman Catholic Church. St Anthony's on Scotland Road became something of a refuge for me by the age of about 6 or 7, especially after one of father's bouts, and I would accompany Mary-Jane to the church in the early hours of most mornings, where she would carry out her duties as a cleaner and I would just stand and stare in wonderment at the pure beauty of the church, as often as not with a rather useless rag in my hand. The iconography used to make me quite literally weep, but in amazement and wonderment that the Lord could have done this for us all. It was all so affective, so emotional and so beautiful. Mary-Jane and I would slowly walk back home, discussing the glory of God, and I would arrive back in time to get ready for school and indulge in a little breakfast: eggs from the Rhode Island Red chickens that were kept in the yard and fresh bread toasted on the big roaring fire to go with them. Butter as well, of course, because of mother's scrupulous pre-war standards, although it had to be that revolting 'Special Margarine' once rationing had arrived. In retrospect, my childhood faith now seems a little cartoon-like; the characters appear and disappear like caricatures, as befits the story perhaps. But at times it was refreshing, invigorating and great fun – at other times less so, for it could fill me with a loneliness that was periodically difficult to shake.

For example, Mary-Jane might, when she could afford it, treat me to a couple of ounces of boiled sweets on the way home, or a few Mojos or Blackjacks from the local newsagent after our early morning pilgrimages to St Anthony's. She detected, I think, a certain void in my life, a nothingness created by the absence of a loving father. I was later told by Mary-Jane that she worried about me. She had noticed that I tended to stare quite a lot, as if I was looking for something or somebody to bridge a gap. I would stare in church, I would stare out of the window at the night sky and I would stare at the rain falling and running down the gutters at high speed, as if it was escaping from something. Many hours of my pre-teen days were spent looking vacantly around me, hoping that something would come to fill the nihilistic visions that covered an elementary loneliness. She saw. I couldn't explain it, but Mary-Jane detected it. Many years later I was reminded of such moments by John Lennon's *Strawberry Fields Forever* and could envisage a lonely teenaged John, staring into space out of the back bedroom of Mendips in much the same way that I stared at the iconography in St Anthony's. For me *Strawberry Fields Forever* has always been indicative of loneliness, with John offering us a private meditational place to share – a wonderfully generous song, I think.

Our walk back from St Anthony's would always take us past umpteen local newsagents. I would stand and stare outside the shops while many dockers and other early birds would be buying their papers and cigarettes for the day ('a *Daily Sketch* and ten Woodbines' was repeated so often it sounded like a mantra). The iconography in the newsagent's windows, the advertising posters, papers, brand labels etc., was just as important for me, in its own way, to that of the church; so too the smells: the dampness of working clothes, the wonderful aroma of pipe tobacco – twist, shag, rough cut – all of which probably came from Ogden's tobacco factory in Liverpool. The physiognomy of the men, all seemingly hundreds of years older than me, gnarled, disfigured, old before their time, but superior, dignified, solemn and proud, very proud: just like the statues and icons in the church. A newsagent's shop at 6.30 a.m. on a wet Monday morning became an extension of religious experience, an encounter of the inspirational kind; something that has never left me. The orthodoxy of the church mingled with these living, secular experiences and created a template of compassionate reality for the rest of my life. Mary-Jane was distinctly moved about my religious fervour, and she often would discuss with my mother the prospect of my becoming a priest. I thought that this was a wonderful idea, and it fuelled my excitement for all things religious even more. Mother nodded her head in a sort of knowing condescension. She knew in her own secret way even at this early stage that if I was to be true to myself I would not be destined for the cloth.

But I loved the Church so much that I fully intended to immerse myself in the ritual as much as I possibly could; making the sign of the cross before bedtime became part of my life. I totally pestered the priest at Our Lady Immaculate in St Domingo Road, Everton, to allow me to become an altar boy, even though I wasn't a member of his church. The queue was simply too long at St Anthony's and I was desperate to do something, anything that would bring me closer to Christ. Poor old Father O'Sullivan held out for quite some time, but was eventually forced to capitulate. He realised, in his goodness, just how much it meant to me. So I was then involved at Our Lady's and St Anthony's. I was collecting churches like another lad might collect ice lolly sticks. It was the great mystery of it all too. The Latin Mass was complete gobbledygook, but mysterious and esoteric. The fact that I failed fully to comprehend it only made it all the more special, I think. It took years for me to realise that I was being drawn to the beauty of the Church and its ceremony, rather than the religious message per se. Once a Catholic, always a Catholic, I suppose … yet I do cringe a little these days, now that I have begun to understand the level of indoctrination of the senses that occurred. I would have gone all the way into priesthood, prob-ably, had somebody in the Church decided that I was a suitable apprentice. Into a system, a set of rules, that I would have only discovered at a much later date I was technically disqualified from by an essential guilt; something which, according to some, precluded me from Christianity altogether. Mother could sense the fallacy; she always knew best.

As previously stated, my actual father was a joiner by trade and his initial jobbing employment turned into a full-scale business as the 1930s moved along. In fact, by the late 1930s his work had expanded sufficiently for him to take a small wood yard in Field Street, in the Great Homer Street district of Everton. At first the bulk of the work at the Field Street yard involved manufacturing wooden crates and boxes for canned meats. There were a number of meat producers in the Everton and Bootle areas of Merseyside and crating the tinned hams and ox tongues became a lucrative order for Flannery's Joiners. In fact, I later discovered that these tongue-and-groove boxes were far more revered than the tinned meat that they contained. The boxes seldom ever ended up as kindling, but came to be used all over Liverpool as ad hoc storage containers. Even twenty years later, as I came to move into my apartment at Gardner Road, I discovered one of my father's boxes staring at me from the cellar. There it was, easily recognisable to me by the stencilled logo on all four sides of the box reading 'Pearson's Butchers' as if time had stood still. I hadn't seen the old fella for a number of years by this time and it stopped me in my tracks. 'I can't bloody well go anywhere without that sod looking over me!' I thought as I slowly and nervously opened the box, half expecting something (or somebody) horribly familiar to be looking back at me. My fears were allayed when I discovered an old, battered, but well-used Tilley lamp inside, which I later renovated and subsequently used to good effect. I even raised a laugh as I read a daft little message on a crumpled piece of paper next to the lamp, a relic from another occupant, another life, perhaps another world even, which curiously read: 'No paraffin, but thanks for the umbrella.'

The shroud of my father was immediately lifted as I tittered with a palpable sense of relief. What the hell was that message all about? I didn't really care, but I knew in that moment that a spell had been broken. My father's constrictions had been released by an esoteric message about a Tilley lamp and a rainy day. Maybe the sort of day that in my youth would have had me staring out from my bedroom window, thinking that it was raining because my life was missing something, when all it was doing was just raining. Maybe the sort of night, those cold nights of my childhood, that would make me believe that I was being punished by God for being my father's son, and then being punished by father for being mother's son; maybe we were just in need of a Tilley lamp. I suddenly felt better than I had for years, thanks to a tongue-and-groove box from Field Street and an old paraffin heater – but back to the thirties.

As his orders for the Epsteins (and others) became more frequent, father moved to a larger premises on Kempston Street behind London Road, which at that time bordered the Jewish sector of Liverpool. The Epsteins had discovered my father's talents as a joiner via the aforementioned wooden crates and also a few well-made cutlery boxes (or at least they looked like cutlery boxes: they were actually strong boxes in disguise), and approached him about the possibilities of providing them with good quality but reasonably priced furniture to retail in their shop in Walton Road. Father, despite his faults, was an extraordinary, self-taught man where wood was concerned, and although he had never bothered a great deal with furniture before, he spent many a long night drawing and designing a range of furniture that would prove economically viable and of sufficient quality to satisfy his new client. He had a fondness for unifying features on wooden items; unlike other small-time manufacturers he did not evade particulars and although his private life tended to depend upon inflated rhetoric designed to frighten rather than reassure his family, his approaches to functional woodwork were very particular. The drawings were duly accepted, and thus began our long-term relationship with the Epstein family, an alliance that lasts to this very day. It was initially a good deal for both parties, father providing them with a small quota of chairs and furniture each week, the Epsteins paying every twenty-eight days.

The Epsteins began with good intentions but they proved to be rather poor payers, and it was often left to my mother to go around to the shop in Walton Road, almost cap in hand for money, when the payment didn't arrive. Despite running the business from hand to mouth, father considered debt collecting to be rather beneath his acquired self-employed status, whereas mother, from a business background, would have no truck with outstanding balances. It was in this way that she came to meet and get to know, at least as far as it was possible, Queenie Epstein who at this stage was the bookkeeper for the furniture shop. Words were usually spoken by my mother about the debt, to which Queenie would remind her of the common business practices of hanging on to money for as long as possible. My mother usually had the last word, however; something along the lines of:

> When I've got enough of my own to hang onto Mrs Epstein, I will do so as long as I can, with pleasure, but I've never been one to keep other people's money about my person. So, in the meantime, I'd be obliged if you could help me feed my children by paying what you owe my husband.

Queenie – she was always 'Mrs Epstein' to us all, in actual fact – came to understand that she was dealing with a formidable adversary in my mother; however, the payments didn't get any more punctual, and mother's regular visits, which she found agonisingly embarrassing, came to be something of a ritual. I think it was all regarded by Queenie as something of a game and possibly one highlight of an otherwise rather boring middle-class domestic existence. The business, and this little ritual, continued unabated between the Flannerys and the Epsteins right up until and slightly beyond the outbreak of the war.

At the very beginning, father turned wood from not only the yard at home but also the front room, which had originally been a shop front. Following his business' expansion and his initial removal to Field Street a portion of our home, his former workshop and storage spaces were left empty. We were living in Walton Lane at this time, very close to the Epsteins' shop. Once father had moved the centre of his manufacturing away from the Walton Lane area, mother immediately decided to flex her muscles about independence a little and, following in the family tradition, decided to open a second-hand furniture shop in father's old workspace.

This would be 1938. Father actually approached her about her selling some of his goods; however, rather defiantly (and not without a certain sense of business acumen), she refused, claiming that she did not want to give the Epsteins any further excuses for delaying payments to him, or indeed cancelling orders. Of course she also wished to express business as well as personal independence from him. In some respects she saw him as a fraud or at the very least something of a 'curate's egg' – good in parts, but unacceptable as a whole.

It was in this immediate pre-Second World War period that I first met the young Brian Epstein. I must have been about 8 years of age when we first met and, as long as I live, I'll never forget that first meeting. Brian was a typically spoilt child and initially I must admit to finding him rather repulsive; but, to be fair, this was principally because our young relationship had got off on the wrong foot. It was sometime in 1937, I think, when Brian was placed in my charge one afternoon at the Epsteins' Anfield/Stanley Park house while Queenie and my mother were doing business. Brian was almost exactly three years younger than myself (born 19 September 1934) and was only a pre-school squirt to me, being all of about 3 or 4 years old and looking very Jewish. He was quite a handful and I thought at the time something of a spoilt brat. So much so in fact that he had me in tears by the end of the afternoon. I had attempted to play with his brand-new toy: a coronation coach (presumably in celebration of King George VI's coronation that year), which was like a piece of crown jewellery to me. Before even getting a whiff of a chance, Brian deliberately trod on the lead horses, breaking their legs, rather than having it distract my attention away from him. I was horrified, but also petrified because I naturally assumed that, being the eldest, I would get the blame for this act of wanton destruction. I need not have worried, however, because when Queenie returned nothing was said at all. Brian obviously always got what he wanted and the ruined coach wasn't even mentioned. Queenie gave me the evil eye all right, but more because she thought I was a rather contemptible gentile rather than evil per se. Her one remark to me was cutting enough, however: 'grubby child,' she protested.

As time went by I did come to endure him a little and as he grew we became quite good playmates over the next twelve months or so, despite our age difference. Curiously, as I look back now, I think I felt rather sorry for him. He appeared to have everything, certainly more than myself, but was always rather unhappy and at times morose. He later informed me that he was 'only ever what his mother made him' – which speaks volumes really.

His social and ethnic echelon defined him before he could define himself – a classic case of cultural capital. For example, before I got a chance to get to know him any better the Epstein family moved to Prestatyn in North Wales for a while once the war began. We lost touch for quite a few years after that as, first in Southport and then at a school named Croxton Prep, Brian began his long and painful journey of definition by others, followed by a self-discovery via a command of detail. This was an odyssey which would lead him back into my company more than once over the next thirty years or so.

Meanwhile, mother's shop had started trading briskly in quality second-hand furniture, plus a little good quality bedding and linen. Mother's new-found assertiveness was in no small way linked to her family background of entrepreneurial know-how. As she began to visit local house clearances and auction rooms she immediately recognised a need in the local market and, having a good eye, spotted some very tasty furniture. She also appreciated our house/shop's position, which was in an area of very low wages and high unemployment, and as such was in the middle of a district which has always been reliant on second hand as something of a financial necessity. Wardrobes, beds, washstands, cupboards were the staple sellers, along with the ubiquitous dining table. Mother was particularly adept at discovering house clearances in the more middle-class, salubrious parts of town, and would often jump a tram to Woolton in order to place her marker or get first refusal on furniture from some of the larger houses out there. Mention of Woolton demands a brief explanation, for it was around this very area that the young Quarry Men and Beatles could often be found, and their experiences of that area of Liverpool form a contrast between their upbringings, and that of my own.

Woolton is another of those districts of Liverpool that was initially co-opted into the corporation. Of course many Beatles landmarks can be found in Woolton, including Mendips (John Lennon's childhood home at 251 Menlove Avenue) and what we knew as the naughty boys' home of Strawberry Field, off Beaconsfield Road. Another one of Woolton's claims to fame is that John and Paul first met at St Peter's church garden fete on 6 July 1957. It would be worth reminding all Beatles fans of this fact the next time they considered them working-class heroes – in fact, wasn't this irreconcilable difference actually what John was singing about all those years ago (i.e. that effectively 'you made me into your working-class hero')? Not every young boy had the opportunity to read volume after volume of *Just William*, that's for sure (I think of myself as one such example).

But enough of the rant and back to the story: quality and value became Agnes' trademarks for families who had little or no spare cash to spend on even the barest of necessities. While mother was providing herself with regular, if unremarkable, income, father and the Epsteins (and the Jewish community in general) were getting on like the proverbial house on fire. Not only from a business point of view, either, for it was about this time that my father and Harry Epstein took to socialising and drinking together – as mentioned earlier – much to Queenie's ignorance and my mother's fear. The Epstein outlet was proving to be rather lucrative for Chris Flannery, despite the late payments, and by the end of 1938 he was even providing their shop with some rather classy Queen Ann reproductions. Most of this stuff was destined for the more salubrious areas of Liverpool's suburbs: Queens Drive, Woolton Road, Menlove Avenue in the south end of the city and also Formby, Waterloo and Blundellsands in the north, in addition to the Wirral, over the water.

However, father's new-found wealth simply increased his desire for booze and freedom. Mother would frequently tell us, when asked about where he was: 'Oh, I don't know … once your father got four wheels and then a little money in his pocket, he was a changed man.' I was pretty glad to see the back of him most of the time for once he had walked back through the front door our own version of a world war would usually begin. A good wash in front of the fire in the galvanised bath, snuggling up to mother to listen to the wireless and smelling that familiar scent of 'Evening in Paris' that she would always wear made us feel safe, at least for a while. If there was nothing worth listening to on the wireless she would sing all of her favourite songs such as *Me and My Shadow, You Made Me Love You* and *One of These Days*.

Music actually became a real comfort; it was at the very least a soundtrack to a degree of temporary peace and stability. Father, of course, couldn't have cared less about music. He was the antithesis to all things musical: he regarded a musician as somebody to be suffered, somebody who could provide a service while he was chatting up his latest bit of 'fluff'. But to mother and myself it was an 'other' world. Radio itself was full of fascination, excitement, entertainment and it became a refuge; a place that we could visit when times became unbearable and father's behaviour became insufferable. It wasn't simply the songs of Sophie Tucker either, but practically any music or show. The wireless became a medium of transportation to other lifestyles, other existences. Excitement leapt from the airwaves to soothe us; there was another world out there!

Not every man was a beast, it seemed – some like Henry Hall, Ambrose, Lew Stone, Roy Fox and Ray Noble actually loved music as I did. My memories of mother washing in the yard, turning that huge wheel on the side of the ringer until it reached top dead centre are forever meshed with memories of sounds reaching out to me from the wireless, with mother singing along to something like *Whispering*.

Looking back to the 1930s after so many years, it seems at times that we were constantly surrounded by music and the smell of carbolic soap. As if, in some strange way, Stan Kenton had something to do with the big tin bath hanging on the backyard wall. But, of course, the memories of my wayward father also at times return to haunt me, returning one's thoughts to reality, and fear. Actually, visions of my father during the war can occasionally make me smile. To his utter astonishment, and my hilarity, he was called up. I thought that this was not only an excellent thing for the War Office to do for the country (in my childish way, I thought that because he was so violent he could sort it all out), but also for mother and myself, because he would be away from home. Initially, he was posted as a Royal Engineer to Devizes and life was heaven without him. He was still alive and I never wished him dead, at this stage, despite his violence, but he was simply not around and almost immediately the atmosphere in the house changed: mother was safe; the Mottrams were free to call; music could be played all day; and we could all live in a little peace. How completely ironic that this threat to the nation could have given the Flannerys so much joy! It was not to last, however, for father was posted back to Liverpool, after his training in Wiltshire to work as a joiner-cum-docker on the Liverpool waterfront. He even came home for his dinner – as often as not with a shoulder bag full of something that had been mysteriously damaged in transit that morning; sugar immediately springs to mind (perhaps he was not all bad, but then again, I wonder which family was being deprived of this precious commodity via his pilfering).

Oddly, and unlike other fading images, such memories are vivid, maybe because other boys' fathers were thousands of miles away fighting for King and Country, and yet my own could jump a tram and be home in half an hour (and according to my mother create World War III back in his own kitchen). I was excruciatingly embarrassed. In addition, he frequently returned home carrying his Lee-Enfield rifle. Other boys would have found this fascinating, but to me it was only emphasising my feelings of foreboding about him and our relationship grew even more strained because of my inability to come to terms with his bringing this symbol of violence into our home. The business was still thriving too. Despite his war work, father was now also able to keep an eye on his profits, and owing to the Blitz of 1940–41 he discovered that he was in great demand. The wood yard was able to provide a boarding-up service for first of all Irwin's retail grocery chain, which was much later taken over by Tesco, and later for many of the devastated homes, and father was paid handsomely for the service. He also took a great interest in reclaiming salvaged wood and reworking it, and this became a very lucrative outlet as the war continued and fresh wood became scarce. On the whole it was a pretty good war for the man.

Following the height of the German bombing in the spring of 1941, mother decided that we were all too much at risk. Everton's proximity to Liverpool's city centre and docklands meant that many civilians from the area were being regularly killed, maimed or made homeless because of the high explosives and incendiaries being dropped by the Luftwaffe. I distinctly remember singing all night long during these interminable raids. There was very little sleep for any of us, and to keep the sound of the bombs away mother would tell us all to sing at the top of our voices. I suppose that she also might have thought that if, God forbid, a bomb should hit us, at least we would never have known anything about it. But enough was enough after May 1941 and she decided that we had to get away. She would not be parted from her young family at any cost, however, and so, forever pragmatic, she began to negotiate with a private landlord by the name of Rubin for a house further away from the city.

In those far-off days, Huyton was little more than a collective on the Lancashire borders of Liverpool. The township of Huyton is actually of ancient origin and, believe it or not, is, like Woolton, also mentioned in Domesday Book. The survey named the settlement Hitune (meaning high town) and a local lord by the name of Dot held the land along with the village of Tarboc (now Tarbock). Such hamlets were part of the land between the Ribble and the Mersey rivers known as the West Derby Hundred. Huyton remained little more than a west Lancashire hamlet for centuries but in the nineteenth century railway development raised the village's profile; indeed, the area was transformed following the successful Rainhill Trials of 1829. Huyton railway station became and remains an important link along this line. Huyton further expanded significantly in the 1930s when large tracts of land owned by Lord Derby were sold to the Liverpool Corporation. Prior to the outbreak of the Second World War housing estates gradually appeared in Huyton-with-Roby and this increase in population meant that further changes were brought to the infrastructure of the area. More redevelopment took place after the war including road alterations and the demolition of some very old properties.

So, by the time we moved to the district some private and council development had taken place, but nothing in comparison to the later post-war rehousing programmes that were to reshape the area and subsequently provide this country with a prime minister (namely, Harold Wilson). After negotiating with Mr Rubin for a tenancy, mother took us all up to Huyton for the duration. We were now living at 94 Dinas Lane and being schooled at St Aloysius' Roman Catholic school. I say 'schooled' but really very little formal education was involved: we turned up, we were fed, we went home. We spent the remaining years of the war in splendid but somewhat unre-markable exile. My life was once again filled with music and theatre for father was spending his time split between his duties as a Royal Engineer and a capitalist in the city centre, and would spend very little time in Huyton, a place which he thought was in the middle of nowhere (well it was in a way). He made sure, however, that the family did not really want for anything, except of course a little love and understanding.

Life had its stranger moments during our stay in Huyton: for example, I remember one morning walking around the area following a particularly heavy air raid; I came across dozens of dead bodies, laid out in rows like a gruesome flowerbed, on what was known locally as the 'Plantations' – an area of prescribed greenery in this new housing area. I took a look at some of the faces of the dead. They were all asleep, as far as I could see. It was unreal and yet very real at the same time, and my young mind couldn't really take it all in at once. Later that week I even gleefully swapped pieces of shrapnel with other boys at school. The utter tragedy of it all only really dawned on me some years later when I came across a list of names in the cemetery of the Huyton-with-Roby church, as I recall. All local monograms read 'of this parish' and a variety of ages could be read, but all referred back to that night in 1941 when a stray bomb had hit a row of council houses. All of the families had been killed outright for no other reason than being in the wrong place at the wrong time: their own homes. It was indeed a strange time in that apparent backwater of Merseyside.

Just a short walk away from our house was a German prisoner-of-war camp. By the summer of 1942 I could be seen walking up to the fences surrounding this camp in the hopes of seeing the 'enemy'; to stare at these warlike creatures and to see whether they were as Wagnerian as we had imagined. On the odd occasion I actually managed to catch a glimpse of a few of these adversaries. I was extremely disappointed to discover that they looked just like us: quite normal, quite civilised, rather young, actually. They also seemed rather pleased to be in that camp, from what my memory tells me, as if perhaps they knew that they were in safe hands, possibly. Moments like these are impregnated upon my mind. I began to come to certain conclusions about the war, ideas that have stayed with me to this very day. Undoubtedly fascism had to be defeated, but these men in this camp, they were just blokes: young men who were being misled, exploited and used – all basically being led by the nose to slaughter. I vowed there and then never to raise my fist in anger to anybody, and I have been lucky enough to have been able to keep that vow ever since, even though at times, especially with my own brother Peter (Lee Curtis), my patience has been sorely tested. One German pilot had baled out over Prescot and came to ground near to what later became the Granada Cinema in Dovecot. We took him food and water and then promptly reported him; he was appropriately taken to the POW camp on Prescot Road. We occasionally went to see him and he appeared very happy to be out of the conflict, just a young German flyer doing his duty; no Nazi, that's for sure.

I soon discovered that there were far more interesting things to do in an air-raid shelter (no, not that – I would have run a mile!) than simply dodge the bombs of the Luftwaffe. I found that they made wonderful amphitheatres, projected one's voice well and could be the perfect rehearsal rooms for a budding vocalist. I had decided, you see, that by hook or by crook I would get into this magical world of wireless. I was also being attracted by the silver screen too: the sheer beauty of the Hollywood productions, the dream worlds that they evoked, the magic that they could weave in my young mind. Wherever and whenever I could, I would get into one of the many local cinemas to watch and be with my idols and then recreate the whole experience in an air-raid shelter. Betty Hutton was the ultimate star for my young self. She had everything: beauty, looks, taste and a pair of legs to die for. She could sing, dance and even perform on the trapeze.

So, for this young boy of 11 years of age, Betty became the archetypal vision, the pinnacle of song and dance, almost a revolutionary character for me, for she made perfect sense. I felt that Betty Hutton kind of embodied me; she awarded me a freedom and by her presence allowed me to seek some kind of identity for myself. Much of my waking day was taken up with schemes to 'sag-off' school in order to pay homage to my icon. At one air-raid shelter I had already begun to set up a shrine to Hutton, when it was actually needed by the general public (How inconsiderate!). I resolved to begin again, but this time in what might laughingly be described as a garage at the bottom of our garden. I decided to open our old garage as a little theatre, where for a small charge – ever the capitalist too, I suppose – I would give the local kids a show. The problem was how to tart it up sufficiently, because I was a very particular child and everything had to be just so. All week I would prepare my little theatre by pinching some of mother's best tablecloths and napkins in order to create a stage backdrop – very conspiratorial.

I distinctly recall wishing that my young friend Brian could be with me because I knew that we were two of a kind, so to speak, and that he also had a great interest in everything theatrical and extravagant. But by this time I learnt that Brian's family had moved even further away from Liverpool and, being absorbed in my fantasy world, I realised that I would have to create it alone. I would announce to a select few of the local kids that there would be a show that Saturday morning and they were invited, but would be charged a penny each. Sure enough, to my great delight, a small line of eager children would form outside our house each Saturday morning. The children would be escorted to the theatre and the show would begin. It might last, perhaps, for half an hour and would mainly consist of me hammering away at a few standards and telling a couple of jokes, until invariably mother would appear, usually looking for her best tablecloth. Clearing the locals out of the shed and clipping me around the ear after discovering that yet again it was part of the scenery, she would say, 'And how much was it this week, Joseph?' Upon which I would meekly inform her of the modest receipts. 'Well, I'm sure that the church will be very grateful for the donation. Now get in!'

Not only was there a German POW camp in the area, but also by 1944 a US Army base, in addition to several British forces camps dotted around that arterial road out of the eastern side of Liverpool. As such, there was a wide menu available to us. Apple pie and custard was always available from the British camp kitchens – yum. We would also find the Yanks equally amenable and receive chewing gum and chocolate, and it wasn't unknown to receive gifts thrown over the fencing at the German camp either from the British guards or the German prisoners. When we might be feeling the pinch of rationing a little more than usual, Gerard and I would traipse around the various camps on the scrounge. Gerard and I 'sold' our sister Jean on more than one occasion! She always failed to turn up, however – I wonder why? We were seldom ever turned away and became good friends with many young servicemen. I have often wondered what became of some of them; they were so young and full of life. I could only hope that they were all able to return to their homes, but many of them obviously did not.

Mother was a great organiser and she would constantly work to ensure that we ate well and properly. For example, our sweet coupons were always sent to a woman from a few roads away in Huyton. Mother actually thought that this person was very lazy because she preferred to have sweet coupons rather than meat coupons. Despite this, mother used this 'friend's' sweet tooth to our advantage, and would exchange our sweet ration for her meat ration, thus providing us with the necessary protein. To compensate for our loss of sweets, mother would then make her own delicious toffee. She had hens in the garden too, and they provided a copious supply of eggs, as well as something for us kids to look after. I vividly recall one sad evening sitting up all night nursing our dying cockerel; it was heart-breaking. While I was preoccupied in my own little fantasy world, father's contract for boarding up the blitzed shops of Liverpool was proving highly lucrative and, his workshop having already expanded into Kempston Street, he now operated fourteen sizing machines working flat out night and day in order to cut and finish the required board. The location of the workshop was also an important feature of father's growing affluence. Kempston Street's position was adjacent to the rapidly thinning Jewish sector of the city (near Daulby Street and Grove Street) and Chris Flannery, despite being a total bastard at home, was also a highly respected gentile.

He was held in such esteem that the Jewish business fellowship charged him with the task of secreting a large amount of documentation (leases, bonds, deeds, share certificates, keys to deposit boxes and the like) in a hidden compartment in the lower reaches of the workshops. Father deepened a large 8ft x 4ft pit driven into the basement floor as a temporary hiding place. He was given charge of some of their most precious and classified information (and, if the worse came to the worst, their lives). Had the Germans overrun the country father's instructions were to destroy all documents, thus eliminating in one fell swoop any records of a property-owning class of Jews in that area of Liverpool. It was assumed that the German occupying authorities would have made middle-class Jews their first easy target for property confiscation and personal elimination. Strange to relate how a man could be so popular at large and yet so cruel at home.

The assistance that father gave to the local Jewish community was never forgotten, and after the war, when all of the papers and keys were duly returned, he was rewarded with a great deal of business. He actually launched a number of projects with a Mr Alexander, after successfully tendering for contracts to remove wooden fittings from scrapped navy vessels in Vickers Yard, in Barrow-in-Furness, and he was able to renew his business associations with the Epstein family once they had returned to the area. Ship dismantling became a very profitable business. So much so, in fact, that it threatened to take over the entire proceedings. Alexander was later offered former War Department buildings in Kirkby, on the outskirts of the city, and it was here that the famous Hygena kitchen fittings company was established. Father, however, pulled out of this project at an early stage, owing to his contractual obligations to the Epsteins, T.J. Hughes and the Owen Owen stores. A pity, I suppose. In retrospect, this Formica-based revolution became part of the growing consumer affluence of the 1950s, and father would have undoubtedly made a small fortune. Still, he would probably have pissed it up against a wall in any case. He preferred road-houses and whore houses to fittings for real houses.

Mr Alexander used to say to father that he would take me away from my family home and educate me. Perhaps to him I looked a little Jewish with my black wavy hair and swarthy, olive skin. Mr Skulnick, another trader, this time in tools and building supplies facing Mr Alexander's shop in London Road, also regarded me as a boy ready for education and training. Mr Skulnick would say that I should have been at home studying – I think he was probably right, for I knew from an early age that my formal education was so lacking in depth that I would at some stage have to supplement it with a broader-based knowledge, probably from the 'University of Life'. But father steadfastly refused to have us educated, and we as his offspring simply had to make do and earn our pennies, as he had so done. In those days I recalled stories of Bing Crosby's family learning that they all had to earn their pocket money individually without any assistance from their parents and this was a similar situation. Father really only had one child: Jean, his daughter. All five sons had to make do; at one stage he described us all as 'five jessies'.

By the time the war ended in 1945 we had left our rented home in Huyton and moved back into the urban chaos that was post-war Liverpool. Mother's family had remained in the Everton area of the city, and she was determined to get back to her roots, despite the fact that living in Huyton may well have saved our collective lives. She once again negotiated a house deal, this time as a swap, and we all moved into a very interesting and little spooky townhouse at 17 Luxmore Road, Everton. The landscape had changed so dramatically in this inner-city area that it took me several days to get my bearings. So much destruction had been wrought that, added to the previous dereliction, something resembling a moonscape had appeared: craters, boulders and empty spaces abounded where once a community had been. From this moment on, in fact, the population of Everton began to shrink and continued to do so well into the late 1980s when, because of a few piecemeal developments such as the splendid Eldonian complex, the population began to slowly expand once more.

Unlike the moon, however, there was still atmosphere and of course plenty of music. I was now just about old enough to sit quietly in a pub without attracting attention from an unhappy landlord, and shortly after arriving at Luxmore Road I was treated to one of the Mottrams' typical 'hoolees' at the Parrot public house on Scotland Road. Music of all kinds was being created on the spot. This was not like the radio or cinema; it was unbounded pleasure for the sake of it: Auntie Katherine with her contralto voice and curious looking banjo; Uncle John Mottram with his strange-sounding parlour songs; and then there were the Whites, great friends of the Mottrams, providing a song and a giggle. Charlie White was father to Priscilla, who as she grew was later always getting into trouble of some sort (usually smoking down the back jigger), but John was so kind-hearted that he could never be cross with her for very long. Priscilla White, of course, became Cilla Black. Cilla was best friends with my cousin, Rita Mottram, and their greatest wishes were to be hairdressers. Rita did – but as for Cilla, that's another story! I tend to think that when confronted with images of war and destruction from around the world on the news today, the question is asked 'how will they begin again?' When faced with such devastation, as those of us old enough to remember the 1940s can testify, there is simply no other choice. All over Liverpool at this time, amongst the devastation, new families were created, such as the Lennons, the McCartneys, the Harrisons and the Starkeys. There is always the promise of a new generation to pull things through, and it was this feeling of optimism and hopefulness, coupled with plenty of shagging, I expect! that abounded as I settled back into life closer to my spiritual home of Everton near Liverpool's city centre.

Even though I had developed an interest in all things popular at our dwelling at Dinas Lane in Huyton, it was when we arrived back in Everton that we as a family seemed to begin to enjoy all aspects of life a little more. I listened to the radio at all times of the day – especially Workers' Playtime, any big band shows and Tommy Handley's ITMA programmes. Curiously

I did not listen to Radio Luxembourg at this stage, for I don't even think I was aware of its existence. By this point my musical education was coming through the local cinemas: the Trocadero, the Paramount, the Majestic and the Rotunda – wherever there was a musical being shown, I would be there. I would regularly buy the *ABC Film Review* and always kept up to date with filmmaking – it was my first real hobby, I suppose (apart from religion that is) and I revelled in it all. Musicals were always top of my particular 'Hit Parade'. *Rhapsody in Blue* was a big film favourite of mine with Robert Alda and Joan Leslie. As for British artists: Gracie Fields, Old Mother Riley and George Formby were OK; but it was the Hollywood stuff that really interested me, aimed as it was to cheer us up after the gloom of war. Optimism does fade, however, and reality has a habit of slapping one in the face. Liverpool came to be largely ignored by central government when the cheque books came out, irrespective of the political leanings of any subsequent government. The years following the war brought a diversification of most cities' local economies, and Liverpool was no exception in this respect: more self-employed people, more young men returning from war wishing to set things up for themselves, even if it was only a window-cleaning round. But isolated somewhat by its geography (despite its links with North America Liverpool's post was geographically in the wrong place to capitalise on rebuilding Europe), Liverpool was not rebuilt as it should have been and the 1947 Town and Country Planning Act did the city few favours.

The Act provided that all development values were vested in the state, with £300 million set aside for compensation of landowners. It was deemed that any land could be purchased by a developer at an existing-use value; after permission to develop was granted, the developer would be assessed via a 'development charge' based on the difference between the initial price and the final value of the land. Such existing-use charges and development charges were theoretically assessed by the Central Land Board, and it was intended that local district valuers would work with landowners and developers to agree a fair value. It was reported in 1949 that 'where [a charge] is payable, the amount has been agreed by the developer in over 95 per cent of the cases'. But in Liverpool landowners refused to sell at the 'undeveloped' price, and even though the Central Land Board had authority to purchase it compulsorily and resell it to the developer, disputes dragged on for years. Furthermore, developers usually found loopholes not to pay any outstanding balances on the value of the land once developed. It was an impasse of vast proportions. Such tardiness was never more evident twenty years later as my young friends the Beatles were posing for their first major publicity shots with the Liverpool-based Peter Kaye studios in 1962. Both the pre-war dereliction and Nazi destruction of 1941 were still part of this photographed Liverpool landscape: a city neglected.

Following our move back to inner-city Everton, I was unable to continue my schooling, and left six months earlier than normal. This didn't bother me in the slightest. I was not a great student, had few pretensions to be, and my mind was always full of schemes to avoid going to school. The only thing that had kept me as a regular attendee in Huyton was a sense of duty towards my brother Gerard. Mother had refused to send him to a special school, and had argued very stridently that he would improve in a classroom full of average kids. This was an interesting strategy from my mother and basically meant that Gerard became my responsibility during term time. I did this without bearing any grudge or malice. I loved my brother and felt duly responsible. In actual fact, mother's ideas worked very well, for although Gerard could never be a normal student (whatever that is), he was able to respond well in a classroom situation and, after leaving shortly before myself, remained in full employment for the rest of his working life. In fact he turned into a very useful craftsman. I had to keep an eye on him, of course, but he became a great woodworker and an excellent sander. It just goes to show that everybody is good at something. I've always been immensely proud of him. So, on the one hand, I was delighted to leave school, but on the other my imminent adulthood meant that I was also expected to begin an apprenticeship with my father at his workshop in Kempston Street. There was no choice: it was accepted that I do this. He was a small-time businessman and had to face the hazards of local conditions. Father was no doubt acutely aware that during the Labour government of 1945–51 he would be subject to what he saw as regulatory 'interference' from a socialist government. It was safe to assume that getting as much out of one's offspring as possible was de rigueur. He was also aware, I think, that he was part of a growing urban business milieu and that such environments tended to create an attentive entrepreneurial type – and there was money to be made. With the notable exception of Gerard, I was regarded as son number one, expected to follow in the old man's footsteps. The problem was, from what I could see, I'd have to become a right shit to do that!

2

IVOR NOVELLO'S POODLES

DE-CAMP BACK TO Everton from Huyton at the end of the war brought about a realisation from mother that she either had to raise her own capital or else go with a begging bowl to father. She still loved him, probably, but she would not be beholden to him for anything she felt she might be able to handle herself or indeed spend any time with him longer than was absolutely necessary. So, Aggie Flannery began to consider moving back into business herself. There were hierarchies of thought at play here. My mother was astute and tended to use at least two types of logic to sort out these recurrent dilemmas. She would usually begin with more general observations of her situation and would arrive at equally wide-ranging conclusions. For example, I recall her saying to me that she would not take a specific instance of kindness from my father as an indication of hope. The usual truth of the matter was that he was, for the most part, horrible to her, so from such everyday experiences derived her general truths. From such generalities she would then deduce the specifics: she also used to say to me 'if the doorbell doesn't ring it usually means that the battery is dead', from which I would infer that it was no use pursuing other alternatives until one discovered whether the battery was in fact dead. In the case of her marriage, she and I presumed the battery was indeed dead; so based on such logic, and for the sake of her children, she would deduce solutions to her problems.

The furniture outlet had proved to be a moderate success before the war. It fed us while father was 'buying a brewery', as Cilla Black might have later sung (*Liverpool Lullaby*), and so it was only natural that she should turn to this once again in order to feed and clothe her kids. In addition to such pragmatic thoughts, she had been bitten by the bug of business which one just has to scratch every once in a while. I still get this itch and I'm sure that many would say the same. So, after settling back into life in Everton, mother began to show interest in a former shop premises that had taken a direct hit from a German land mine. The entire building had been blown out, leaving a skeletal frame that looked eerie and ghostly against the Everton skyline. Local children would explore the debris and were constantly warned about the hazards of playing in this dangerous area – all to no avail, of course. The fact that a family had been literally blown to pieces where we played had little to no effect on the kids whatsoever, except to increase their morbid curiosity. Mother was also fascinated by this site, however, and we could detect from the glint in her eye that she had decided to act. She was warned away by most locals. Yes, there might be potential there, but the finances required to refurbish would be astronomical. Father, of course, discouraged the whole project for he wanted mother to be tied to the kitchen sink for as long as possible.

Nevertheless, unbowed and certainly undaunted, mother began to make tentative enquiries about the bombsite that stood on the corner of Luxmore Road and City Road. After much scouring of the local press and libraries, she discovered that the property was freehold and after further local enquiries that the then owners wanted nothing to do with it, owing to its advanced state of dilapidation. But these property owners had missed a trick: in 1946 mother approached local public authorities with the idea of rebuilding the property. The new Labour government had appointed Aneurin Bevan as Minister of Health, with a remit that also covered repairing and expanding the woeful housing stock. The responsibility for instituting a new and comprehensive National Health Service was complemented by proactively tackling the country's severe post-war housing shortage. Bevan handed over funding and responsibility for these urgent repairs to the local authorities. I'm not sure these days of its proper title but I seem to recall something we described as 'War Damage Funding' being made available for rebuilding; it was based on the proviso that commercial use was guaranteed and that the owner would occupy the premises. Upon a promissory note stating that the shop would indeed open for business, mother managed to obtain a small mortgage on the building to buy out the previous owners. Within a matter of weeks, work had begun (costing mother next to nothing) and within months she had begun to trade: bedding, furniture and fancy goods, as well as a few essential lines. Ever the resourceful one, she soon began to turn a profit, clothing and feeding us from her own pockets without having to rely upon 'his nibs' for anything.

Following the immediate success of the shop at 90 City Road, our house at 17 Luxmore Road had to be placed on the market. The Luftwaffe had ensured that property was in short supply and absentee landlords were on the prowl looking for a quick buck. Mother decided that she wanted a family to move into our old home and was pleasantly surprised that an old school friend eventually seemingly came to live there. It was only a matter of weeks, however, before mother discovered to her horror that she had been had and that this old friend had been acting as a fence for an unscrupulous local agent. She had inadvertently allowed the property to be taken into the hands of an absentee landlord and never forgave herself. This sort of opportunism became common practice all over Liverpool during the 1940s, not the least in the Toxteth/Liverpool 8 district where most of Liverpool's black community were at first bombed out of Pitt Street, moved to the Myrtle Street area, only for the University of Liverpool to evict them forcibly in the 1940s in order to expand: we were all shocked at such discoveries. After all, wasn't this the 'new Jerusalem' that so many people had fought and died for? We were discovering in no uncertain terms that the immediate post-war period was one of utopian optimism, yes, but mixed with considerable monetarist backsliding; it seemed that Jerusalem would have to wait. No wonder the dual arrival of Bessie Braddock and Margaret Simey, those immensely strong local female politicians, seemed a genuine attempt to bring Liverpool out of the Dark Ages, politically. By the immediate post-Second World War era Agnes Flannery, spurred on by Braddock and Simey, had also become a very independent and free-thinking woman.

One example illustrates this well: in acts of both contrariness and good business acumen, she refused to sell almost anything that was made by my father's factory. It made good business sense, for my father's goods were now becoming very mass-produced, up-market items aimed at the new middle classes colonising Liverpool's suburbs (but not the inner city areas such as City Road). The Epsteins purchased more and more of father's furniture to sell at their store in Walton Road during the 1940s. Epstein's shop was situated in Everton, but was dealing almost exclusively with the new growing suburbs and, as a family, we were once again beginning to see a little of them now they had albeit briefly returned to the area.

Queenie Epstein and my mother began to get to know each other once again, but to tell the truth, Queenie found that the locals of Everton were a little beneath her. Following the end of the war, the Epsteins had a lovely house to return to overlooking Stanley Park, near to the Anfield Road end of Liverpool Football Club's stadium. However, by the late 1940s, they took little time in removing themselves to the leafy suburbia of Queens Drive in south Liverpool. Not that there was anything wrong with this, you understand, but Queenie in particular seemed to find the early Edwardian suburban districts such as Anfield, Walton and Everton perhaps just a bit too plebeian (and old fashioned) for words. Mother found this outlook rather aggravating and eventually had little time for the woman (in addition to the fact that she was still unwilling to pay any of Harry's furniture bills to my father on time).

Queenie did like to spend her Wednesday afternoons (the half-day holiday in Liverpool) in the local picture house on Walton Road, however. The Astoria Cinema building in Everton has long since vanished, but it was here that she would often take the young Brian to a matinee. Brian and I were beginning to get reacquainted as well, and he would occasionally invite me along. Even at this young age we were both aware of parallel traits and, despite the two-year age difference, began to get on quite well (perhaps like all children at times we merely suffered one another, but there was something there from the beginning). There was a very special relationship between Brian and his mother, however, and word soon got back to me that even though Brian wanted me to be there, his mother most certainly did not. I was Mr and Mrs Flannery's son: a gentile and rather low class as far as Queenie was concerned, and so I was never privy to these special treats (I was working in any case).

Brian and I were in our early to mid-teens by this time but living in largely different worlds that might occasionally collide. Nevertheless we recognised some kind of bond between the two of us, but our friendship was beginning to grow when it was acutely disrupted. It was about this time, the mid to late 1940s, as I recall, that Brian was having a particularly unhappy time at a school in Aigburth, Liverpool: the Wellesley school. Having discovered he was being bullied, Harry and Queenie decided that Brian was to be sent away to a Jewish boarding school in Sussex. Mother and I were suitably horrified: how could anyone simply pack off their children in this way, especially at such a difficult time in the boy's life and to what seemed like a secluded school hundreds of miles away? But, of course, the situation the Epsteins found themselves in must have been complex, to say the least. Brian was a very delicate child; by his teenage years he was also in a great deal of mental turmoil about his differences from other children. On the surface his parents perhaps presumed that his unhappiness was caused by his Jewishness, and that it was this that led to the inevitable bullying; but surely they must have also suspected that this particular sense of self was simply one strand of a far more complex web of identity-giving signifiers.

Even though Liverpool has always been a great melting pot of culture, this has never prevented the city from also containing and condoning elements of racism. And even in the post-Holocaust climate of the 1940s, being a middle-class Jewish schoolboy frequently meant having to endure a great deal of bullying and taunting from gentile contemporaries – hence, perhaps, the need for the King David grammar school by the 1960s. So, for Harry and Queenie it is perhaps understandable that they thought a period of time spent away at an exclusive Jewish boarding school might have delivered a lesson about identity together with a hardening-up process. These days this all seems a terribly hard step to take; however, we must remember that the Epsteins were not alone in thinking this way. In Liverpool a young boy, of any religious persuasion or ethnicity, if he aspired to be a 'real' man, had to develop this gist of masculinity at a pretty early stage or else suffer the consequences. Brian would later inform me that as a youth he was constantly troubled because even at a relatively young age he instinctively realised there was a deeper underlying reason for his demeanour; something that could never be toughened out of him. He recalled to me how deeply unhappy he was at being unable to make friends at Wellesley school and how he was also unable to explain to his mother and father just how he felt. He once told me that standing up to the boys at school calling him a 'yid' was actually less of a problem than being attracted to one of those conducting the bullying. I sympathised and identified with this dilemma. We were both young males who had yet to realise or at least fully come to terms with sexuality. Believe me, it can be a tortuous experience – especially within that cultural environment of post-Second World War Britain. One day my own father casually informed me that he thought that all 'queers' should be lined up against a wall and shot. According to my father, queers behaved the way they did because they were perverts. Even by the time I had come to terms with my own sexuality never a word was ever spoken about it between mother and myself; as time went on she probably knew. Whatever the case, at this stage she thoroughly disapproved of the Epsteins' treatment of their eldest son.

As for myself, I recall being very sorry for him and thinking that I would miss our occasional meeting. But I never really refracted any of this into any personal significance. It was only later that I came to question my own mien, a little.

Although there is a great deal to feel nostalgic about regarding these days of innocence, it would be wrong of me to develop a sense of overblown nostalgia about a period of the twentieth century when it was considered rude to discuss sex, wrong to have sex, and both illegal and perverted to love somebody of the same sex. It can be seen quite clearly that the repression of homosexuality was in fact a crime in itself, and tantamount to slavery of the worst kind: slavery to a system which refused to acknowledge the potential of the individual; slavery to a system which refused to consider that one's body and one's psyche was one's own affair; slavery to the idea that a relationship with another human being was based upon the stylistics of marriage. Nostalgia is, indeed, disingenuous. Nostalgia creates gross over-simplifications. I cannot get nostalgic over a period of time when I neither understood myself nor the reasons why my young friend was vilified for being 'different'.

But back to business: by the end of the seemingly endless 1940s Flannery's shop on City Road had become renowned for its bargains and its good quality, second-hand furniture. Hartley's Auction Rooms was mother's main source of supply and, via her Everton shop, she had identified a niche in the market. The terrible poverty that had blighted so many people's lives after the Wall Street Crash of 1929 right up to the outbreak of the war was now consigned to history, and although certain Liverpudlians continued to endure a poverty trap in those immediate post-war years, unemployment had dropped considerably and there did appear to be a little more disposable income floating around. The pubs were doing well, the two football clubs and dance halls too; young people appeared to be looking for new forms of entertainment and there were just enough pennies to cover the costs of such extras. There was a little more to spend on home improvements, too, and Flannery's was the place to go. Everton was still a largely deprived area, mind you, but items such as quality second-hand furniture could certainly be sold there in the late-1940s, whereas before the war one might as well just chop it up for firewood – according to my mother 'it was the sticks that sold in those pre-war days, not the good stuff'.

Hartley's always had a line of horses and carts outside of their sale-room, on which they would deliver sales from their auctions, and I have fond memories of these carts arriving at City Road when a sale had been arranged. A new delivery of second-hand furniture for the shop was quite an event, and I would, naturally, be looking for a few bits and pieces for my bedroom: 'Oh, that looks nice, mother, can I use that until somebody wants to buy it?' I would declare, to which mother might say, 'Joseph, how do you expect anybody to buy it when it's stuck up in your bedroom?' 'Exactly,' I would whisper to myself under my breath. So for that short time before we had moved from our Luxmore Road home to 'over the shop' there was a constant two-way stream of furniture, bedding and ornament traffic between our house and mother's shop. Shop stock would go missing, only to be found in my room and equally items would often vanish from the house only to be discovered in the shop, sporting a 'sold' ticket. Brass knick-knacks, starched tablecloths, small offcuts of carpet, even pieces of brightly coloured linoleum might be removed from our living room to be sold in the shop. It was a battle of wits in which mother would always say: 'It all comes around again, don't worry. We'll get a better one. The cash will come in handy, and we'll see something else at the auctions.' Finally the inevitable happened: one evening we were having dinner when mother came in declaring that somebody desperately needed a dining table. We were all told to lift our plates while mother removed the tablecloth and the table was duly carted away, sold from underneath us. Eating from one's knees took on different connotations in the Flannery household.

Following the arrivals from the salesrooms, the best part of the evening was usually taken up by mother, Gerard and I setting to work, polishing the stock for display. After a day's work in my father's Kempston Street workshop the lovely smell of lavender polish would fill the air around us, mingling with the sweet sounds coming from the radio as we three would polish away to our heart's content. We had to tell Gerard when to stop, otherwise he would have carried on throughout the night, but with the old man out of the way we were all in heaven. That smell, plus the splendid tintinnabulations of Ted Heath and his band blasting away will never leave me. There are special relationships our memories have with music. Some simply define it as nostalgia for a bygone age, but it is much more than that. The sound of music in the air has such an important effect upon the listener; it can make ordinary memories seem so special and stand out over others apparently more momentous. Simple everyday incidents, when connected through music, can take on enormous significance. Those moments in the shop were galvanised by the sounds drifting out of the radio – the primary medium of the day, no doubt about it. I will never forget just how important music has been in my life and to this day I constantly remind myself how it has contributed to my entire world view.

When the so-called post-war affluence began to rest on debt I'm not very sure, but in the fullness of time it surely did. My first recollections of this are the arrival of the great catalogues to our area: Great Universal Stores, Littlewoods, Empire Stores. Catalogues had been in existence far earlier, of course – after all Sears, Roebuck & Co. helped to build the Wild West – but the appearance of credit-based catalogues in the Everton, Anfield and Walton areas of Liverpool, allowing ordinary working-class people to buy goods on the never-never (and for locals to become agents and earn commission) was noteworthy. The Littlewoods business empire was Liverpool based and run by Mancunian John Moores, who had also established and made a million from the Littlewoods Football Pool in the 1920s. In 1932 Moores started up the Littlewoods Mail Order Store and this was followed by several department stores. But as I recall it was not really until the post-Second World War era that mail order catalogues came to make an impact right across the class and employment spectrum in north Liverpool. Home shoppers came to spot bargains in the catalogues and even though the quality might be lacking, probably because some materials were in short supply in the 1940s, conditions became favourable for all kinds of mail order operations. In addition to the catalogue revolution of the post-war era, I also distinctly remember the arrival of that other great boon to mankind: Formica – that plastic veneer that revolutionised home improvements forever! Both catalogues and Formica seemed to arrive at roughly the same time to me, and both were slavishly snapped up by the locals. Formica was marketed as a new, clean product, and anything new at this time also began to mean preferable. 'New' began to replace words such as 'good' or 'best' and also became an antithesis to second hand, so even the good people of Everton were a little coerced into believing that if something was a. new, b. cheap and c. available on H.P. it was highly preferable to a. second hand, b. quality and c. available for cash only.

The 1950s witnessed the growth of decorative laminates such as Formica, first popular in the United States where they were used widely in espresso bars and dinettes – how very exciting, I thought, as I leafed through the latest US paper or magazine brought back to Liverpool by the local 'Cunard Yank'. At the same time, a machine for moulding an extremely toxic melamine formaldehyde resin was delivered to my father's yard as he too recognised that such materials were becoming widely used as components in plastic veneering. I saw from second- and third-hand copies of US and Canadian papers that even plastic tableware had become popular alternatives to china; it was all quite amazing, and I was fascinated by all of these new materials and designs. In retrospect it could be argued that these were rather shoddy and disposable goods based on the ideology of all things new, but at the time I loved the colours, the designs and the feelings of the future stimulated by such products; many are now considered highly collectible retro items. Naturally not everything new was of a poor quality (rock 'n' roll immediately springs to mind) and such items, ways of purchasing and the like came to indicate change: change came to challenge austerity; change invaded most people's thoughts. The mechanisation of plastics meant that a great deal was gained, but I think in the long run a great deal was also lost in regards to craftsmanship. My mother certainly had to rethink a little about her stock in trade, that's for sure. Of course, PVC really took off during the 1950s. By the early to mid-1950s it could be used, for example, to make records – how marvellous! Mother never really dealt in records and those that did come into the shop from perhaps the occasional house clearance were usually shellac 78s and were promptly snaffled by myself before my mother could move them on, as it were. But the PVC discovery was particularly well timed considering the boom of the popular music industry in this era. Notwithstanding records, Flannery's Stores began to deal in these quasi-luxury items and, once again, profit from that trading. Travellers would be lining up, vying for business. Mother would treat them all to a cup of tea and then inspect their lines, as they were called. Men who were representing companies from seemingly all over the world would attempt to sell anything from pairs of plastic maracas to fish-shaped vases; from cheap toys to sticky-backed plastic. All were attempting to cash in on the new-found relative (or perhaps illusory) affluence of the working classes.

Agnes Flannery was always on the ball as far as such changes were concerned and she, albeit rather reluctantly, began to stock the new plastic-based goods in order to combat the onwards march of catalogue shopping. It was a good move and predictably the items sold very well, especially when she also bit the bullet and set in motion credit facilities. She not only operated a tontine, but also dealt with the Provident Loans Company and the locally based Frost Loan Company. With austerity giving way somewhat by 1950, fancy goods began to move very quickly. Income that was previously used for furniture was now being temporarily withheld by customers because they were able to purchase items on credit, leaving the locals with even more disposable income in their pockets. Notwithstanding this small involvement in the credit revolution, mother never encouraged her children to take advantage of this new system, emphasising that it was really just spending money that one did not actually have. Many people began to purchase small ornaments for the home: daft little things like vases, china dogs, egg timers, plastic flowers and the like, alongside cheap dress jewellery and Hong Kong-manufactured plastic toys for the kids at Christmas time. Many such items were put away by mother in the storeroom until Christmas and she worked her magic via her tontine club. Items were kept in the store after a small deposit was handed over, after which small weekly amounts would be paid into the tontine by the customer. Most customers would try to overpay for their purchases so that a little money might be left on hand; this could be taken out as a cash bonus closer to Christmas.

Furniture sales had changed dramatically by the beginning of the new decade and were increasingly based around what we might describe as 'occasional' items. Basically, this was an expression used for describing furniture that served very little useful purpose other than to adorn an otherwise rather staid parlour or bedroom. Working-class pragmatics of previous generations concerning house adornments were being phased out for the sake of aspiration, and having time and funds for anything vaguely occasional was likely an uplifting experience for many. To be able to afford a little luxury item was to contribute gradually to the altering of ideas about values. Britain had a long way to go to catch up with the kind of mass-consumption economy we could see coming from America, but these were the early shoots. As the old declined so the new emerged: electrical goods and petrochemicals were here to stay in the shape of radios, record players and fridges; vinyl, nylons and plastics.

Father, meanwhile, was also a very instinctive business instigator, of that there was little doubt. The immediate post-war period was a good one for him, financially and socially, and it must have been satisfying for him as a Flannery to move up both the business and social ladders. His businesses certainly prospered and I suppose that we, as a family, also fared reasonably well – but we never really knew one way or another. A genuine wanderlust fuelled his selfishness and we were left in no doubt that his first priority was himself. Of course we were not left starving on the street, you understand, but if things were going so well, why were we always relying on mother's income? If father was prospering, why weren't we? The answer was gradually becoming obvious to me. I was now 15 years of age and I could plainly see that whoring and drinking, together with not a little gambling, effortlessly ate into a great deal of time and money – it also began to eat into my dwindling respect for him.

Just prior to my joining him in the workshop, however, he pleased me greatly one day by turning up at our latest home in Everton with a new-fangled van. We children were simply amazed – decidedly chuffed – for all vehicles were in short supply just after the war. Those vans that were being manufactured mostly went for export (Britain exported more vehicles than the USA at that time), so for a family in Everton to have their own means of transport was quite the thing. Mother, on the other hand, saw the arrival of this ex-Liverpool Echo delivery van a little less enthusiastically. As we were all leaping about in celebration, she continued to dry the dishes, declaring under her breath her memories of father's pre-war mobile sojourns: 'Four wheels again … we'll never see him now.'

This was a mantra that in her more contemplative moments some years later I would often hear repeated, as if this came to be a particularly seminal moment in their fracturing relationship. She was perfectly correct, and in due course father's four wheels indeed signalled an even greater expression of personal freedom for him than mother had previously known and their partnership further dissolved accordingly. For the meantime, however, we were all offered a run in the red 10cwt Morris Commercial. Mother naturally declined, but we kids piled into the back, picked up our friends Alfie and Tony Rice from the corner of the street, and were soon popping along the East Lancashire Road at the speed of light – well, 25mph, at any rate. The drive became very exciting at one point when we suddenly veered off into the car park of the Cherry Tree public house. Father parked the van and promptly waltzed into the pub for a few pints. Initially rather lost for words, we kids were then provided with a packet of crisps and a bottle of pop each while the by now struggling engine cooled off a little. Father, however, was heating up as quickly as the little Morris side-valve engine was cooling down. After about half an hour he emerged from the Cherry Tree only to notice a trade union strike meeting being held in the pub car park. Mixing his anti-Labour sentiments with probably four pints of best bitter and a couple of Scotch chasers, he soon began hurling verbal abuse at the trades unionists gathered around their shop steward.

What began as good-natured banter soon deteriorated into heated abuse: father calling them 'Commie bastards, leeches', and the like. I must admit that I have never subscribed to his form of politics; more often than not the only weapon that working-class men had in the Liverpool of the 1940s was the strike. Nevertheless, it started to get more than a little frightening when the van's engine, which was probably still a little overheated, would not fire up, and the crowd of angry, baying men gravitated towards us. Father reached for the starting handle, and we all thought that blood and guts were going to be spilt. However, in our innocence we failed to appreciate that the starting handle was actually for starting an engine rather than hitting people, and as he gave the front of the van another quick tug the engine flew into life. Just as we were about to be set upon, our former Echo delivery van lurched away into the sunset, and we were safe. I was excruciatingly embarrassed but this was moderated somewhat as we sped off back towards Liverpool, singing at the tops of our voices: 'We're off, we're off, we're off in a little red van, 50 Dockers are after us and they'll kill us if they can!'

Although I was full of trepidation about starting an apprenticeship with the old man, I was quite excited about the prospect of working with wood as my just-so tendencies were drawing me towards joinery and carpentry. While father was away from the workshop everything was fine and I found the job enjoyable and the camaraderie excellent, but when he was present the atmosphere would change; in truth things were very bad between us. I was also trying to keep my eye on Gerard and look after him. For example, I would carry a teaspoon with me at all times – something to flatten his tongue and keep his airways exposed just in case he suffered from a fit while at work. He had started at the workshop a little before me and had been given a variety of mostly menial tasks to do. Some jobs Gerard would cope with and enjoy: as for more complex work involving different tasks, he could not cope. One morning I found Gerard in a flood of tears and I accused my father of taxing and then teasing my brother to breaking point. To be challenged like this in front of his workforce was far too much for the man's inflated ego and the next minute I found myself covered with boiling hot Croydex wood glue – you might remember the sort, horrible smell, made from fish and animal bones and kept liquid in an electrically heated woodworker's pot. I screamed in pain and ran from the building trying in vain to remove the rapidly solidifying glue from my skin. Mrs Riley, a wise and good woman who lived across from the Kempston Street yard, helped to bathe my skin and soothe me; she even wanted to call the police. Eventually I ended up back at home, where my ever-rational mother calmed me further and repaired my external wounds. There was nothing she could do about the internal ones, however, and from that moment on a war of attrition between my father and myself cemented, and was only resolved some years later when I decided for the sake of my mother to move away from the family home.

In spite of constant battles with my father, I rapidly became an accomplished veneer joiner during my time at Kempston Street. I simply enjoyed the basic creativity of the work. I think father purchased all of his new wood stock from the local supplier Letherens, but quantities of reclaimed and demolition wood were constantly appearing: for example, the parts of a mahogany staircase from Blackler's Department Store which survived a German incendiary bomb. From Supermarine in Barrow were purchased wood fittings from scrapped navy submarines. Father rented a small shop on Great Homer Street and stocked it with such surplus ex-Royal Navy wood fittings that could not be reprocessed, making a packet in the process. My greatest pleasure was in seeing finished articles from these reclamations move out of the yard to the retail shops, such as those owned by the Epsteins. Even to this day I can still occasionally recognise a piece of my own work when I see it. Gerard, too, was becoming something of a craftsman. His work with walnut veneer was very artistic and he would bevel and shape wood quite beautifully. But in my mind's eye I could see that my father had essentially written off both of us. Gerard for being somehow substandard by father's specifications and me for being, well, just me, I suppose: my mother's son. So nothing either of us could do would ever please him. I was a constant reminder to him that he had responsibilities – a family, a home – and, as I have previously suggested, these were very painful mnemonics for a man who appeared to want none of these things in his desperation to rise through Liverpool's entrepreneurial ranks. The city has much to thank entrepreneurs for, but my father's selfish, perhaps almost obsessive, behaviour gave neither himself nor his beliefs any credit. He would particularly like to antagonise me and insult my intelligence by sending me on message runs to one of his many women.

For example, on one occasion he sent me to a local, private dwelling with a message in a sealed envelope. When I arrived a voluptuous blonde was there to meet me. It was quite obvious that this woman was one of father's mistresses. She was acutely embarrassed, but opened the letter in front of me and read the contents. In an attempt to break the ice she casually said to me: 'Well, Joseph, you are certainly a good looking boy, just like your father.' 'How dare she?' I thought. This was probably one of the worst insults that I had thus far endured, being compared to my father by one of his fancy women! Even though her comments were simply small talk

I could not stand it and retorted, 'No I'm not like my father at all, thank you very much ... don't ever say that I'm like him. I'll never be like him. I have four brothers and one sister and we're all like our mother!'

My diatribe contained not a jot of bad language and I was never one to blaspheme in those days, but what followed was familiar, for I ran. I always ran. I ran for what seemed like an age, and eventually ended up back home. Mother could see that I was upset, deeply hurt, and she also realised who was to blame, but I spared her the gory details. I later discovered that, shortly after this event, father had unceremoniously dumped the blonde for being indiscreet, just like he dumped everybody else in his personal life. I felt curiously sympathetic towards her; after all, hadn't she also trusted him? What a mug she must have felt (just like his own family, I thought). Some years later, on a return visit from my National Service, I was feeling rather magnanimous and so I decided to give him one last chance. He had been reasonably pleasant to me over the weekend and the atmosphere had improved. I wanted him to like me and I would probably have forgiven him anything, if I could only have gained his confidence. It was at the time that Eddie Calvert, 'the Man with the Golden Trumpet', was riding high on the British and American playlists with *Oh mein Papa*; this, I think, would have been 1954. Full of good thoughts, I purchased the record and gave it to him on the Sunday before my return to camp. He evidently didn't like my taste in music for he promptly broke it over my head. I didn't think it was that bad a number! Those 78s were rather brittle affairs: just like my relationship with my father.

By the time I had reached the age of 17, in 1948, I had become a regular performer, of sorts. It was all on a strictly amateur basis, but my confidence was growing tremendously through being regularly asked to sing at the impromptu get-togethers in the Parrot pub on Scotland Road. Those of us who were old enough would fill the tables in the parlour to listen to each other sing or recite, or whatever took one's fancy. It was discovered that I actually had a rather appealing voice (although not to my father: he would usually go to the bar and cringe in disgust and embarrassment). So, although I wasn't really old enough to be in the Parrot in the first place (21 being the age limit in those days), the landlord turned a blind eye; after all, it was good for business in these pre-jukebox days. Mother would be surrounded by her family on these occasions and was clearly in her element. Uncle Henry, Auntie Liza, and cousins Mary and Mick on the banjo would all be there, as well as the Whites from Taliesin Street, and we would rattle through some of the great classics of the day. *The Gypsy, Apple*

Blossom Time, Back in Your Own Backyard, My Yiddish Momma and two of mother's favourites, *One of These Days* and *Margie*, all became part of my growing repertoire as I found that a few people expressed an interest in hearing me sing. Even the kids outside the pub would listen attentively to the songs and occasionally join in or applaud from the street. After being informed by my own father that I was basically a waste of space, this all came as a very pleasant surprise to me and I came to dream, as I had done as a child in Huyton, about the possibilities of show business.

In addition to this, I was getting very brave and actually making regular visits to that great Liverpool institution (and in those days one of the best dance halls in the country) The Grafton Rooms on West Derby Road. I was a pretty good dancer and at the Grafton never found myself without a partner for too long. I also ventured into Liverpool city centre on the odd occasion and came to discover the delights of a new genre of music that was gathering something of a cult following in Liverpool, namely country and western. I had never previously heard much of this strange-sounding stuff, other than by watching some of the singing cowboys on the silver screen (guys like Roy Rogers, Tex Ritter and the Sons of the Pioneers) and I discovered a liking for a little-known singer (at least to me) named Hank Williams. I distinctly remember listening to a couple of singers in a pub behind the old Liverpool Market – an area that I was later to frequent – called the Duck House, knocking out an odd song called *Move It On Over*. It was a really different style of music altogether, very spartan, stripped down, lean-sounding; I thought it was one of the wildest things that I had ever heard, and I loved it.

I was also in this pub under false pretences, but alongside my older cousin Peter I was generally ignored. The pub was often full of Yanks from the Burtonwood Airbase near Warrington, and I thought the whole scene was terrific; some of them even came back home with us, along with their female appendages. We would talk at some length, and they might tell me romantically of all the exciting places they came from: New York, Los Angeles, Denver in Colorado, Chicago, Detroit and Memphis in Tennessee – all names that seemed very quixotic to me and the differing accents of the men were alluring to say the least. Eventually they would be unceremoniously turfed out of the house when mother caught a couple trying to head off into the sunset of an upstairs bedroom, but despite these little embarrassments we all became firm friends in the months that followed. I was also to discover, that first night in the Duck House, the occasional merchant seamen returned from their trips to the Unites States with a few country and western discs. These were the 'Cunard Yanks' of Liverpool's post-war history and although they were later incorrectly cited as greatly assisting the growth of the Merseybeat scene, my memories of them were from these pre-rock 'n' roll days, and more associated with records by the likes of Hank Snow and Jimmy Rodgers rather than Elvis Presley and Chuck Berry.

However, these growing interests in music genres, film and theatre further ruffled my father's feathers. Once again he saw, I think, something decidedly 'unmanly' in his son. He would have preferred a drinking, womanising 'lad', but instead got a rather effete but musically inclined boy. Even when I actually made him a great deal of money by suggesting that we turn a lot of waste wood into small children's toys for Christmas, he found this somewhat 'girlie', despite enjoying the profits. The aforementioned developing market economy of the late 1940s greatly assisted his cash flow as first T.J. Hughes and then Owen Owens in Liverpool placed firm orders for small wooden cars, rocking horses and jewellery boxes. This perpetual lack of acknowledgement, coupled with my father's increasingly aggressive disposition on the very few occasions when he actually graced us with his presence of an evening, plus my own hormonal changes as a teenager (a new expression that came to be coined about this time), increased my own potential for rebellion. Although I actually enjoyed the work, I knew that a Mexican stand-off had been reached between my father and me. The workshop was now too small for the pair of us, and I began to make plans to get away. My younger brother Chris and my cousin Peter, who was also my best friend after the young Brian Epstein had left the area, joined the Merchant Navy and had started sending letters home, telling (probably tall tales) of exotic climes and gorgeous women.

The main priority for my young self was to get away from father as soon as possible. I visited the Merchant Navy recruitment offices and informed them of my desires to be a waiter – preferably silver service. In my mind I had decided that if I wanted to move amongst the rich and famous – movie stars, singers and the like – then my best opportunity was to be seen amongst them. After their laughter had subsided I was curtly informed that I was too young and was told to go away and 'get some experience'. One could see their point: was there ever a less experienced, more naive Liverpudlian in the entire history of the city? On my way out of the recruitment office I was told that if I applied for a job at Liverpool's premier hotel, the Adelphi, I could then apply to be listed on a pool which would give preference to those who had already worked at good standard hotels.

This sounded like just the thing. After an extremely stringent round of interviews, which involved discussing the merits and demerits of certain types of knives and forks and correctly folded sheets, I was accepted on to the panel at the Adelphi Hotel. I was dispatched to the local tailors in order to buy my cardboard shirt fronts with the fly-away collars and then told to report for duty as a commis waiter. I was given the dubious pleasure of serving the 'nobs' with their bread rolls. I didn't care – I was now going to be in direct touch with not only the stars of the silver screen who might periodically stay at the hotel, but also the lords and ladies of the country. They were bound to be different, weren't they?

Prior to my first day at the Adelphi, I received a letter from the hotel which astounded me. I was given the opportunity, out of all the new recruits, to serve a six-month apprenticeship at the Caledonian Hotel, Edinburgh, which also included duties at none other than Holyrood Palace. At first I thought that it was a wind-up, that I was the subject of a witty initiation ceremony, but sure enough, after hurriedly making my way over to the Adelphi, I was informed that the letter was indeed correct, that I had shown myself to be the perfect type for such an engagement, and that I was to travel immediately to Scotland. I was delighted; mother laughed her head off! I don't think she believed me even as I boarded the newly nationalised British Rail train for Scotland, but it was strangely true. However, after all that fuss it was something of a let-down, to say the least. Apart from actually serving the then queen, our now dear departed Queen Mother, with her breakfast – which was a great thrill for me – I spent one of the most uneventful periods of my life in Edinburgh. As beautiful as the city was, I was rather isolated and apart from the ageing staff, I was mostly alone rattling around an empty Caledonian Hotel for six whole months. It made me realise that I was truly a people person and that mixing with others was my forte, despite my father's displeasure and discouragement. So, somewhat chastened but having learnt a lot (especially about myself), I couldn't wait to get back to Liverpool. Maybe the authorities thought that if I could put up with six months of that then I could put up with anything. Whatever, I returned to the Adelphi desperate to meet some real people again.

I was more than delighted to be back on home territory, and cele-brated with a visit to the Grafton Ballroom. If I remember correctly, the Oscar Rabin Band was performing on the night of my return, and I won the dancing prize with a lovely bit of stuff from Wavertree called Olive. The work began in earnest at the Adelphi the following week, and sure enough, I found that I was placed in close proximity to several big stars, serving them their bread rolls and coffee. I remember meeting the then very young 'Nabob of Sob' himself, the late, great Johnnie Ray. He was perhaps on one of his very first tours of the UK. He took something of a liking to me and was a very generous tipper. It all seemed rather innocent until I was told by my fellow waiters that he had been prowling the dock road that evening, looking for young men. I must confess that I never felt the same way about him after that. Not long after the onset of my new career, I was informed by the head waiter, the phlegmatic Mr John Tournefant, that none other than Ivor Novello had personally requested that I attend to him in his room.

At first I was thrilled; I had absolutely no idea that he may have fancied me. This time I was given the nod by my friends at work about the possible scenario, and sheepishly asked Mr Tournefant if I could be excused. However, his reply was brusque: 'Do it, or lose your job.' I scuttled off to Mr Novello's suite in a confusion of delightful apprehension and paralytic fear. I knocked. 'Come in darling', was the articulate and effervescent reply. I opened the door and crept in. Mr Novello was waiting for me, and it was quite obvious, even to me, that he was very interested in getting to know me better. In fact, at one stage I found myself being backed into the bathroom, with only a couple of yapping poodles between the great man and myself. Seeing that I was literally going out of my mind with stress, Mr Novello's ardour began to diminish and he became rather contrite, taking pity on me. I was greatly relieved when he suddenly changed tack, informing me that I was to look after his poodles, one named Black, the other White, if my memory serves me correctly, while he was at the Empire Theatre, day or night, and that it was my responsibility to see that they were fed and taken for a walk. Phew! Anything was acceptable after what I took to be his other plans and so I readily agreed. Even the ignominious act of walking two miniature poodles around Liverpool city centre was preferable to what seemed like a fate worse than death.

Not surprisingly after that near miss, I could never really feel the same way about his music either; it was always a little middle brow for me, in any case. Some time later I read that he had eventually and unfortunately picked on the wrong guy and had been questioned by the Metropolitan Police for homosexual activities: poor man. These were very dangerous times. I remembered that he had been a somewhat overgenerous tipper, which, even in my innocence, suggested to me that he was far too free with his affections and affectations – an overt 'luvvy', to be sure. It was probably only a matter of time before somebody tried to compromise him or extort money or favours from him. The tips gave the game away, really, but as far as I was concerned these were the only advances that I would ever have admitted to, despite being scared shitless at the time. As strange as his behaviour had been, it didn't seem to me that it warranted insinuation, never mind criminal proceedings. There was so much misunderstanding in those days about male relationships as male affection, love even, was too readily substantiated as sexual deviancy.

I was looking for a level of excitement and, sure enough, I was getting it. I was young, naive and learning about life. Looking back I can see now that I was attracting a great deal of male attention because of my attitude and countenance, but I simply thought that this was the way to behave around famous people. Noel Coward even propositioned me over a bread roll, but I had to be quietly informed of the fact by my colleagues:

'Joe, you're just so innocent, don't you realise what Mr Coward has just asked you?'

'He just wanted to know whether I was busy this evening, that's all.'

'Joe, he said … "and what will you be doing with yourself this evening, young man … fancy joining us? Would you like a ticket for the Playhouse?" … that's not quite the same thing!'

'Oh. I don't quite get your [pause for thought]. Oh, I see what you mean …'

And so it went on. Basically, the seemingly esoteric nature of the signals meant that they failed to get through to me. God knows where my full sex education was to come from. I was practically innocence itself when I began working at the Adelphi, but I did gradually learn, painfully slowly, that the rich and famous have their weaker moments as much as, if not more than, most.

Not only were the internationally rich and famous eating at the Adelphi, it was very much a status symbol for the local middle and upper classes too. Often I would be serving prominent local business families or perhaps even the lord mayor and/or lady mayoress with bread rolls. I was on duty most Friday evenings, which was a very busy time for the Adelphi restaurant, for many middle- and upper middle-class non-residents would treat themselves to a meal perhaps before an evening's entertainment at the theatre or the pictures. I was always glad to be busy and enjoyed briefly discussing the latest movies and plays with the diners as they ate. It was at this regular Friday evening serving at about 6.15 p.m. that I once more bumped into the Epsteins. They began their Friday evening ritual of eating at the Adelphi before going to the theatre, and on the first such evening they discovered that their commis waiter was none other than Aggie Flannery's son, Joseph. Mrs Epstein was suitably unimpressed, although Harry seemed genuinely pleased to see me. Even more delighted, however, was a youthful but rather ashen-looking Brian. This must have been the very early months of 1950, the year I was to begin my National Service, for I believe that the family had finally given up on a private education for him and had brought him home to Liverpool to start working in the family business. I had heard on the grapevine that he had been attending a place called Wrekin College, but I had no idea exactly what or where this place was – another obscure, elitist establishment no doubt.

In between serving the Epsteins with their bread and coffee, and much to his mother's annoyance, Brian and I struck up a good friendship once again. I was amazed to discover that he was working only a short step away from our City Road home, in the Walton Road branch of Epstein Furniture, and we arranged to meet occasionally, going to the pictures or for a cup of tea, or even just to mooch around Crease's record shop on County Road. It was on these occasions that he would tell me of some of his experiences away at public school. He was a very unhappy boy, and even via my own state of innocence I could see that he was desperate to talk to somebody about himself. He was quite clearly very troubled about who he thought he was and, perhaps of equal importance to Brian, what other people thought of him. I could see that he needed a type of affection other than that which could be provided by his family. But where it was to come from, God alone knew. He reminded me somewhat of characters such as Mr Novello and I do believe that, as a consequence of my 'Novello incident', I was probably the first of his companions to at least question his sexuality, although I didn't quite understand the full consequences of this for I had no real understanding of sexuality at all, let alone that of the homosexual variety; let's face it, had I done so, I might have seen something of myself in this troubled youth.

Brian must have been about 16 by this time, but looked rather young and skinny for his age. I always felt terribly sorry for him, too, because he never looked very well and I always thought that he appeared to need a good dinner inside of him. He never consumed a great deal of food at the Adelphi and, in fact, I think the only real enjoyment he derived from that part of the evening was talking to me. While playing around with whatever was on his plate, he would avidly inform me of what performance he was going to see that evening, who was on in the forthcoming weeks and why he expected that evening to be a good or indifferent experience. Nine times out of ten he would be going to the Playhouse Theatre in the Queen's Square area of Liverpool. I remember informing him about the Duck House pub, which was in the vicinity of the Playhouse, and the country and western music that was played there.

He was immediately interested, although obviously too young to go himself. Brian displayed a total lack of knowledge about American country and western music and admitted that it was far from his favourite. He loved classical music, show songs and a little modern and traditional jazz, but he also stated to me on more than one occasion that he expected hillbilly music to be successful in Britain, given time. I found this quite amazing coming from a boy just out of public school – perhaps he had a pal or two interested in popular music? Probably not, for he was a loner. I eventually discovered that he was an avaricious reader of the British 'inkie' the *Melody Maker*. Thus far I had not really dipped into this British popular music weekly, so on his advice began to read (at least parts of) *Melody Maker* alongside my *ABC Film Review*. From what I recall neither the *New Musical Express* nor *Disc* were in print at this stage. This proved interesting for me for, at least up until that experience in the Duck House, I had been transfixed by show songs, big band crooners and ballads, and was ignorant of practically any other musical styles. It was clear to me that Brian and I had a connection; at this stage it was just something to talk about, I suppose.

Even though it could also at times be a little embarrassing, I enjoyed serving the Epsteins. It continued for a few months and I would look forward to my Fridays working in the Adelphi French restaurant. Queenie was forever the social animal and, although she found my scrupulous professional attention to detail at the table quite acceptable, she tended to look down upon me from her elevated social position. This proved a little disconcerting when she might deliberately interrupt a brief conversation between young Brian and me by asking for more coffee or tea in a thoroughly patronising tone. In that instant I was relegated from a position of equal with her son to one of servant or lackey. Still, used to the job as I was, this sort of behaviour was actually par for the course for the Adelphi and so I was able to let it ride. I've never been a vindictive person, in any case; not like many of my colleagues at the Adelphi, who would pour, spill and generally slop food all over those customers who attempted to pull any kind of social or at times military rank. There was actually a hit list in the kitchens of offending regulars, and I must admit that certain members of the Epstein family were occasionally placed upon it. No names, no pack drill, however!

This dining club relationship with Brian was eventually short-circuited by my own inherent stupidity, as my show business fantasies came to impinge upon my sense of reality. Donald O'Connor and Margaret O'Brien had arrived in town; I loved both of them. O'Connor was an American dancer, singer and actor who shot to fame in a series of movies in which he co-starred alternately with Gloria Jean, Peggy Ryan, and Francis the Talking Mule. But he was best known for his role a little later as Gene Kelly's sidekick Cosmo Brown in *Singin' in the Rain*. O'Brien was a child star turned serious actress and I had particularly liked her film from 1951 entitled *Her First Romance*. They were staying at the Adelphi, but were having all of their meals delivered to their suite, and on this occasion I hadn't been the lucky one to serve them. But I was still determined to see them. They were performing in Liverpool all week, but all the evening shows had been sold out months in advance. My only chance was to catch them at a matinee, but that meant playing hooky. In my child-like way I simply thought that it was just something I had to do. I phoned into work, informing Mr Tournefant that I had eaten a stale meat pie that had made me queasy and that I wouldn't be available that day. It all seemed harmless enough; after all, who doesn't do this sort of thing at the age of 19? I duly saw a wonderful show. My head was spinning; I was so enraptured with the performance. I made a mental note to tell young Brian the following week at our Friday night meeting, and sang my way back to Everton a very happy bunny indeed.

Reporting for duty the very next day I was ordered to the manager's office immediately on arrival. I was tersely informed that I had been seen at the Empire that afternoon by a member of the management and that my erroneous absenteeism constituted a sacking offence. I was sacked with immediate effect, and was also instructed to pick up the balance of my wages from the accounts office 'forthwith'. I was obliged to be off the premises within half an hour. I loved the job yet had screwed it up for myself through my own simplistic gullibility. Once again I returned home with my tail between my legs. I had really enjoyed the experience at the Adelphi, and I suppose that it was unfair to sack me without giving me a second chance; however, I had laid the trap for myself. My interest in all things theatrical had been my undoing and my fantasies had taken control.

If I was to get involved in some way in this fantastic business I would have to hold on to reality a little more; I had to be able to return to earth without such a devastating crunch. I decided to become more pragmatic, and it was around this time that I was given the chance to do a little bit of singing myself.

It soon came to pass that I discovered ways to get involved in showbiz that didn't involve being either chased around a bedroom by a composer and his two poodles or being sacked by an angry manager for eating mythological meat pies. For the time being, however, mother was not pleased. Father was titillated and demanded that I return to the workshop immediately. I ignored him and presumed, probably correctly, that he just wished to reconvene his glue-throwing competition – with me as the prime target. My memories of the Adelphi aftermath are of spending the following few weeks endlessly polishing our radiogram and playing all of my records one after another, trying to work out some sort of system for my life: something that involved music, dance and laughter. The occasional evenings out with my parents at the NUPO Club also took place at this time, and will be explained in due course, although I would have to say at this juncture that they were something of a lifesaver for me, for I was very depressed for most of the time.

What little money I had left from my wages was spent at Crane's and Rushworth & Draper's music shops on a host of 78 records. Occasionally I would discuss the purchases with my young friend Brian when I met him in the Walton Road area of town. But mostly I would take the records back to my room and play them all day. Mother would inevitably call me into the shop to help her. Not that she really needed any help, but simply because she could see that I was very low in spirits. I picked up all sorts of stuff on those old 78s, some of which had been deleted and were going for a 'tanner': Oscar Rabin, Steve Conway, Ted Heath, Dickie Valentine, Alma Cogan, even some Bob Wills records that were in the back of the deletion box, which reminded me of those country and western songs at the Duck House. All of these artists had suspended my grasp upon reality: they were my reality, and that was probably at the nexus of the crisis. I was saved from what appeared to be a fate worse than death for a young man – depression and boredom – by three important events: one, the first real relationship of my life; two, at least something of a part-time career in singing; and three, my papers to join His and then Her Majesty's Forces.

3

A DUTIFUL ENGAGEMENT AND NATIONAL SERVICE

THE GRAFTON ROOMS was an entertainment centre in Liverpool. The venue opened on 2 February 1924 as a purpose-built dance hall able to accommodate 1,200 dancers. It had a beautiful oak sprung dance floor and in its day played host to the best band leaders from Armstrong and Ellington to Loss and Sylvester. The Grafton became a real haunt for me, and it was here that I met the lovely Pat: that's Pat as in Patricia, by the way, not Pat as in Patrick. This Liverpool dance hall was one of the few regional venues that, by the early 1950s, still attracted some of the biggest bands in the country. Also, the resident band, led by Mrs Wilf Hamer, that brave and independent woman who led her husband's band after his sad and untimely death in the 1930s, was a very strong outfit and attracted a good deal of attention. By the late 1940s the most famous of the pre-war band leaders had decided to move on to rather safer areas of show business such as management and the scene began slowly to change. The likes of Ambrose, Jack Payne and Jack Hylton had become agents and impresarios, and the tours that proliferated before the war had ground to an abrupt halt after 1945. It was all becoming a rather expensive business for them, hawking a band around the country, especially if the venue was half empty by the time they got there (as was often the case, for by this time a younger population was looking for other musical soundtracks). In addition, age was simply catching up with some of these big names of the thirties and, with the death of Al Bowlly in 1941, there wasn't really a personality vocalist to speak of – or at least until Ted Heath brought his band together.

It was left largely to the regional bands to provide non-London music fans with entertainment.

This became something of a problem by the late 1940s, especially when the younger rough element, which had come to be called teddy boys, began to voice their disapproval of the musical fayre dished up by many rather substandard local bands. The Grafton, however, was very different. It still had tremendous pulling power, especially for ballroom and old-time dancing, and we were very lucky to be able to see all of the great bands in Liverpool after the war. They would even occasionally re-form just to play the Grafton. Of the newer outfits, my favourite had to be Ted Heath's fantastic big band, but Heath was not a regular visitor. Other smaller units such as Harry Gold's Pieces of Eight with Betty Driver as vocalist, George Webb's Dixielanders and the ubiquitous Joe Loss Orchestra all played the Grafton to packed houses. It was at the Grafton one Saturday night, dancing to Harry Gold and the great Grafton resident band of Mrs Wilf Hamer (the best band in Liverpool by a mile) that I met my future fiancée, Pat. I suppose that she was able to share that great sensory dance-hall experience that I loved so much, and this brought us together.

It was one of those evenings when you think that practically anything was possible, that you could easily transcend this world to another given half the chance. We both seemed to share that moment in some way, on the dance floor, and so Pat and I were immediately drawn to each other. She danced well too; had to, actually, for I was a very particular dancer. We won a spot prize for our dancing, hit it off right away and things began to blossom thereafter. Not until, however, that first, important Liverpudlian question had been asked: 'what school did you go to?' Why ask this? Well, it was quite simple. I would never have considered going out with a Protestant! As ridiculous as that sounds today, it was inconceivable to me that I could ever consider being involved with a woman of a different denomination, let alone religion. Of course, even in the early 1950s Liverpool was ravaged by this sort of religious bigotry and although it embarrasses me to admit, my religious zeal was probably but one step away from bigotry. This is one of the eternal contradictions about my past that I have to face when I think of my anxiety over young Brian's treatment at the hands of religious bigots as a schoolboy. I regarded myself as a liberal sort of guy, but I would still have refused to date Pat had she been an Anglican or Protestant. Little was I to realise, in any case, that I was being even less prudent by beginning a relationship with a member of the opposite sex, but that was all to be recognised some time later. I came to realise the error of my religious ways too. Religion is personal; I prefer to call it faith and I have retained a great respect for the Jewish faith in particular.

I often wonder, now after all these years, just how much in love I really was. Even to this day I probably don't know much about love. With the notable exception of my mother's love, I've never been too familiar with it; even though I think it's a good idea, I find it difficult to locate. They say that 'falling in love with love is playing the fool', but I don't think that this was entirely the case for me. But I did love the concept of loving Pat very much and I must admit to the fact that I was very taken with the idea of actually being in love. Father thought the whole thing was a case of the vaguely hilarious bordering on the faintly ridiculous. I didn't understand his allusions of absurdity, but mother was very keen to see the relationship prosper, and it was about this time that she opened my 'bottom drawer' in the belief (or was that hope?) that a wedding would ensue. Looking back, I think her thoughts were most likely based on aspiration rather than confidence – perhaps too a show of solidarity in the face of father's sarcasm. In my oblivion, I began to prepare myself for wedded bliss. The land of make believe was now enveloping my life fully and Pat and I became at least for the moment unofficially engaged. I had not proposed as such, but in my thoughts I was going to be married. I wanted to be a father – wow!

Yet, perhaps like my own father, I was mentally careering out of control, determined to embrace an institution that I thought was custom made for me, when I really ought to have been asking myself some pretty severe, self-reflective questions. Unlike father, however, circumstances soon dictated that I was to discover a little more about my partner and, as a consequence, myself, before taking the plunge. For the moment, at least, Pat and I became inseparable. I had decided to help mother in her shop on a pro-tem basis, rather than lounge around in my room or work back in father's joinery trade, and she paid me a small but acceptable wage, so I was able to open a small savings account at the Post Office. Pat worked as a checker at Littlewoods, and also began to put money to one side. I have to admit that I found it very difficult to save. We spent our money and time holding hands at the cinema and quick-stepping at the Grafton as we danced our way towards my 19th birthday with glee. Very quickly we decided that we were so compatible that marriage was the natural step to take and we duly made our engagement formal. My lasting memory of that engagement party is of my father pissed out of his mind licentiously cheerful about what he thought were the improbabilities surrounding the potential scenario, and attempting to chat up my future wife (to no avail,

I might add). Naturally, I didn't understand why he felt that the whole thing was so droll.

Pat was a beautiful young woman, and enjoyed being seen with a good-looking young man, such as myself. For my part, she sort of completed an equation for me. There was therefore a certain shallowness to our relationship that I can only now appreciate in retrospect. I was attempting to view myself as others did. So a consort on my arm was an acceptable image, especially as I was also becoming known locally as something of a crooner. There we were: two lovely young things together, enjoying each other's company, looking and feeling great. It took my mind away from the debacle at the Adelphi (which I regretted more than anything at that time) and the 'I told you so' looks from my ever-loving pater. Pat and I were of the same generation – I was a little older but by very little – and we enjoyed the same things. Ipso Facto. That was what it was all about, wasn't it? It was all so natural, so accepted, so instinctive – but was it?

For example, sex, that long-standing taboo stretching into the 1950s, became a troublesome part of the equation. I began to worry. I had no idea what to do and Pat had no idea how to tell me. When she told me she was a virgin I didn't really comprehend. The only virgin I had heard of was the Virgin Mary and she'd had a baby, so I wasn't over-confident about my role in all of this. Temporarily, at least, our blushes were saved by the Catholic faith. The creed dictated that unless we wanted to be burned on a furnace in hell after our deaths, we were not recommended to indulge in sexual intercourse before our marriage. Phew! This news came as something of a relief for me – anything for some kind of postponement of the fateful moment. I presumed that somebody would let me in on the great secret at least by the time I was wed. We were told that, as a couple, we could always go to the priest if worse came to the worst. What sort of advice he would have given God alone knew, but I regarded this as a good safety net for us both, and I cautiously heaved a sigh of relief.

My naïve concerns about sex would not simply go away. In all honesty, the very thought of sex scared the living shit out of me. Her naughty bits were different from mine, I knew that when I first placed my hand on her breast. But, after that, I still thought that one's belly button held the secret to the life-giving process. Picture, if you will, a young man of 19 years of age considering placing his penis in a woman's belly button. Not only that, but from what I had been told, I wasn't even sure if we actually connected during the act at all. I had been informed, behind the bike sheds at school, that as long as one sought sexual gratification in the presence of a woman a baby was bound to follow. Despite my growing knowledge of the Ivor Novellos of this world, I had still not really heard anything specific since to contradict this information. I was also reliably informed at one stage that sitting on women's lavatory seats had to be avoided in case babies ensued (this was why men and women didn't share toilets apparently), but I wasn't sure about this either, as it failed to explain to me how I could use the same loo as my sister and mother.

Great ethical complications ensued for my young self. For example, to my way of thinking the first of these two pieces of information amounted to masturbation in the company of a female. This presented such a religious boy as myself with two great dilemmas: firstly, I was painfully shy and could never do that in front of a woman, and, secondly, according to the Jesuits who taught us at school, it would also mean that I would be damned and go blind (some fellow pupils decided to 'go blind and be damned' if my memory serves me correctly). I might be a father then, but one with diminishing sight. I'd have to sell matches outside the cinema instead of watching the movie. So it seemed to me that I was faced with a three-headed predicament by the whole issue of sex. Firstly, the prospect of eternal damnation if we got carried away before the rings were on the fingers – which wasn't very likely; secondly, progressive blindness if I decided somehow to attempt to make a baby in the same room as my wife; and, thirdly, if contact was actually allowed then there were the odds-on chances of my sticking my member in the wrong hole altogether. Problems, problems, always problems! And, of course, to repeat, I dearly loved the idea of becoming a father. I was starting to get cold feet about the whole thing when I received a letter from the king. I was curtly informed that I was to report for a medical at Aldershot within the next two weeks. If healthy, I would be allocated a regiment of my choice. I couldn't get out of it by telling them that I was a homosexual, because I didn't know that fact myself. Anyway, I was engaged to be married. Also, as the time arrived, I have to admit that I was pretty relieved to be going. There were just too many grey areas at home and one thing that you can say about the army in 1950s Britain was that it was pretty straightforward. Eighteen months of National Service had intervened. The Cold War was at its height, the Korean War was about to begin and I was glad to be joining the army. Nothing has ever been straightforward in the life of Joe Flannery.

I kept in close contact with Pat during my first six months in the army. In a curious move, paying some sort of homage to my father, I elected to become a Royal Engineer. I was stationed at Aldershot and began to enjoy the life. I did miss my fiancée, of course: I had placed her on a pedestal and she was a sort of icon to me. So I wrote home regularly every week as well as arranging as many weekend leaves for myself as I could get away with. The army's discipline actually managed to push all of the previous mental anxieties to one side, at least for the time being, and I began to look forward from a sort of artificial distance to the vaguest ideas about marriage and settling down; later rather than sooner, perhaps? I discovered much to my great relief that it was also quite amazing just how much one could learn about sex from a barrack room full of squaddies. Before too long I'd discovered all about it: what to do with it and, perhaps more importantly for me, where to put it. I even managed to join in a few smutty conversations without giving my innocence away, and the rest of the lads just presumed that, because I was engaged and in love – in other words a rather sad bastard – I wasn't one for going into Aldershot trying to put a tail on a young lady. To be honest, the whole crux of the matter was slowly becoming rather more complicated than simply issues surrounding fidelity, now that I had learnt of the correct orifices in which to place my virginal member.

Despite still not having officially proposed (what was making me defer?, I pondered) I was still resolutely determined to go through with the marriage, but I was having some serious doubts about engaging in the act of sex itself. I just wasn't altogether turned on by it, to use a later expression. It didn't revolt me, it was just that I failed to get excited in the same way as my fellow squaddies. Very occasionally I would question myself, but I just put it down to being either religious or loyal or old fashioned or a combination of all three. I had previously wanted to be a priest so I made some rather dubious connections with this piece of ancient history, I think. It wasn't long before my just-so attitude to dress and deportment, and the army itself, came to the attention of the officers at Aldershot and I was made up to the rank of corporal. I was also given the task of helping to parade new recruits and, I must admit, I enjoyed this promotion tremendously. I was now dually treated with both a level of cautious respect together with being regarded as one of the lads, and so this link in the command chain appealed greatly. I wrote home telling everybody about this great event in my life and passed on the good news to my bride-to-be, who was delighted also. Or so I thought.

My new-found authority led to a little more leeway on the camp for weekend compassionate leave, and it was a good job too. Life back at City Road had taken a severe turn for the worst, and a letter arrived from mother informing me that, after a particularly vehement discussion between her and my father about one of his many women, he had beaten her repeatedly. This time there had been a severe facial injury sustained by mother. I was absolutely devastated. Mother had refused to be seen by a GP because of what she saw as a stigma surrounding the circumstances – this was 1950s Liverpool, of course – but the wound must have been grim, for she closed the shop for several days and went to Auntie Winnie's house just to recuperate and get away from the scene of what she viewed as her utter humiliation. As far as I was concerned this was the worst yet. Father had injured both of us previously, but it was never really what we considered to be permanent damage. To me, hundreds of miles away in Hampshire, mother's very life appeared to be in danger.

Yet, despite everything, by the time I had been able to arrange a weekend pass, there she was back home again with that man with the split personality. As soon as I could get her alone we talked, and talked, and talked some more. In fact, my memories of leave from Aldershot are littered with kitchen table discussions with mother as I spent many hours during 1950 and 1951 trying to persuade her to leave him. At first it was all to no avail, she insisted on staying but as time wore on her resistance to change began to weaken and eventually (sometime perhaps in late 1951) she slowly came around to the idea, at least in theory. However, she also placed a time limit on the agreement by telling me that 'yes, she promised to move away from him', but only when her youngest (Peter) had grown into adulthood. Until that time she felt duty bound, as she put it, to see it through. The fact that she was placing her own life in jeopardy she discounted. I was not exactly over the moon about her decision, but I had to accept it as the best I could get under the circumstances. However, I was to remind her of her promise to me over and over again during the next few years just in case she placed it too far on the backburner, making it thereby conveniently inaccessible. As far as I was concerned she had finally agreed to make the break and, come hell or high waters, I was going to make her stick to this agreement.

Ironically, mother was very pragmatic about my own situation within the Flannery household. She was sad but also glad that I was no longer around. Obviously father's errant behaviour had worsened, and for me to witness it first-hand would have inevitably caused great friction and potential danger. I was now a strapping man of 20, well trained by the army and very fit, and it was becoming obvious that I would have been a physical danger to my father had I have lost my temper with him. Fortunately,

I was able to control my anger long enough to see a weekend pass through to an end, but the aforementioned incident with my father and the Eddie Calvert 78 record certainly tried my patience to the very limit. I could see that mother was very frightened when we came together in the house. On more than one occasion I did feel like doing him in, I would have to admit. Whether that would have ever occurred is another matter, but I agreed then, as the best solution for all concerned, that yes, I would carry on visiting as and when I might but would basically use the leave opportunities to see Pat as much as possible. Diplomacy was considered to be the greater part of valour. I also needed to keep an eye on the local entertainments scene when I was back in town. You see, prior to my National Service, things had been looking up in that quarter; allow me to explain.

In between my sacking from the Adelphi and only shortly prior to joining the army I had commenced singing a good deal and with some small measure of success, too. In actual fact, the money earned from these small gigs around the city supplemented my meagre wages from my mother so much that I was in no real hurry to get a proper job, especially with the inevitable cloud of National Service looming on the horizon. It had really all come about when my Uncle Alfie had been the first to encourage me to sing a few years earlier, telling me that I had a modicum of talent which ought not to be wasted. It was Uncle Alfie who would call on me to sing at the Parrot pub when I was in my early to mid-teens, and it was also he who suggested one day, when I was at a loose end, that I should join mother and father one evening at what was known as the NUPO Club. As strange as it may seem, mother and father still went out together on an occasional evening. Unbelievable, but true! Typically, father wanted everything to appear normal from the outside and would invite mother to accompany him to this small working-men's club on the outskirts of Liverpool 8, in Canning Street. Had it been in Liverpool 8 itself, the black district of Liverpool, we would certainly have not gone at all, for this was considered by many white Liverpudlians to be a rather dubious and transient area, full of what my father called women of the night. I was somewhat reluctant to go with them, for it all seemed so false, but for the time being at least I agreed to go with my mother and father to this odd little drinking club. My main reason for going, to be honest, was to ensure that mother was safe, for when father had 'scooped a few jars', as we might say in Liverpool, he could get especially nasty (the aforementioned Cherry Tree incident, for example). But funnily enough I discovered that his behaviour in the NUPO Club was for the most part distant yet exemplary.

I was delighted by this, and often daydreamed about the possibilities of us all becoming one happy family, based on the evidence from the club. But these fantasies didn't last too long. The following night father would be out on the town once again, probably with a bit of stuff (another woman) on his arm instead of my mother, and the Flannery version of normality would be restored very quickly. Still, the dream was good while it lasted.

The club was situated in a very large cellar in Canning Street. I had no idea exactly what NUPO stood for at the time but I later learnt that it had been established in the wake of the police strike of 1926 and had something to do with the police. In the best Liverpool club terms, it could have been initials for something rather enigmatic, anything ranging from a works social club to a Catholic parochial club to a local branch of the Masons. Whatever, I knew its origins at the time. The cellar was divided into two areas, with a bar at one end and a billiard table at the other. OK, admittedly not very salubrious, but nonetheless very exciting for a teenager such as myself. I shouldn't have been in the place at all, of course; the licensing regulations were very stringently enforced in those days and such licensed premises were technically restricted to over-21s, but the club committee knew my father well and he enjoyed a surprisingly good profile in the city generally. Furthermore, when it was discovered that I could sing a bit everything was immediately deemed acceptable. Even if it meant placing the club's licence at risk, the chance of a little live entertainment always came first.

Right up until the beginnings of disco, Liverpool thrived on live entertainment. In any case, I soon discovered that the club was very close to the Hope Street police station, and that after hours the local police would come in for a drink. They weren't going to bust a handy local watering hole for the sake of one underage singer. When an invitation inevitably went out for someone to sing a song towards the end of the evening, which might be about 10 p.m. (not very late by today's standards), the billiard table would be covered with an old piece of board. A one-legged pianist by the name of Legs would appear as if by magic to man the old 'joanna' in the corner of the room. If Legs happened to be unavailable it was at that stage that the Flannerys would effectively take over the performance duties; it was on one such evening that my name was put forward by Uncle Alfie and mother (much to my father's disgust), and I proceeded very nervously to lead the entire club in a raucous sing-along of old favourites. After overcoming my first bout of butterflies I truly loved the experience, and it was decreed unanimously amongst the club regulars that in future order had to be called when the young Flannery took to the boards because 'a splendid time was guaranteed for all'. After a few successful nights at the club I actually began agitating mother and father to take me to the NUPO to perform on a regular basis. Father was most displeased. Not only had he realised that I had elected to go in the first place in order to keep an eye on him, but he was now also discovering that I was more popular with his cronies than he was. It was all highly amusing in an ironic kind of way.

There was another lad at the NUPO who was also a very popular singer there, and his name was Roy Edwards. He was a little older than myself, and had been treading the boards around the pubs in Liverpool for some time. The NUPO Club actually paid him to sing, and I was most impressed by this, together with his behaviour once at the club. I considered him at this time to be the consummate professional because that was exactly how he behaved. I observed him very closely. He would arrive at the club early, disappear, and change into a clean shirt and tie, especially for that evening. He would always have band parts with him, in case there might be a different musician at the club or perhaps a number of musicians who wanted to jam. He would ask the customers for requests and was able to sing whatever they asked of him. His repertoire was vast, and he could turn his hand to anything from popular hits of the day by the likes of Frank Sinatra or Steve Conway right up to light opera and arias and then on to Irish songs in the Count John McCormack mould, who was always very popular on Merseyside. I wanted to be like Roy, I decided. Inevitably, Roy Edwards was spotted whilst doing the rounds of the local pubs and clubs. An agent for none other than Ken Mackintosh, a great band leader during the 1940s and 1950s, signed him and Roy was soon to leave Liverpool to commence a long singing stint with this very successful outfit. Not before we had become friendly, however. Once the news was out about his transfer to the Mackintosh band he encouraged me, suggesting that I tout myself around his old haunts in an attempt to give myself the experience that my voice demanded. He advised me:

> Look Joe, I can make a reasonable living out of this, why don't you get yourself around my old gigs and see if you can do the same … you've got the voice for it, and I'm leaving town anyway, so the gigs will be there for the taking … go on, you won't regret it.

Very often that's the sort of encouragement one needs. You know in your own mind that you have some sort of ability, some sort of noticeable difference, but when what seems to be a seasoned professional announces to you that he feels you might possibly have something to offer, you listen and listen good. Roy Edwards' advice proved to be something of a lifesaver to me for it came within a few weeks of being kicked out of the Adelphi Hotel. I mentioned to you that I had been playing all of those deleted records in my bedroom at home and had discovered that I could remember all of the words and phrasing by heart. Roy could hear this and also knew that I was a bit desperate. His heart was certainly in the right place.

I immediately did as he suggested and charged around the venues (or dives, take your pick) that he had left behind. I auditioned for some and was just taken on spec at others, and before too long I discovered that I had a diminutive circuit of engagements, ranging from the NUPO at one end of town (who were now paying me in lieu of Roy's departure) through to the Olympic and the Sandon public houses at the other. A few were little more than holes in the wall and the money was duly pathetic, of course. But it was all a real thrill for me and the experience was fantastic. For a shy, somewhat withdrawn lad such as myself it all proved invaluable. The money even helped me clothe myself in the style to which I wanted to become accustomed: the best suits and shirts, the most expensive ties and hosiery. And at last I was beginning to feel the part of somebody involved in show business. In due course I also had an adoring female companion by my side, and Pat and I would really look the part as we turned up for an engagement, looking the bee's knees.

You see, I suppose that this little performing experience broadened my outlook so much that it directly led to me chatting up Pat at the Grafton (it didn't lead to much else beyond this, mind you). This was something that I would have previously been far too frightened to have done at any earlier stage. Older women, especially relatives, were OK, but talk to women other than my mother or a member of my own family? Not bloody likely: that would have scared the living shit out of me. But this albeit limited singing episode made me into a more sociable and amiable person. I began to feel better about myself generally, and after my two false starts on the job front my self-esteem received the required shot in the arm that it needed. I enjoyed looking good – I took a great pride in my appearance – and now I was involved in something that made that particular vanity an absolute necessity: singing. People seemed to like me. Pat liked me. Perhaps life wasn't so bad after all! The gig that proved to be the most important for me during 1950, prior to my call-up papers, was the foremost engagement procured from Roy Edwards' circuit at the

Sandon pub, near to Liverpool Football Club's ground in the Anfield area of the city. I sang at the Sandon every Thursday night and came to share the bill with another up-and-coming local. He was a comedian, but not the usual run-of-the-mill stand-up that I was used to seeing in the pubs and on variety bills at that time. He was a very intelligent man, somebody who had obviously practised his art, and who took a great deal of interest in the world around him, for his routine was not one of actually telling very many jokes, as such, but rather observing people's idiosyncrasies and commenting upon them in a very ironic manner.

During the day Ken Dodd worked as a hardware salesman (door to door, I believe) and it was here that he apparently picked up a great amount of material from the people that he would meet 'on the knocker' and in the streets. He adopted silly personae, stepping in and out of characters that were all very familiar to us, but unfamiliar and unusual as fodder for a comedy routine. Comic characters such as Dickie Mint were used as smokescreens to disguise the fact that really he was ever so gently poking fun at us all. This comedian and I became good friends as we began to work the Sandon regularly. At this stage I would usually perform twice; opening the evening, very briefly, with a couple of songs and then introducing the locals to this brash young comedian: 'Ladies and gentlemen, may I introduce to you, the "King of Knotty Ash", Mr Ken Dodd.' Ken would then usually appear either trailing a load of pots and pans behind him, in his role as an Aunt Sally man, or else begin his spot by marching into the Sandon lounge banging a massive bass drum like some demented boy scout, singing something like *Silent Night*. I found his act to be hilariously funny, even in those far off days, but the audiences were often rather puzzled, being used to the likes of either ITMA (*It's That Man Again*) on the radio (Tommy Handley) or else a smutty barrack-room comedian like Max Miller, and they would vary greatly in their responses to this radical sort of humour; Ken would not always win them over. From time to time he too (just like myself) could get depressed.

You see, it was never easy performing anything in the boondocks of the Liverpool variety circuit. From time to time there would also be a bad atmosphere at the Sandon: trouble of a tribal nature might spill over into the evening's entertainment and barracking Ken became an occasional and cruel diversion for the ill-tempered adversaries. We all had to face it, of course, it was part of our apprenticeship, but the comic would very often come off worse. Trying to be funny when nobody wanted to laugh was an incredibly difficult vocation. The pub could house literally hundreds of people and on the occasions when the atmosphere did markedly deteriorate, Ken's work became very hard and seriously dangerous to his health. Sporadically, I found myself having to take to the stage again, together with the pianist, in order to rescue the middle of his act. I would sing a few old favourites, the sort that would guarantee a singsong like *Marta* or *One of These Days*, and gradually calm down the enraged crowd. In the wrong atmosphere the angry punters most certainly were unable to get to grips with Ken's oddball humour at all. He was undoubtedly a comic genius in the making but the world simply had to catch up with him, which, in due course, they did.

Nevertheless, and despite the gang warfare, Ken and I became a real attraction at the Sandon, and surely enough word began to spread. As something of a loose double act we pioneered the Merseyside Artists Association at Cabbage Hall in Anfield – a development of the local Ossie Wade's Showcase that we both played of a Sunday afternoon. The idea behind the MAA was for an organisation where initially anybody could play or sing, if they felt so inclined, and it later developed into an important and influential body of people attempting and largely succeeding to keep performers in work on Merseyside. And, as for Ken Dodd, as you all must realise, he never really looked back. His professionalism increased in direct proportion to his confidence as he was determined to make a living out of his art. As I recall it was Ken, in fact, who suggested to me one evening, after a particularly successful gig, that if I left the money matters to him we would both benefit. It went something like this:

> Look, Joe, I like working with you, you're always well turned out and you take things seriously … we work well together. But I know that I can get more cash out of these buggers if I handle the deals for the two of us, rather than allow them to make separate deals with each of us. Leave the cash side of things to me OK and I'll see you right.

True to his word, things did improve for him (and how). I never asked exactly what he had negotiated – that was his business. All I know was that he was able to strike a far better deal than me and yet I ended up with more cash in my pocket. He was very astute, even then.

Those first few semi-professional steps of Ken's were marvellous to witness and will always stay with me. The Sandon proved to be a great local rostrum for him as he battled the innate conservatism of the audiences and expanded his brilliant comic genius. The natural ability to make people laugh, this zany quality that very few have and even fewer have under control, was God-given. As unlikely as it seems, this natural comic talent came to my attention again, many years later, when it manifested itself in, of all places, Hamburg. I was in Hamburg and working with a Merseybeat band by the name of the Midnighters, which contained a fair-to-middling singer by the name of Freddie Fowell, soon to be known as Freddie Starr.

Ken Dodd was not as manic as Freddie, and his humour much less outrageous and deranged, but nevertheless Starr, like Dodd, often left people for dead intellectually. Freddie added even more influences to his madness, bolting on the humour of the Goons and Michael Bentine to his repertoire. After witnessing at first hand these two naturally gifted comedians I came to realise that it takes time for people to understand a revolutionary comic. Some members of the audience initially, at least, feel very insecure, threatened even, by the constant barrage of sarcastic wit and caustic diatribe, and can take offence until they find a connecting point between the comedian and themselves. Of course, in my view Freddie Starr when we first met in Germany was not really a comedian as such, but his wonderful insanity as a performer was rarely ever far away from permeating his only average competence as a singer. His mimicry, however, was already at an advanced stage of delirium in Hamburg and my brother frequently recalls how Starr was able to impersonate every singer at the Star Club with consummate ease, including my brother Lee Curtis. Eventually his manic approach to showbiz came to intercept his desire to become a kind of second Elvis and addict him, like Ken, to the genius-like irrationality of professional derangement.

So it was Pat and the Grafton, Roy and the NUPO, Ken and the Sandon, and together with helping my mother out at the shop in City Road, life had improved immeasurably. Still, there were days of depression. There was something I was still unsure about; there were feelings I could not pin down. Hanging around during the day, waiting for things to happen, feeling as if everything was in a sort of freeze frame; father treating me like some kind of second-hand dishcloth. And then my constant worries about my own sense of self: who was I exactly? In truth, I was actually becoming a little tired of Liverpool. Sure the local gigs were great, having a girlfriend was 'great' too, but things always appeared to be rather grey. As much as I loved my home city, it began to feel rather lifeless for me, parochial even and although I could escape reality with my fiancée for at least a couple of times a week and then sing a little with Ken or at the NUPO, I was itching to do something more with my life, but what?

What the hell was I going to do with myself in Liverpool for the next two score years and ten: sing at the NUPO; get married and have kids; work an endless stream of dives like the Olympia? There had to be something more. And what about the music? I was certainly finding it increasingly difficult to get turned on by having just a piano playing behind me. I wanted to sing in front of a band, but how? And although I dearly loved my music, even I was beginning to feel a little bored with the same old balladeering-style stuff. Doddy liked it and, after he had persuaded me to work with him in this unofficial double act, the money and venues improved, so the punters must have liked it too. He and I both knew that crooning was still popular, and it was all I could actually do musically, I suppose, but whereas he was a devoted fan of the old stuff, and was to soon realise that he could do far more than merely carry a song, I think I was growing less and less fascinated by the standard thirty-two-bar ballad.

I wanted something else, but what exactly? As usual for the young Joe, I had no idea! I couldn't be satisfied but couldn't pin down the roots of my restlessness. Surely we ought to live at peace with ourselves and at peace with others. After all, we are social beings. But how was I to remain harmonious within and maintain peace and harmony around me, so that others I loved could also live peacefully and harmoniously? In order to be relieved of my uncertainties, I had to know the basic reasons for them: the cause of my mental suffering. However, as I investigated the problems I couldn't really get to the bottom of them. Why was I generating negativity within? Unwanted things had happened and I created tensions. Wanted things had not happened as I had completely wished, so obstacles always stood in the way. However, that wasn't simply 'it', for surely everybody has these reservations in their lives. The roots of my problem seemed to reside in the fact that I surrounded myself with negative thoughts about everything. What made things worse was that I knew that this was not because I was a negative person, but more to do with the fact that I felt deep down that I still did not understand who I actually was.

Before leaving for Aldershot I came to be drawn back to the sounds that I had witnessed as an onlooker at the Duck House: those bizarre, simpler forms of music based around twelve and eight bars rather than the complex patterns set by the big bands. This became part of my musical itch and I simply had to scratch it. So I ended up spending my last evening in Liverpool, prior to getting the train to Aldershot, not singing, but listening to the sounds in the Duck House. I was alone, for Pat didn't like goodbyes, so here was I leaving for Aldershot at 10 p.m., listening to honky-tonk music for my long goodbye – how apt that now seems. By this time the scene in the Duck House had developed even further and was very exciting. Not only was this hillbilly country and western music being played, still attracting several US airmen from Burtonwood, but also other odd styles of music were being performed in the pub. Somebody in the bar described one tune as 'black music'; another called it 'jump'. One drunken sod described to me how he was going to jump a tramp steamer that night to New Orleans so that he could get involved in something he described as 'Dixieland jazz'; I'd never heard of it, apart from George Webb's Dixieland Serenaders. He probably ended up getting the bus back to Knotty Ash just the same. One sad man left the pub, in a huff, calling it 'coon' music and shouted back into the Duck House that it should stay in Toxteth where it belonged. I didn't really get any of this, but I was fascinated.

It all sounded a little out of tune to me but was highly infectious and, upon enquiring after one of the sources, I was told that one song was originally by a black guy called Louis Jordan. The song was *Ain't Nobody Here But Us Chickens*. It certainly sounded a million miles away from *Shrimp Boats*. But I made a mental note as it was all a little late as far as my repertoire was concerned: I was off to the army. I also made further note of the allusion to Toxteth and left the Duck House for the last time as a civilian, at least for the time being. I was singing, was supposed to be in love and engaged to be married. All of these things I thought that I wanted, but I was a very restless young man by the time I was boarding the train for Hampshire and the army was offering at least a change of direction. I'd become a little stale, worrying about mother, angry at father, frightened about my relationship, anxious about my singing. I felt a degree of relief as I spent my first night in a redbrick blockhouse in Aldershot.

So within a few short days, there was me, getting some in. It was hardly paradise, but unlike many other unfortunate souls who really did endure their National Service, I was finding it all rather enjoyable. I was awarded a stripe after my hut was awarded a banner for the best on the parade ground. After about four to five months as a corporal in the Royal Engineers I was even asked by the authorities whether I wanted to make a career move towards sergeant and then sergeant major, and actually join the army on a full-time basis. I was regarded as a potential career soldier by my commanding officers and they were in favour of my going further. I was amazed and rather flattered. However, although there was a degree of enjoyment on my part, I realised I was part of a system dependent upon hierarchy and I wasn't really sure whether I liked that or not. I was also becoming conscious of being an object of a certain amount of odium from the new squaddies, and I certainly didn't like that one bit. I get a high from meeting people and I like being liked by people; I have always been sympathetic towards people, too, no matter who they might be or what they become. The journey improves when you enjoy people, and life's a long, hard road in any case. I have always thought that to live solely for some future goal is rather shallow. It's the presence of other people that sustain your life – as the sides of a mountain sustain the top, as a wise man once said.

Being a parade corporal meant that I was in charge of some under-standably reluctant young men, half awake at some ungodly hour of the morning, rightly resistant to an expensive, antiquated system that was actually quite appalling and utterly irrelevant to most of them. I soon dis-covered that, although I could give and receive empathy and wit from the lads who had come into the army with me and simply regarded me as a mate, albeit a lucky bastard, it was quite naturally a different picture with the later recruits. I soon became a living figure of repression to those that followed in the wake of my contemporaries. I hated their antipathy because it really mattered to me that I was liked. I didn't want their respect if it meant that I had to endure their loathing as well. It all came to a head, as I remember, on one particularly windswept and godforsaken morn-ing in the middle of winter, as I was parading a bunch of new recruits into ranks of three, and discovered that one of the third rank was missing, probably still in his pit or else AWOL. I shouted to the platoon on parade: 'Where's the third man, then?' As soon as I'd opened my mouth, I real-ised my mistake. A rather stupid thing to ask, considering the famous film of the same name had only recently been released; I should have known better. 'He's gone to get his fucking zither, Corp,' came the curt reply from well to the rear of the ranks. Well, what could I do or say? I had asked for it, after all, and it was actually a pithy remark; within seconds the entire platoon crumpled into a fit of laughter, shortly followed, I have to admit, by yours truly.

I could only keep my rectilinear authoritarian face for so long and once one guy had started, well, that was it. It soon became obvious to me that I had lost the co-operation of this new batch of national servicemen. That not only was I a pre-established figure of malevolence, but also something of a figure of fun, it seems, for following this episode my authority was shattered. I appeared rather droll to those who took my laughter as a level-ler, but also rather soft to those who would exploit this laughter as an act of weakness. I realised that I was on the horns of a dilemma. I couldn't foresee a life as a hated sergeant major after this. I would have had to have torn into them, put them in the guard house or some such ritual, and I wasn't that much of a bastard – honest! But I knew that the army wouldn't have appreciated this rather commensurate parade ground experience. Any mark of authority that I once might have represented merely by my presence as a corporal had now eroded over a quip about a movie. It was evidently time for my young self to rethink a little. Perhaps even time to move on, I thought.

Once the humour of the incident had worn off, the whole thing made me think harder about the impending offer of an NCO promotion. I liked being liked and I enjoyed the banter, but I wasn't supposed to engage in any witty repartee with a shower of sappers, as they were called. If I was to collapse in a fit of laughter every time my authority was challenged, while at the same time be regarded as an 'army bastard', I really wasn't going to enjoy life as I'd expected. I decided there and then to graciously decline the army's offer, and ask for a transfer away from the parade ground ethics of Aldershot. Surprisingly (or perhaps not, given the circumstances), I was dispatched without further ado to an army medical centre at a camp just outside Abergavenny, Wales. I was now a trainee medical NCO with two stripes in a little place called Crickhowell. This seemingly distant medical unit had been established in a rambling old eighteenth-century mansion to cater for the adjoining general-purpose training camp. The mansion actually housed the local doctor, whose duties also ran to medical parades for the army. He must have been on to a good thing, for the army paid handsomely for this service. The affluence showed, too, for the mansion was beautifully furnished and painted with best quality Ministry of Defence paint.

To my relief I soon discovered that I had landed myself possibly one of the softest touches in the army. My job was to call a medical parade for the doctor every morning and that was just about it. There was little else for me to do: just to roll-call some malingerers every day and in the process discover which ones had crabs or the clap; call them into the doctor's surgery with a degree of authority; see them out and point them in the direction of the pharmacy where they would pick up their jars of mysterious ointment or liver pills; and then have the remainder of the day to myself. I was even billeted at the lodge adjoining the mansion. It was a lovely little gatehouse, just enough room for one, with all mod-cons. This suited me down to the ground. I could be as particular as I wanted to be, and there would be no exchanges of the 'delightful odour' surrounding damp or dirty soldiers. I didn't have to slum it at all, and I soon discovered that even the officers' accommodation was inferior to my own.

The advantages of this posting were obvious: a great deal of free time. After the doctor's parade, which was, just like everything else in the army, first thing in the morning, my time was then my own. Typically, however, I soon found myself becoming increasingly bored. Even though the threat of war was never really very far from a national serviceman's thoughts in the 1950s (somewhere there always seemed to be a limb of the empire fighting for its disconnection or else the phobia of the Red Peril to scare the living daylights out of you), Abergavenny seemed a million light years away from such trials and tribulations. The equally bored CO came to visit me one day and, acknowledging my general state of enforced mental redundancy, suggested that I do what I could to relieve it. I took this comment as a figurative blind eye and began to think of how I could alleviate my boredom.

My daily routine already involved slipping away into Abergavenny most mornings (I was never missed), and the day after the CO's revealing statement I happened to be passing the local Woolworth's store when I noticed that they wanted some part-timers. Retail! This seemed like an opportunity not to be missed for a young Flannery with time on his hands, and so I went into the store and asked to see the manager right away. With my own shop background, added to the stripes on the sleeve of a well-pressed uniform, I instantly landed the job as a part-time warehouseman, with the proviso that I could be called away to the camp at any time. Perhaps not the most thrilling of occupations, you might think, but to me it was just the sort of boost that I was looking for. In any case, it's more often who you work with than what you are doing that makes for a level of job satisfaction, and they were a great bunch of people in that Woolies in Aber. I must admit that I also felt it was important for me to keep in touch with any new developments within the changing world of the retail trade. Perhaps I always assumed, deep down, that this was the sector where my real living would eventually come from, despite my theatrical and artistic leanings.

In the short term, the job proved to be very lucrative for me, both mentally and financially. It gave me something extra to think about during the week and I was also earning a decent part-time wage on top of my meagre army salary; in addition, I was able to indulge in a little wholesaling myself on the camp, with the approval of the shop manager and my CO, you understand. Woolworth's were renowned for their record department and even a tiny store such as the one in Aber stocked all the hits of the day.

So I would purchase them at wholesale price, plus a little staff discount, and flog them on the base. After my first six months in Abergavenny I was so independent that I was also able to get a regular seventy-two-hour week-end pass whenever I wished. The general inactivity at the camp between Friday and Monday meant that I had effectively become a part-time soldier as well as a part-time packer. This meant that I could either put in some extra hours at Woolies on a Saturday or, more usually, take a trip back to Liverpool to spend some time with Pat and my family, returning to camp on the Sunday evening. My army pass meant that I didn't have to pay any train fare, and so I was quite the toff once I had returned back to Liverpool, splashing a little money about, as was my wont. Pat especially enjoyed these visits. She liked me to spend money on her, as I did, and we revelled in each other's company, two young things together. It was assumed by all that, as soon as National Service was out of the way, we would be married. Little did I know that Pat was beginning to lose interest.

Although the warehouse job at Woolworth's kept me sound in mind and pocket and reasonably busy, tins of processed peas and luncheon meat were not exactly taxing my brain and, after the end of my first year of army service, the job too began to bore me as much as the army did. My thoughts were always turning back to music and entertainment: my return trips to Liverpool inevitably led to tours of the picture houses, dance halls and theatres with my fiancée; however, upon returning to Abergavenny there was very little for me to get excited about. There was a cinema, but it was rather behind the times as far as the latest releases were concerned, having a curious devotion to Abbott and Costello that, even to this day, I cannot understand. There was a local dance hall, too, but with all due respect to the resident band, the music was about as exciting as a wet kipper in the face. I decided that for my final year I should get involved in organising something musical at the camp. The CO was all for it. I think by this time he was working his way through the entire NAAFI quota of Scotch whisky just to assuage his own indifference, and so anything that I might suggest was greeted with a rather sozzled enthusiasm.

I suppose that was my first real venture into the entertainment industry from a commercial point of view. I was given a sizeable budget to work with and decided to go the whole hog and book the best band in Britain at this time (1952): the Ted Heath Band. By this time Ted Heath was just about the most important band leader and arranger in the country; not only that, but his vocalists were also becoming singing stars in their own right. Dickie Valentine, The Stargazers, Ruby Murray, Alma Cogan,

Lita Roza, and Dennis Lotis all sang with Heath, who was an enormous catalyst for their careers. This was the year of the first *NME* charts in Britain, and one look at the successes of those singers following their arrival bears a wonderful testament to the power, appeal and throughput of the Ted Heath Band. Certainly, to experience a massive orchestra like Heath's bashing out, say, *Skyliner* to a packed auditorium of dancers, as I had already done back in the Grafton in Liverpool, was truly something to behold.

The army paid for everything. All I had to do was make sure that we could cope with the massive amount of interest that the band's arrival would create. It must have been a real event for such a prominent band to pay a visit to this part of Wales. I was very nervous about the whole thing, of course, but handled all of the personal arrangements for the band myself, so that I could be as near to my heroes as possible in case a little bit of their magic might rub off on me. By the end of the night's proceedings, Ted Heath, who apparently was never a man to pass compliments lightly, did chat about the evening and he congratulated me on the whole event. I remember his words to this day: 'So you're the young corporal who sorted everything out for us? Well, this was very well organised – and that is speaking from great experience, I can tell you; you might have found yourself a vocation there, my friend! Well done, we had a great time!' I was delighted, ecstatic even. A vocation, eh? Very interesting; at the very least it was concrete proof to myself that I could organise something, and organise it sufficiently well for the leading band leader in the country to be well pleased. Surely this was something I could dip my toe into in one form or another. I had also girded up my loins to say to Mr Heath, '… Er, I can sing, too', but remained rather dumbstruck, a little too awe-inspired by the great man for my own good. 'But once my National Service is over, that's when I'll give it a go!' I thought. 'But, then again, what about Pat?' Maybe I already half knew that things would not be going according to plan. Perhaps something in the back of my mind told me that I was never going to be a husband and father. Another event that same evening rekindled those thoughts of self-doubt, already set in motion in my mind prior to my leaving Liverpool.

After the dance, myself and a private who had been helping me with this successful evening decided to put the tin hat on it all by picking up a couple of local girls who had attended the dance. I felt really powerful that night. You know what it's like when things really go according to plan, when things are a success: you feel as if you are on a roll; nothing can stop you; you're unbeatable. You also feel that you've got to share your success with somebody. I've stated before that I love being loved, and there's a feeling of success that people can pick up on. More often than not people can enjoy the vibes actually coming from you. Success not only breeds success from a commercial point of view, it also breeds success personally. Wilf and I were a roaring success that night. Everybody wanted to know us. We, or rather I, had brought the famous Ted Heath Orchestra to deepest Wales; it was like the second coming: we could do nothing wrong, and under those circumstances one just wants the congratulations to go on forever. So be it, we decided; a night of raw lust and passion was added on to the agenda. In ordinary circumstances, the words 'raw lust' and Joe Flannery don't really go together very well. I was also an engaged man at this stage: where was the guilt? Hiding under the veil of my ego, no doubt. Perhaps this is all the more reason why this evening is particularly memorable for me. What could possibly go wrong?

We took two local girls back to one tiny cottage in Abergavenny and enjoyed an evening of unbridled carnal knowledge. I use the word 'knowledge' deliberately here, for it was indeed an awakening as to the intimacies of the female body. I discovered, for example, that belly buttons were not as useful as I had previously thought! It was the usual scenario of me and my partner in one room, with Wilf and the other girl in the adjoining room. The cottage actually only consisted of two rooms, in any case, with a bucket for a loo in the equally tiny back yard. It being a Friday evening, I wasn't really expected back on camp for the following morning and so I settled back into the arms of my passing stranger and let the show commence. She knew a great deal and soon enough I had become a fully qualified survivor. By the time we had exhausted all sexual possibilities dawn was beginning to break.

Daylight hadn't poked its head into the room sufficiently to illuminate it (there was no electricity), and my erstwhile seductress was rooting about beside the little bed looking for her cigarettes, telling me she was 'gagging for a fag'. I thought she had told me that she was 'gagging for a shag', which scared the shit out of me because I'd already spent myself. Fortunately, she discovered her ciggies and matches under her knickers and when she struck a match to ignite Willy Woodbine, the room also became incandescent. I turned over to watch her smoke by the light of the Swan Vesta and immediately noticed an unsteady gleam on the walls and ceiling behind her head. I asked her what it was. At first she didn't really have any idea of what I was talking about. She then took a long drag on the cigarette, removed it from her mouth, scratched her left tit and in a state of knowing comprehension said, 'Oh, these old places are riddled with bugs. They come out at night to breed, I think, but don't worry, Joe, they'll not hurt you. Now, where were we?'

What? Bugs? Joe Flannery has been shagging in a room, a cottage, entirely covered in bugs? I felt a cold shiver of revulsion traverse my body as I launched myself out of the bed on to the quarry-tiled floor. Reaching for my dress uniform, which had been worn for the gig, you understand, I shook it hard, trembling at the thought that my best bib and tucker was also infested with God knows what and I hurtled towards the door with the sound of the woman's laughter ringing in my ears. She evidently considered it all hilarious: the sight of my white backside heading out of the door probably was. From Abergavenny back to the camp was exactly 4 miles and I reckon it was me who shattered the 4-minute mile in the early hours of that Saturday morning (and for the most part, barefoot), and not Roger Bannister; a little later I crashed through the gatehouse door without searching my infested uniform for the key and immediately removed what clothing I had managed to put on in the escape. I dived into the cold bath, and began scrubbing.

Eventually what seemed like an entire nation of little insects breathed their last before descending in a steadily clockwise motion down the plughole and into oblivion. I reeked of carbolic soap all day, my skin was raw with scouring and my dick was also raw for a different reason. This was supposed to have been my greatest success so far. It had turned out to be a night to remember all right, but not the sort that I had expected. Later that morning Wilf turned up, totally oblivious to the events of that morning. I began to chuckle to myself. Maybe it had to end like that. Maybe I was being enlightened by God or something. Dipping one's wick as an engaged man was bound to lead to misfortune (any priest might have told me that), but the whole experience seemed to inform me of other priorities and issues in my life. Was it worth it? Wilf was a tad perturbed when I told him about the little rascals – I mean, who wouldn't be? But he was far less concerned; his first priority as a red-blooded man was to get his end away in any set of circumstances, come what may. I, on the other hand, found the whole incident far less worth the effort and I pondered over this all week as I waited for the weekend pass to arrive for my usual visit home to see mother and Pat back in Liverpool.

I couldn't bring myself to draw any firm conclusions. I probably wasn't quite ready to confront these issues in any depth. Maybe it had just been a warning; maybe I just wasn't the kind of red-blooded male that most squaddies appeared to be. After all, I was still engaged to Pat and I was fully intending to become a married man, so the disgust and guilt could be attributed to that; but this undercurrent raised by my night of carnal lust would not go away and all the way back to Liverpool I pondered over my own sexuality, my own 'macho-ness', my own Homo sapien inclinations. I concluded that it was something of a grey area. I thought, 'Well, Joe, you're just particular, that's all; you just aren't drawn to shagging under any conditions. There's nothing essentially wrong with that, is there?'

As it turned out, the incident that I have just described coupled with the following visit to Liverpool irrevocably altered my perceptions about personal relationships between men and women for many years to come. I went home that following weekend feeling very puzzled and not a little guilty. I had let her down; I was full of remorse together with a high level of disgust, and was actually prepared to tell her all about it just to see if I could wipe the slate clean, like a sort of confessional. It's a good job that I never got the opportunity, because ideas like that, attempts at total honesty, seldom ever work out how you plan them. That weekend, late in 1952, I returned home ostensibly to meet my best pal and cousin Peter, who was also home from sea on leave, and I hadn't contacted Pat to tell her I was home. I thought that it would be a pleasant surprise for her to discover I was back in Liverpool unannounced. It had been two years since Peter and I had met and, although we had sporadically kept in touch, I had missed him. He was never a great writer and the few communications I had received from him while at sea were very brief and rather vague, and whenever I had written back my letter always seemed to arrive months too late.

Peter and I duly met up, had a good chin-wag and went to the movies on the Saturday. Afterwards we were walking happily down Renshaw Street in the city centre when I spotted a girl in a very familiar brown gabardine coat walking towards us linked arm in arm with an American airman. My heart stopped beating for a moment. There was no mistake: I instantly recognised the girl on his arm was Pat. I felt sick and light-headed, even though I had already violated our relationship the previous week. I allowed them to walk practically right up to me, and greeting the happy couple I remarked to the airman, 'Excuse me, if this young lady would like to take off her glove, you will find that she is wearing an engagement ring … and I gave it to her.' Pat looked mortified; the American airman looked embarrassed and ashamed. They looked at each other, and then at me, at which point I turned and simply walked away. I told Peter to go home and immediately jumped on a bus to Pat's house to inform her mother. Her mum was at first delighted to see me, but then realised that something was terribly wrong. I asked her if she knew of Pat's whereabouts: she said that as far as she knew Pat was out with a friend by the name of Peggy. I then informed her of the sad meeting on Renshaw Street and she broke down in tears. We were both very upset together by the time Pat arrived back home about an hour later. She was also in quite a state. I suppose, if anything, matters were made worse by me sitting in the front parlour waiting for her return. But I was of one mind only: the engagement simply had to be called off, and immediately. Was it just the incident of that day that had led me to the conclusion or was there more to it? I think, in retrospect, perhaps there was.

For example, I immediately instructed her mother that all of the engagement presents, which had been stored at Pat's, were to be returned. I was quite sure that there would be no turning back. Something else was probably driving me to this decision and I can see now that it was not simply the chance meeting in Renshaw Street or the shenanigans in Wales the previous week that were motivating me to this immediate verdict. The clue to this ending of our engagement is evident via my next conclusion: if my corporeal fantasy had been extinguished by my fiancée, I would not run the risk of it ever happening again. I declared that I was to be forever unmarried. I was quite certain about this decision; nothing could have made more sense to me at the time. Despite my desire to be a father, it has stayed that way ever since. I explained to my mother that evening that the engagement was over. She was obviously terribly disappointed. She knew me and realised, I think, that this might have been her last opportunity to consider this particular son an eligible bachelor. She evidently understood in her usual silent and thoughtful way. Curiously, it was a peaceful night in the house, with no signs of trouble from the old man. He was not his usual loutish self and everything fell rather silent. After three weeks Pat sent her friend Peggy to visit me while I was again home on leave in order to arrange a meeting, which duly occurred at the Hippodrome Cinema.

Afterwards, we went for a meal in town at that famous old Liverpool Chinese restaurant, The Cathay, and Pat asked me whether I could consider giving it another go. Foolishly I agreed, but I had to return to the army and the reunion lasted only a further three weeks. Nothing remains the same, everything changes, and while these few weeks on the one hand furthered my hopefulness and optimism, they conversely made me very miserable. I could not trust her. Once trust has gone a relationship cannot move forward, it merely rambles and lurches from mini-crisis to mini-crisis. It simply could not work. Trusting anybody of the opposite sex again in such a close relationship became one of my biggest qualms. We split up once and for all as the year drew to a close. To this very day, however, I still believe that I would have made a good husband and father.

My remaining few months or so in the army drew steadily and unremarkably to a close. I continued to arrange a few concerts and socials at the camp, and in Abergavenny itself. I continued in my work for Woolworth's as well; but my memories of this era have now become rather blurred and are strangely at odds with any sense of reality. I was very depressed and I remember it as one does a dream: only fleetingly. Every so often something springs to mind, but it was as if everything was suspended, as if things were going on around me from which I was oddly disengaged. I can't honestly remember anything of any significance except what was going on in my mind, which was, for the most part, thoughts about what I would do with myself once I had left the services. I do think now that I probably experienced a small but significant breakdown. I also recall, however, that I was offered a very cushy commission at the end of my National Service: Joe Flannery, whose spelling was always abysmal, was being offered a position as a pen-pushing junior officer in His Majesty's Forces. The post, however, was back at Aldershot, and what with the bugs, boredom and bawdiness of Abergavenny, the prospect of shuffling paper at a desk in Aldershot seemed about as attractive as pushing water up hill in a wheelbarrow. I graciously declined the Royal Family's kind offer and prepared myself for civvy street.

So, perhaps after everything that had happened to me over the previous few years, I had come to something of a mental impasse. I was beginning to pose some important personal questions to myself. I was beginning to emerge from the self-imposed religious-cum-idealistic catalepsy. While my last few weeks in the army became a period of time involving neither great highs nor deep lows, looking back, this time has also come to represent for me a sort of emergence from a chrysalis. As if, up until that cataclysmic moment with Pat, I had been little more than a pupa. Henceforth, my existence would be more closely related to the imago. I certainly kept that one important promise to myself, and I neither approached nor dated any female in the ensuing period. It was as if, after those two combined episodes, a further chapter of my life had closed.

4

ONE OR TWO HOME TRUTHS

UTTERLY CHASTENED BY what I considered to be my own failure in love (I blamed myself, of course), I returned to Liverpool from my National Service perhaps not lacking in self-confidence, but certainly lacking in a confidence in other people. New beginnings can be productive, but one is frequently left with a melancholy derived from that previous era that filters our existence from that moment onwards. I occasionally feel that life is a journey through realms of sadness, and you never truly leave that sadness behind; some of it sticks like glue, and every so often it can overwhelm you again, leaving you drained. This was such a time. It was as if my search for beauty and happiness was to be thoroughly illusory, and at the very least highly transitory.

Back home with the family once again, my day-time work continued with mother, but, as the weeks turned into months and the seasons began to remind me of my times back in the army, my thoughts also turned to my little job at Woolworth's in Abergavenny. I had been relatively happy there, and it occurred to me on a number of occasions that I should return. However, the constant tension in the Flannery household was always present as a pertinent reminder that I should not leave my mother alone with father for too long a period; it was a potentially dangerous situation. As he had aged, so his drinking had taken on gross proportions and I decided to forego another adventure, at least for the time being, in fear for my mother's life. It began to dawn upon me that perhaps I ought to seriously consider opening a small shop of my own. I was only 22 years old but felt eminently capable of turning a profit, if only I could find the right premises. I determined to keep my eyes and ears open in case a small property might come on to the market. I was actually earning most of my money after dark, in any case. No, not like that, but singing. I'd returned, at first, to the NUPO Club and, having brushed up on my technique, I eventually started to receive a few bookings in and around Liverpool. I was brought together with Ken Dodd again, but things had changed in Ken's life since my sojourn in the army.

By this time Ken was beginning to create quite a stir for himself and had even been asked to do a little radio broadcasting. From memory, I recall his big break coming in September 1954, when he made his professional show business debut at the now-demolished Nottingham Empire. He later told me that he was so nervous that he sat in a local milk bar for most of the afternoon, going over his lines before going to the theatre. By this time Ken was already receiving bookings at some of the more salubrious theatres in and around the north-west of England. He had clearly shifted up a gear. My time in the army had evidently held me back, artistically, while Ken had used the intervening time well, further developing his creativity by working on an already good singing voice. It was evident to me that I wasn't really needed to bolster this increasingly dynamic act. However, at the Napier Club on the East Lancashire Road, sometimes twice a week, our paths did cross; also at Ossie Wade's club in Walton Lane of a Sunday afternoon. There were no hard feelings and I simply continued to build up a repertoire of the most popular songs of the day in the hopes that I might attract a little attention myself. Jealousy in the popular music business of the 1950s and 1960s did occur, of course, but from my own limited experience I have found it to be over-exaggerated; more often than not people were genuinely pleased for each other when somebody began to rise in the ranks. I wished Ken all the luck in the world.

My own repertoire consisted of my favourite ballad-style numbers from this period: the popular songs of the day such as *Tell Me Why* by Eddie Fisher; *Too Young* and *Pretend* by Nat King Cole; *High Noon* by Frankie Laine; and one of my mother's favourites, *Here in My Heart* by Al Martino. For a while I was quite fanatical about Tony Bennett, and his rendition of *Stranger in Paradise* is still a great favourite of mine. I continued to be very particular in performance, always giving any resident pianist or trio my key and any band parts that I could lay my hands on and, in doing so, I built up a good reputation amongst the musos in Liverpool. I was known to be reliable and professional and, although work seemed a little infrequent at times, it kept the wolf from the door and kept me in touch with the business that I loved.

You might recall that I had originally applied for a job at the Adelphi with a view to becoming a seaman, but things had not gone according to plan. My National Service had been far more successful and so I signed on in late 1952 to see if I could hack it at sea. It was a while before I received notification from the New Zealand Shipping Company to join a ship, but a letter arrived in due course informing me that I was to join the Newfoundland in Southampton. I was a little disappointed to discover that I had to travel down to Hampshire. I did have some rather romantic visions of being waved off from the landing stage at the Pier Head by my adoring family, like that Hollywood image of a conquering hero ('a man's gotta do' etc.). Oh well, never mind. I nervously informed my father that I would once again be leaving (this time) the Mottram side of the family business. He responded in his usual aggressive tone in his accentuated Liverpool accent: 'your mother lets you do nothing all day anyway – I don't know why she even pays you. You should be working with me in a man's job. You won't last five minutes out there, you'll be back cryin' for your mam, and whingeing for your job back.' Thank you father, no change there then.

Evidently knowing something about me that I was unaware of myself, he kindly informed me that I was going to be in for a shock and would be crawling back to him, tail between my legs, all in due course. I really didn't know what he was talking about, but I took it to be a case of sour grapes and left it at that. My mother was very supportive, as usual, and realised that some kind of real, physical distance between me and the old man was essentially a sound idea, if nothing else. She certainly didn't want to see me leave Liverpool, but she was wise enough to recognise potential flashpoints if I were to stay. I was incredibly nervous about the whole affair and, to tell the truth, had a number of misgivings; however, with suitcase in hand, I set off for Southampton with my cousin Peter, who was returning to the port after leave in Liverpool, boarding the southbound train at Lime Street station.

After a rather gruelling journey down to the south coast, I arrived at Southampton docks to find that the ship I had been instructed to board was laid up for a week of repairs and loading. I was given a bunk on board the vessel and then spent that week loading the ship with essential supplies. I had signed on as a steward, and was informed that I was to serve the officers with their meals, as well as any paying passengers (there were to be a few but not many: the ship was principally for cargo). It was hard graft, that week, but we were bound for Auckland, which fascinated me, so I began to get over my homesickness as the days wore on and started to look forward to the trip. I had noticed that a number of seamen had taken a particular interest in me: they had given me tea, cigarettes (which I didn't smoke) and had enquired about my background etc. I presumed that they were simply being friendly with a fellow shipmate-to-be. I felt quite proud of myself that I was being regarded as an 'old salt' and thought nothing more of it. On the Friday, before the tide was about to change and as the tugs were lining up to escort the ship into open sea, I was approached by an older deckhand and, as it happened, a fellow Scouser.

'Listen young Joe,' he whispered. 'Do you realise exactly why those guys are taking such an interest in you?'

I replied that I just thought that they were helping me to adjust.

'Adjust! You're the one who will be adjusted. This is one of those kinds of ships. You are a very good-looking man; Joe, those men are … well, do you know what "queer" means?'

I said that I had no idea.

'They are doing you favours at the moment, but you'll have to pay them back …'

'Well, that seems fair enough,' I retorted.

'Do I have to spell it out to you, Joe? They will rape you as soon as we're at sea. They will all fuck you, Joe. They want to have sex with a younger man … and you're it! Don't you know nothing?'

Apparently not! I was not utterly innocent, but I had never realised that it could actually happen to me. George Melly was later to write that 'wine, women and song' was often converted into 'rum, bum and concertina' once the voyage was underway, but we hadn't even left Southampton yet. I decided there and then that my seafaring days were over without even leaving port. I ran to my bunk, grabbed my still-unpacked suitcase from my locker and jumped ship. I literally hurdled the dock railings and leapt on a bus bound for the station. I had just enough money for a single ticket back to Liverpool and within a few hours I was walking along the platform at Lime Street station in a complete daze, wondering what on earth to do next. The old man had been right, damn him. The bastard knew there would be a problem. How did he know? What did he see in me that I was unable to see for myself? Was I that stupid? What was the matter with me?

I meandered back to Everton and finally arrived at Luxmore Road, soaking wet and bedraggled, with, as father predicted, tail well and truly pointing towards my orifice. Mother was pleased to see me, of course, but immediately suspected that something was terribly wrong. I told her that I had just become very homesick and had jumped ship. I couldn't begin to tell her that my arse was on the line. How do you tell this to your mother? She packed me off to bed and I slept for almost two days. I developed a fever and the doctor was called. At one stage it was thought that I had contracted pneumonia; however, I pulled through OK. This time my nerves and my self-confidence had taken a tremendous blow. I was now clearly in something of a mess. I wasn't very sure who I actually was. After all, hadn't father predicted this unfortunate outcome? He knew something, but what? Had I not been so headstrong, maybe I could have learnt something about myself from him. But why did he know and not me? And why did mother not say anything? From the moment I walked back through the door she had been very supportive, but because I wasn't prepared to discuss the overtly sexual nature behind my homecoming, she had left the matter there, so to speak. But I needed her to tell me why I attracted these seamen. Did she know? Did I want her to discuss it? Looking back after all this time it has all the elements of a black comedy. After all, I later realised that I was gay. Not that this would have prepared me for a homosexual gang bang, you understand, but, rather, I can see just how naive and innocent I really was. Not only did I not have any idea about the sexuality of others (it just wasn't discussed at all in our household), but, more than this, I was not even in touch with my own sexuality. Even being occasionally called a 'sissy' meant very little to me, only perhaps that I might have been rather more polite than other teenagers. My father, on the other hand (a man of the world if ever there was one), certainly realised that there was something different about me, but he derived a certain grotesque pleasure by keeping me completely in the dark.

The next few weeks following this shock to my system were ones of rebuilding confidence. I was a very sensitive lad and objectionable behaviour of any description left me with a bitter taste in my mouth; in fact, it still does. I can take it, you understand, but I also tend to dwell on it. I appear to deal well with tragedy: from the outside it seems that I am holding up well, but inside I am often torn to pieces. One positive decision made during this period of convalescence, however, was not to return to the wood yard under any circumstances. Father had been to see me once during my illness, showing little sign of any compassion, but had left me a note attempting to lure me to work with him as soon as possible, apparently because he was busy. No chance! It was his behaviour that had led to this impasse. There was no way that I was going to allow history to repeat itself.

I went to the afternoon matinees at the local picture houses when I could, sitting alone in the Majestic or the Trocadero watching my dreams pass before my eyes. This was what I wanted: something to do with those characters on the screen – but how? I didn't mind so long as it was in the entertainment business (it didn't cross my mind at this stage that there was a music business, as such, for all roads appeared to lead to the Rome of the movies and theatre). How could I possibly imagine that I could involve myself in this glamorous world? Here I was, in an old northern city which was fast becoming a backwater, unemployed, unqualified and feeling remarkably useless. The only people who thought anything of me at all seemed to be my mother plus half a dozen randy Southampton sailors who wanted to shag the arse off me. This was clearly not a good phase of my life, which was especially disappointing considering that it had all promised so much only a few weeks earlier. I resolved to do something about it, without quite knowing what. My paranoia was further increased by my mother entering yet another of her entrepreneurial phases, needing me less and less. I was pleased for her, but further saddened by my own apparent uselessness. However, one thing that cheered me, and put me on the local entertainments map a little, was that a very short time later I had the pleasure of witnessing the fabulous Betty Hutton at the Liverpool Empire.

Her career as a Hollywood star had recently ended due to a contract dispute with Paramount following the Oscar-winning *The Greatest Show on Earth* and *Somebody Loves Me* (1952). The *New York Times* had reported that the dispute resulted from her insistence that her husband at the time, Charles O'Curran, direct her next film. When the studio declined, Hutton broke her contract. So by the time I saw her Hutton had been working in radio, had appeared in Las Vegas and she was now on a long, arduous tour of British theatres and US bases during 1954, and arrived in Liverpool towards the end of October that year. Together with the great vocal group the Skylarks, Betty played a full week at the Empire, and it was in the middle of the week commencing 27 October that I witnessed her performance. She was very tired and quite ill but battled through the evening in redoubtable fashion. At one stage of the performance, the Skylarks were laughing and joking with Betty about her inability to perform one of her hits (it might have been *It's Oh So Quiet*). I was so enamoured of her that I called to her at one point from the audience: 'Go on Miss Hutton, you can make it!' To my utter astonishment she immediately stopped the show and asked me to come out of the audience. We then sang a little duet to rapturous applause and this was followed by me singing alone, with my arm around her waist, *Good Luck, Good Health, and God Bless You*. By the time I was escorted back to my seat Betty was crying buckets. She then sent a note inviting me to meet her at the Adelphi the following day.

Some of the chaps I had worked with at the Adelphi were still there, and so when I arrived the following morning they were dumbfounded to discover that I was in the lobby in order to meet one of the world's biggest stars. 'That's it now, Flannery, you've made it!' cried one of my ex-oppos just at the point when none other than Mr Tournefant turned the corner; he just looked at me rather sniffily, refusing to be drawn into any conversation, but I felt I had exacted my revenge. Betty Hutton and I talked for ages at the Adelphi and she was so taken with me that she invited me on board for the rest of the week's engagements as her companion. I soon discovered that it was little wonder she had been exhausted. In between her performances in the theatres she had been playing at as many US bases as possible, which were still manifold in Europe at this stage. I suppose I became one of the very few British citizens to enjoy a performance of Betty Hutton from the wings of a converted hangar in a highly restricted US air base, namely Burtonwood. Because of Betty, I was also able to obtain a long-term pass on to the base as a visiting performer and received a handful of lucrative bookings as a cabaret act there. The pass also became very useful once the Mersey sound arrived in the early 1960s, for I was able to take a few groups on to the base to entertain the Americans.

Both the *Liverpool Echo* and the *Liverpool Daily Post* reported our impromptu performance at the Empire, but the press was unable to follow her, as I was, into the nether regions of American air force performing. She performed a different, far more sexy act at Burtonwood (after all, she was playing to airmen a long way from home) and played to both black and white audiences, although they were segregated the night that I was with her. Much later, when I was in the USA for my 50th birthday, I held a wonderful banquet at Essex House in New York – the same suite where Grace Kelly held her party before leaving for Monaco. Betty came along as the guest of honour and was a real delight. If one just thought of Betty Hutton as one of those 1950s commodities who sang for her supper, I think the point would be sadly missed about her contribution to popular music. I witnessed real affection and fandom from those US airmen. In fact, the music business, film, radio records and television failed to capture the whole of Hutton – for me, she was a real one-off.

Apart from singing of an evening, plus the occasional visit to the theatre or movies, my social life was practically non-existent. I was still very withdrawn and prone to bouts of sadness, but one afternoon in 1954, I rediscovered my childhood acquaintance, the young man who also tended to suffer from a great deal of melancholy. By sharing our doubts and insecurities over occasional dinners in the room behind my newly acquired shop, we became once again firm friends and each began to help the other redefine the rest of his life. Once again, Brian Epstein and I crossed paths. During the summer of 1954 I had finally managed to get a small, empty shop unit on Kirkdale Road. My mother had already suggested to me that it might be better if I moved out of the family home in City Road. This was not because she didn't want me around – far from it, in fact – rather she thought that my father's deteriorating behaviour might lead to a rather messy criminal act on my behalf. Basically, she was of the informed opinion that I might seriously injure or even kill her husband if things were to get out of hand. After all, I was now a strapping ex-army squaddie. Had I hit my father in albeit an unfamiliar fit of rage the chances of him getting up again would have been slim to say the least. Mother naturally recognised this and, being perturbed about this impossible domestic situation, asked me to move out. My father actually took my mother out to the pictures one evening in the spring of 1954 to see *The Robe*; this allowed me a few hours to move my bits and pieces to the little empty shop unit on Kirkdale Road. It was all very exciting, and rather than feeling any overt sadness at leaving the family home, I was rather thrilled. Time alone would tell whether it was to be an upswing in my day-time fortunes, but it was an experience not to be missed. Things were very bad at home between my father and me. He was drinking profusely and couldn't even bear to be in the same room as me by this time. So, with my mother's reiterated promise of leaving him as soon as Peter was deemed old enough, I set off into the wild blue yonder of self-employment in the fancy goods trade.

My mother's sister, Auntie Jane, owned a furniture shop on Kirkdale Road, so she was close enough if needed in an emergency. The Epsteins also had a shop on Walton Road and, between these two friendly furniture traders, I felt a little more secure. To begin with I furnished the back room of the shop with former orange and apple boxes: my joinery skills came in handy there! I did, however, succumb to hire purchase and bought myself a decent bed-settee from one of my father's contacts, the Gerrard-Kelly clearance house on Walton Road. This long-established family firm was only too pleased to help me, because I was a Flannery; strange to think that the very bed-settee that they were letting me have on the drip was part of the master plan to avoid me battering Mr Flannery Senior to a pulp. Having been successful with the Gerrard-Kelly connection, I then made full use of my father's other wholesale contacts in the trade and I discovered, once again, that he had a marvellous reputation as a good business man. My father's Jekyll and Hyde personality was actually proving to be very beneficial for me. Owing to his sterling business reputation, I was allowed a much higher level of credit from the fancy goods wholesalers in and around Islington than other young men might have obtained. Mr Applebaum, in particular, a well-respected Jewish jewellery wholesaler in Islington, was especially kind towards me, and I shall remain eternally grateful to him for his flexibility, encouragement and advice. However, after hearing of my leaving the family nest and setting up a business on my own, my father one day waltzed into my little shop wielding a hammer, threatening to smash up the place and me along with it. As momentarily frightening as it was, it all proved to be a load of hot air: he was drunk and I managed to remove him from the shop. Father ended up outside on the pavement, mouthing idle threats and rather inebriated ramblings. He had now taken on a different disposition and had become little more than an embarrassment to me.

Brian Epstein was also at home with his family at this time. It soon came to my attention that he had joined the Royal Army Service Corps for his National Service, after having been refused entry to the RAF, but had then been discharged altogether on medical grounds. Apparently, he had been considered emotionally and physically unfit. This sounded like Brian, poor thing. He was now back with his family and, in due course, we began to run into each other in the Walton Road area. Epstein and Sons were, of course, the kingpins on that road, highly regarded and well respected, and I was delighted that Brian should seek me out as soon as he realised I was in business in the area. We would often meet for a little lunch on a Wednesday afternoon, which was the traditional half-day closing in Liverpool, and discuss life's little successes and tragedies. Brian was not always in the Walton area of Liverpool because he had been placed in charge of another family outlet, Clarendon Furnishing in Hoylake; however, we did try to see each other at least once a week. It was at Clarendon Furnishing that Brian really blossomed as a salesman and manager. The writer Ray Coleman later claimed that the young Epstein essentially got his business chops together at NEMS, but this was not strictly the case. NEMS at this time was Harry's concern, not Brian's, and the young man was farmed out to a subsidiary on the Wirral to develop his skills. My memories of him from this time are of a very fragile but rather elegant person. He was somebody who looked both the perfect young man about town as well as a rather exquisite piece of porcelain. His dress sense was immaculate and I knew that style was one of the few things that he felt confident about. I realise now that my friendship must have been incredibly important for him at this stage because I do believe that I was probably the very first person, including his family, to whom he confided that he was homosexual.

It was one rather wet Wednesday afternoon on Kirkdale Road. There was not a soul to be seen – it was after all half-day – but the whole Kirkdale Road/Walton Road area could be incredibly depressing on a day like this and, knowing that Brian would be feeling low, I expected a knock on the door after closing time at one o'clock. I'd already prepared a little light lunch for the two of us in the back of the shop, just in case. Sure enough, just after one o'clock came the tell-tale light rap on the frosted glass of the door. This time, however, he was even more distressed than usual. We sat down and I made him eat a little and watched him very carefully. He was a bag of nerves, physically shaking and extremely emotional as I asked him what on earth was wrong. Was it something to do with work? No, work was fine; in fact he was a big hit in Hoylake where, for him, the class of customer was different and his gentility greatly appealed. What was the matter then? No reply. He muttered something about feeling very frustrated, that he couldn't begin to explain how he felt; but then there appeared an enormous well of emotion, a massive burst of energy: 'Joe, you must not tell a soul, but I just have to tell somebody, and you're my closest friend; I'm attracted to men rather than women, Joe. I want men, not women … do you understand?'

To be perfectly honest I didn't immediately get his drift, but in the very next moment I realised what this terrible anguish was all about. Brian was homosexual. Things were beginning to add up. Following his confession, he appeared a little more relieved: he had at least told somebody. He then began to explain that he had been experimenting with his feelings a little. This sounded a little dangerous to me but he continued that to begin with he wasn't really very sure exactly who he was attracted to, but the more he visited the Playhouse Theatre and then the pubs in and around Queen's Square, such as the Magic Clock and the Royal Bar, the more he had realised that it wasn't simply the theatre that attracted him, but the people, the lifestyle and then, more particularly, the male actors. He also stated that the whole scene around the area was to his liking. That it was not only theatrical, but also based around some gentlemen friends who were similarly inclined. Brian enlightened me that he saw the theatrical lifestyle as one that would appeal to his homosexual leanings, that it was probably the least prejudiced of all professions.

I was not overly concerned for him at this stage for, despite my relative innocence, I was aware that there was a homosexual community that existed in and around the Playhouse Theatre and Queen's Square area in Liverpool city centre, and I also knew that it was very protective. However, he also admitted that he was attracted to what he described as 'rougher boys', and this began to worry me. It was common knowledge that blackmailers and thugs enjoyed an open season on indiscreet male homosexuals and, with Brian coming from a very prominent Liverpool family, misdemeanours could prove tortuous and expensive. He told me he couldn't yet tell his family for fear of shame. What the hell was he to do? Frankly I was pleased that he had come to me, but also a little bewildered. I had, of course, the utmost sympathy for him, but I was not his father, neither was I his rabbi. He had admittedly turned into a charming young man, but also one who was intent upon experimentation. I already knew, for example, that he was on some form of medication and I had previously tried, to no avail, to persuade him not to depend on it so much. Whatever anyone advised him would probably be of little use in the long run, for Brian was headstrong and intent upon trying anything in his search for the happiness that had thus far eluded him. Therefore, what advice could I give him? The only thing that sprang to mind was what the local priest had always told me in St Anthony's on Scotland Road: 'to thine own self be true'. In the long run, all I could tell him on that wet afternoon in Kirkdale Road was to be as honest as he could. Living a lie might have to be part of one's outward presentation in mid-1950s Liverpool, but that didn't mean that the lie had to extend to the people who loved him. Brian's mother was devoted to him and even though his brother Clive and his father Harry might find it difficult to bear, there was nothing else to be done. When the time was right, I suggested, he would have to come clean; otherwise he risked serious nervous problems by bottling it all up. Of course, society in the 1950s dictated that it could go no further than immediate friends and family.

This was truly the kind of repressed culture that we lived in during that immediate post-war era. Homosexuality was, after all, still an illegal act, and for such a prominent Liverpool family to have a 'queer' was tantamount to sedition. I would like to think that, looking back, Brian took a lot of strength from that afternoon; perhaps it was something of a galvanising experience, being able to tell at least somebody, if not a member of his family, and I was happy to be of service. He knew that my own family background had been fraught and that I had also had to deal with some very important issues as a young man. Little did he or I realise at this stage that I too would have to agonise over the very same matter some months later. We parted that afternoon extremely close. From that moment forward our already strong friendship would have a bond that could not be broken by others. Even though my own lifetime partner was soon to come on to the scene, Brian and I had developed a firm attachment. To my knowledge Brian didn't actually tell the Epstein family immediately. In fact, he took what he later described to me as a 'soft option' for a while and kept any apparently sordid details from them a little longer. Yes, he continued to see his 'rough element' and, yes, he received a couple of good hidings from one or two and was actually blackmailed by another for a while. What helped Brian through this time was the company of myself, many of the actors and actresses at the aforementioned Liverpool Playhouse, together with the 'gentlemen's' scene that operated in the same area of Liverpool, to one side of the Playhouse: Queen's Square.

I saw a good deal of Brian Epstein during this period of our lives and he managed to get me out and about on many occasions visiting theatres and picture houses from Liverpool to Wallasey to Manchester. In fact, my own live performances reduced somewhat at this time owing to the socialising that went on between the two of us. We were also frequently seen together in the Queen's Square area and were considered by some to be an item. We were extremely close but this was not the case. If the truth be told, I was still very confused about my own sexuality and about sex generally, but perhaps as a consequence I was very curious about this scene. The company was great and I was befriended by ace photographer Albert Marrion: we became firm friends right up until his death. I thought of Albert as something of a mentor for the rest of his life and consulted him on many occasions on issues ranging from business decisions to personal preferences.

There was a vast variety of men and women from the Playhouse, such as Brian Bedford, John Gay, Patricia Routledge and even a young Rita Tushingham, and with interests bordering upon what could be described as the artistic, I felt in my element. Some, like young Brian Epstein, were also interested in fine arts and classical music; others were more like me, interested in popular styles and cultures, film and theatre especially. A few were academics; there was the occasional solicitor, a barrister or two and several businessmen and artists. The majority of the clientele were what we now call 'gay', of course; however, it was by no means an exclusively gay scene. This was a company of friends and some of those friends were evidently heterosexual liberals and were there because they simply enjoyed the company of their good friends whatever their sexual orientation. Some who bonded through shared interests were actually branded by outsiders as 'queer', when their curiosity actually lay in the arts, not necessarily in gay sex. What really fascinated me was that they were all genuinely interested in each other as individuals. They talked to each other without any ulterior motives. It was, indeed, a very genuine, honest and vibrant community. Some, as it turned out, were actually the City Fathers, responsible for upholding the law in the city of Liverpool. And yet here they were breaking the law by merely being themselves; how ridiculous it all was and how antiquated it now appears! Years later my mind would occasionally drift back to these formative days. Films such as Dirk Bogarde's *Victim* or much later *Scandal*, which depicted the unfortunate Stephen Ward, would bring to mind just how our intolerant British society found such friendships abhorrent. It is all so tame by modern standards, yet the pain and suffering inflicted upon those of a different sexual persuasion by the post-Second World War establishment remains unforgivable.

As for then, it was as if for the first time in a very long time I felt relatively at ease. This didn't appear to be the case from my new friends' point of view, however, for both Brian and I were labelled 'The Untouchables'. But this wasn't a derogatory remark. In my case it was actually a signal to those men and women who might wish to flirt with me that I was not certain about my own sexuality, and that I should be left to my own devices. This nickname stuck to the pair of us for some considerable time, for I didn't even consider the possibility that I might be homosexually inclined for at least another eighteen months, and it was probably evident to my new friends that I was attempting to work things out for myself on a gradual basis. They were very thoughtful, in actual fact, for the 'Untouchable' emblem kept everybody at a convenient length.

The locale named Queen's Square no longer exists, as such. In those far off days, that area in the city centre now adjacent to St John's Precinct was a market, and to the rear of the market was the epicentre of the Liverpool wholesale fruit and vegetable trade. Barrows were in and out of the market square like the proverbial fiddler's elbow, with their own warehouses being but a short walk away, across Whitechapel, in two rather dingy streets called Mathew Street and Harrington Street; hence perhaps the Cavern

Club retaining that smell of cabbages. This latter street was yet another city centre back-street area that I came to frequent by the time the sixties were under way.

I was beginning to question my own feelings towards men and women during 1954. There was one man who also drank in the Magic Clock and the Stork Hotel who I viewed from afar. I thought he was rather pathetic and looked as if he needed looking after. I felt rather sorry for him but thought no more about it, really. This was to be my first sighting of Kenny Meek, my future partner for many years. At this time I also had to fend off Brian a little, for he had developed one of his schoolboy crushes on me. These came in waves and would continue until I departed for Hamburg in 1963. We did share a love but I had no desire for any closer attention. There was more than one stage during this process of gradually coming out that frightened me, however. For example, a still well-respected solicitor in the town took it in his head to attempt to seduce me by following me home in his car. He stopped his motor as I approached home, opened the passenger door and gesticulated to me that I should step in. The cruelty of the man! I just ran and ran and ran! This, together with the growing attention of Brian at this stage, were the first real indications to me that I was attracting attention from members of the same sex; and I must admit that I was petrified.

Even today responses to homosexuality can be frightening, but imagine, if you will, what either being gay or just wondering if you were gay meant in the mid-1950s in a city such as Liverpool. These days it is widely acknowledged that there are male and female elements in all forms of human behaviours. But in those days a northern sexual spade was most decidedly not a shovel, and for those of us who began to question our sexuality it was a particularly startling experience. You might be beaten, you might be jailed; you might lose your job or have to lead a double life. One could fall foul of a blackmailer or even be sent to a mental asylum. In fact, a friend of mine voluntarily committed himself to spend some time in Rainhill Mental Hospital in a forlorn attempt to rid himself of his homosexual inclinations. He was given heterosexual pornography in an attempt to stimulate his seemingly dormant heterosexuality and drug aversion therapy when shown homosexual pornography. Naturally enough, it was all a complete waste of time.

Meanwhile trade was brisk in my little fancy goods shop. So much so, in fact, that towards the end of 1954 I decided to move out of the rear of the shop and into a well-appointed apartment at Alexander Terrace, 30 Princes Avenue in Toxteth. Mother was a little worried about this because she saw Toxteth as a rather transient area, but I was attracted not only by the flat, which was for these days, relatively sumptuous, but also by the district of Liverpool 8. You might remember that I was interested in the music coming out of this area of Liverpool and situating myself in Princes Avenue meant that I was close to the various tribal clubs and 'shebeens', the latter being a term for those illegal drinking clubs established in and around Liverpool 8, also known to this day as blues parties. I could now get my fill of jazz, blues, calypso and anything else that might be about. I was surrounded by music. Princes Avenue was and still is a beautiful, broad boulevard stretching from Upper Parliament Street to the gates of Princes Park, one of the first municipal parks in England. In Victorian and Edwardian times it was the height of opulence and the massive terraces built along both sides housed Liverpool's elite. By the mid-1950s, with the housing crises continuing, many of these ornate and expansive properties had been turned into rabbit warrens of pokey flats. Not so number 30, however, for this house had been laid out in far more extravagant apartments.

It was part of a large row of beautiful terracotta-fronted properties named Alexander Terrace and was either owned or subleased by a Mrs Wydett who, with the help of a full-time maid, kept the house in immaculate condition. As soon as I entered the property the smell of lavender polish took me back to City Road and I was hooked. I quickly discovered that the reason why this house was in such good condition and appeared more sumptuous than many other properties along the boulevard: it was an upper-class knocking shop! Mrs Wydett was a high-class tart who offered her own services while also employing another two girls under her wing at number 30; quite an arrangement, to be sure. Their clients were mainly professional, Jewish businessmen who looked after the girls' every need. The rates, their clothes, food, electricity and gas bills etc. were all taken care of by the clientele. In fact, the three women were wonderfully provided for. Once I had discovered that the oldest trade in the world was being plied in the house, I have to admit that at the time nothing could have concerned me less. These days, as I drive past my old apartment on a regular basis, I wonder what happened to them and feel guilty that I did not at some point attempt to intervene in their lives and their professions. I was delighted with my own home, though, and felt that I was on my way up. Life, however, was to take yet another turn during the early months of 1955.

5

'DON'T WORRY MR LOSS, I WON'T LET YOU DOWN'

WHEN I WASN'T working for the evening, or visiting the cinema, theatre or enjoying the company of the coterie from Queen's Square, I might be found having a quiet drink with my cousin Peter. If that were the case, I would invariably find myself entering one of the many talent nights at pubs in and around Liverpool and, more often than not, would win a fiver for singing. In actual fact, I had been singing professionally less and less over the previous twelve months owing to day-time commitments and night-time social life. So whenever the opportunity might arise, I would always give it a go to keep in vocal trim. I had even gone out as far as Southport in my search for that fiver.

One evening early in 1955, Peter and I were in the back parlour of the Olympia Pub, on West Derby Road. This pub was, and remains, opposite the Grafton Ballroom and the Locarno (the latter of which was formerly known as the Olympia). We hadn't actually planned on going into the Grafton that evening and were just enjoying a bit of a sing-along after having deposited my winning £5 with the barman when a famous face popped into the parlour for a quick drink. It was Rose Brennan, well-known vocalist with the Joe Loss Orchestra. The Loss band was an extremely popular attraction in Liverpool and was playing a few nights at the Grafton Ballroom. They were one of the most eclectic bands in the country and Loss was a man who always kept his eye on the best-selling lists. He would change the repertoire of the band on a week-by-week basis if necessary, just to keep up with record and sheet music sales.

Although his band had been in existence before the Second World War, the Joe Loss Orchestra was one of the most successful acts of the big band era in the 1940s and the early 1950s, with hits including a cover of *In the Mood*.

Back in April 1951 Elizabeth Batey, then lead female vocalist with Joe Loss, fell and broke her jaw. Joe was badly in need of a replacement and remembered hearing Rose Brennan on the radio during a visit to Ireland. Within days he had located her and, before a week was out, she was in Manchester rehearsing with the band. She stayed with Loss for fifteen years, before giving up show business in the mid-1960s. She wrote many of the songs she recorded with Joe Loss under the name Marella, and co-wrote songs with John Harris. Her co-vocalist with the orchestra from 1955 was Ross MacManus, but he left temporarily – I seem to recall that it was to join the Black and White Minstrel Show, although his young son Declan (aka Elvis Costello) had also been born the previous August. Either way, it was Rose who made it possible for me to progress in the music business. I'd just finished singing a 'ten to ten' special (the song intended to extend things once time had been called at 9.50 p.m.) when Rose came up to me and told me: 'You have a wonderfully powerful voice. I can arrange an audition tomorrow at the Grafton, 11 a.m., for a vocalist to replace Ross MacManus who's leaving for a while. It's only temporary – are you interested?'

Interested; you bet I was interested! 'I'll be there,' I exclaimed enthusiastically. 'Come on Peter, we're going home, I need to get my head down tonight.' Following that excited utterance we immediately left the pub, leaving a happy Rose Brennan (who hadn't even asked for my name) together with a rather bemused barman waving my £5 from behind the bar. The next morning I arrived at the Grafton at 11 a.m. expecting to find hundreds of prospective vocalists waiting to sign with the famous Joe Loss. However, when I walked through the front doors of the ballroom I was shocked to discover that I was the only one there. Rose came over to me and I remember her words to this very day:

Good morning darlin', let me know your name and I'll tell Mr Loss that you've arrived. I'm sorry to have sprung this on you but there isn't an official audition. We've only just discovered that our other vocalist Ross is leaving for a while and we need a replacement as soon as possible. Mr Loss left it to us vocalists to search out potential singing partners. When I heard you last night, you sounded just right for me. Now relax a little and we'll get something organised.

Well, amazement was compounded upon astonishment. Sit down? I couldn't stand up! After the pianist was found and a delay ensued waiting for Mr Loss to arrive, my nerves were about to completely shatter when everybody suddenly seemed to be ready. Loss was very charming but also non-committal. He asked me what I would like to sing. I said Nat King Cole's *Pretend* (it was all I could think of, to be honest) which pleased him immensely. I later discovered, via Rose, that this was one of his favourite songs: thank goodness for that. After a rather wobbly rendition of *Pretend* we sat down at the piano and Mr Loss began to speak.

'Not bad; how do you learn your material, Joe?'

'Well,' I replied, 'I just listen to the radio or buy a record and learn it from that. I try to get somebody to tell me the key so that I can let the pianist or the band know what key it's in, and that's about it to tell the truth.'

'You don't read music at all?'

'No, I'm afraid not.' My heart sank.

'Well, most people tell me that and that could be a problem with this set-up. We are on the road almost all the time and don't have time to listen to records in order to learn songs. If you were to work with the Joe Loss Orchestra you have to learn to read sheet music.'

I had not enjoyed the privilege of an ordinary education let alone a musical one; I had realised that this problem might come to pass. Little did I envisage that it would be with such a prominent band. Mr Loss looked thoughtful, however. He evidently did need a replacement, and urgently.

'Listen Joe, I like your voice, so does Rose, which is just as important, and you look good. Ross isn't leaving until the end of the month. If you can learn to read music by the beginning of next month, I'll take you on. My musical director will let you know about a couple of tutor books that you will need to pick up. I don't want chapter and verse, just keys and triads. It might be worth your while to contact a local music teacher too.'

I was stunned. 'I'll do my very best. Don't worry Mr Loss, I won't let you down.'

Joe Loss seemed pleased with himself, relieved even: a chance meeting had brought about the possibility of a temporary replacement for Ross MacManus, his popular male vocalist. We shook hands; as I began to walk back to the foyer of the Grafton the band members were assembling for rehearsals. He hadn't asked me about my occupation, my family or my availability. I supposed he assumed that if he offered somebody a job, they would readily accept if available – he wasn't wrong. As I approached the edge of the dance floor he shouted to me, 'Joe, I'll give you a guest appearance tonight. Put on your best suit, stay in the audience and I'll pull you up on stage during the second half. If you can do it in front of a crowd, then that should confirm to me whether or not you've got what it takes to replace Ross.'

'Yes Mr Loss, and thank you.' I was onstage that very night! What about wages, money, clothes, travel? My shop? Nothing was discussed. Well, why should it have been? This was what I'd always wanted, wasn't it?

That evening at the Grafton everything seemed to go according to plan. The band was very hot and went down a storm, and halfway through their second spot they called me up from the floor. There was no announcement about my being the new singer in the orchestra; Joe Loss simply stated that they had discovered some local talent. The whole point of the spot was that they wanted to prove to themselves that they hadn't made a ghastly mistake. I stepped on to the stage and sang Al Martino's romantic *Here in My Heart*, which went down very well, and the nod of acknowledgement from Mr Loss suggested that I was hired. Provided, of course, I got the important matter of a bit of music theory under my belt.

I quickly sorted out my affairs. The shop would have to close for the time being. It was only on a rental basis, so there were no long-term commitments to renege on. The family were also informed of the good news and, with the exception of father who scowled at the very idea, were naturally delighted. Mother dutifully reminded me, however, that the work was only to be short term; that Ross MacManus would return and that I ought to keep a clear head about future prospects. I tried very hard to take on board what she was telling me, but truth be told, I was far too excited. I now had a month to learn a little theory and so I purchased a small red theory book (I think it was *The Rudiments and Theory of Music*) from Crane's in Liverpool's city centre, booked myself in with a qualified music tutor on the top floor of the Bluecoat Chambers and proceeded to learn a little of the verities of notation. In actual fact I found it rather easy; so much so that by the time the Joe Loss Orchestra was back in town with a twelve-month contract for Joseph Flannery esquire, I could read popular music sheets with relative ease, recognising the thirty-two-bar formulae right away.

Following the week's engagement in Liverpool we played a few dance halls in and around the north-west of England, ending up in Blackpool. To tell the truth, I remember little of the engagements. For the most part I was rather panic-stricken for the first two weeks: the assistance of the lovely Rose Brennan was absolutely seminal and without her I wouldn't have been able to cope. During the day we would rehearse, followed by lunch. We would then pile on to the coach, be given sheet music to read, packed lunches to eat and a chance to catch forty winks before the next port of call. It was all very exciting: I loved travel and being surrounded by musicians, but I was very nervous. As far as wages were concerned, I was rewarded handsomely. We were all paid cash on a weekly basis and my salary was between £25 and £30 per week. I sent a lot of it home. There was really very little to spend it on in the north of England in the mid-fifties: a few shirts, socks and undies, a pot of Brylcreem and the odd suit were all I needed. I made sure, however, that I stayed away from the customary card schools that the band held. Some real money changed hands on the coach and I didn't intend to lose my shirt to a trumpet player at this early stage.

By early summer we were ensconced in the Villa Marina in Douglas, Isle of Man, a very beautiful part of a very beautiful island, to be sure. The Joe Loss Orchestra was resident for the season and was attracting hundreds of dancers each evening. Owing to the recent success of Bill Haley, the band began to incorporate a little rock 'n' roll into their repertoire that summer and the response from the dancers was phenomenal. After one frantic evening of jive dancing, I remember remarking to Mr Loss: 'That twelve bar stuff that we played went down better than anything else. I wonder whether this new rock 'n' roll is going to see off the balladeer?' Joe turned to me with a determined look on his face, as if he had already considered this possible scenario, and firmly informed me:

> Rock 'n' roll will stay young Joe. It's just too exciting to be a passing fad. I've seen lots of dance crazes in my time, but rock 'n' roll is much more than a dance craze, believe you me. Whatever happens, I'll *make sure* this band plays it. The Joe Loss Orchestra is about *now*. It always has been and always will be.

On the evidence of history, this can be seen to be a very good decision. Joe Loss always had his finger on the pulse. What he had recognised in the summer of 1955 took the British media almost a further twelve months to detect. Indeed, Loss' band was still playing pop hits for dancing in the late 1960s, almost fifteen years later and long after other band leaders had hung up their batons. This was my first real association with something approaching live rock 'n' roll, albeit big band style via Joe Loss, but it was while in the Isle of Man that it became evident to me that the music and dances associated with rock were bringing throngs of younger teenagers back into dance halls. Thanks to rock 'n' roll, the dance-hall business on the island really began to spring to life.

As a dancer at the Grafton, I hadn't previously really noticed any decline, but as a singer, travelling around with Loss, I was surprised to find many halls only half full, with kids filtering in, staying for an hour or so, and then aimlessly filtering out again. There was a younger audience waiting for something to happen, dissatisfied with the staple fare of the big bands. Rock brought excitement and rearticulated the jive. There had always been plenty of jiving, even before the arrival of rock: I well remember the US GIs jitterbugging and lindy-hopping all over Liverpool. But the combination of the jive, which was relatively sexy for its day, coupled with the revolutionary music of rock swept across British dance halls like a breath of fresh air. My time at the Villa Marina was a busy one indeed, as Joe Loss recognised and pandered to the repeated calls for rock 'n' roll that summer of 1955.

Our digs in Douglas were quite palatial. In fact, neither food nor money nor sex was rationed. But I kept myself pretty much to myself – at least as far as the latter was concerned – for I still didn't really think of myself as a full member of the band by any means. I kept reminding myself that I was just a replacement, a substitute. I was also, of course, still confused about my own sexuality. In fact, I determined neither to worry nor think about the matter of sex for the entire time I was with Loss. My days off were usually filled with a bit of sightseeing: cups of tea on the promenade at Douglas or a bus trip to Ramsay or the Laxey Wheel, and of course rereading my music theory book. Life seemed simpler that way and I was able to get on with my job. I did become friendly with the girls from the Ivy Benson band: a very famous British jazz band consisting entirely of women, who were a big draw on both the swing and jazz circuits. Their stories were amazingly raunchy considering this was 1955 and they used to get up to all sorts of high-jinx. Even though Ivy Benson thought she ruled the band with a rod of iron, evidently there were ways and means to get what you wanted as a female when on the road month after month. I considered myself very privileged to be asked by Ivy to make a guest appearance with the band one afternoon. It was an open-air event in the gardens attached to the Villa Marina and, in need of a little male vocal crooning, they asked if I might moonlight with them. This beautiful amphitheatre in the gardens played host to a number of bands during those hot summer afternoons. I mentioned this to Joe Loss and he had no objections 'just this once'. So I also briefly fronted the Ivy Benson band for a matinee that summer and it was indeed a great experience. They were so professional and it gave me an interesting insight as to what it must be like for a female vocalist to appear in front of an all-male band. For example, I distinctly remember two female horn players discussing the verities of my backside while I was singing a Perry Como number. Isn't role reversal a wonderful thing?

I became very pally with some of Ivy's band, although the great woman herself was a little more difficult to deal with. She tended to come over rather like a cross between Margaret Rutherford and Jackie Pye, the wrestler, at times. However, I don't blame her for this at all. It was the likes of Ivy who helped to break down the barriers between the sexes during this very inflexible decade. Some of her girls were gay, too, which made the whole entourage a very interesting sight to observe. Rather like a fly on the wall, I would witness different kinds of role-playing within the band: matronly and masterful figures; little girls lost and 'baby Jane' types, plus, of course the long-suffering and experienced musos simply plying their trade – a truly wonderful mix. I learnt a lot about life simply from observing a female band on a night out. I sat in with them a few more times before the season drew to a close and attended their farewell party – what a riot! Who said that women cannot party as hard as men?

We spent most of the autumn in London and on the south coast. Our main venue was the Hammersmith Palais, but we played a lot of private functions too. Joe Loss was a great draw on the 'debs' circuit – you know, the upper-class twit brigade of the 1950s. We might play the odd hunt ball or a 'gay young thing's' coming-out party or a ball given for a visiting diplomat; I even remember playing at a posh do for members of the Royal Family. Very little, as I remember, was turned down by Mr Loss' agent. The band, including myself, was on a wage and had to be paid and Mr Loss was always keen on balancing the books and making money. By the mid-fifties keeping a band fed and watered for the best part of a year had become an expensive luxury, so work, any work, was welcomed. He was very generous with charity functions, however. We would usually play at least one of these every couple of weeks: perhaps a matinee somewhere for the Water Rats, the Variety Club of Great Britain or some such artistes' charity. This was double edged, of course, for if we played a charity gig further paid bookings would roll in for the next few months simply because Mr Loss was considered a good egg. He was all heart, was Joe.

By the time our Christmas party dawned at the Hammersmith Palais, I must confess that I was absolutely knackered. My voice had been giving me trouble since the latter part of autumn and, having visited a doctor in London, I was told to rest – it wasn't up to the constant torture of professional work. But there was no such thing as rest for a vocalist in the Joe Loss Orchestra. We might have been extremely well paid for the mid-1950s but we never had a chance to spend any of it; my bank account had never looked so good but my voice was being worked to a frazzle. After a second visit to the doctor in December I was further informed that only immediate rest would prevent the dreaded nodules appearing on the vocal chords, but what could I do? I loved to sing; I loved the life, and wanted it all to continue. Little did I realise that Christmas Eve 1955 would be my last ever performance with the Joe Loss Orchestra.

We were given a month off over Christmas and I immediately made plans to head back to Liverpool. I remember my farewells at Euston station seemed to be especially poignant. Rose Brennan was there to see me off and it all seemed a little overwhelming for us both. We had gelled very well and I think that Rose expected to find herself in a rather invidious position the following spring when Ross MacManus' return was anticipated. Rose needn't have worried, for the spectre that hung over my relationship with my father was to rear its ugly head once more that Christmas, forever preventing me from any professional singing. When I returned home for the Christmas of 1955 the family was in some degree of turmoil. Mother's relationship with father had deteriorated further. Father was drinking very heavily and was in various stages of drunkenness most of the time. He was neglecting his business interests, and when he wasn't at home boozing and insulting us, he was out on the road in his fancy new motor with a floozy by his side. It all reached a critical stage on New Year's Eve. We always tried to spend the New Year together, despite father's wanderlust; however, during the early evening of the 31st, he suddenly announced to all and sundry that he didn't want to spend another moment in our company and was going out. It was quite obvious to me that this had already been planned. I was furious. He treated his wife, my mother, like dirt; he was evil in the way that he treated his family. Only young Peter was spared this man's wrath. I challenged him there and then to be honest with us all:

You've had this planned for a while … you don't want to spend New Year with your family, because in your eyes, you haven't got a family. All you want to do is go out, get rotten drunk and have your way with the

nearest piece of skirt … well if that's what you want, you may as well go
out and get it … we know you father … you're nothing but a lush, a
waste of space!

There, I'd said it: 'a waste of space', the very words he would throw at me,
and now he had at last got them back in return. He stood and stared at me.
I knew he wanted to kill me. This waste of space was telling him now, and
the truth hurt, by God it hurt. For me he was nothing but a lush; the son
in whom he always appeared so ashamed was the one to inform him of
it. He suddenly launched at me and grabbed my throat. His grip was like
a vice, he had such strong and muscular hands. I tried to pull away but he
wouldn't let go. I could feel his breath on my face, it stunk of whisky and
of all the foul deeds he had been involved in since I could remember. He
was squeezing the life out of me; he was pressing the space in my throat so
heavily that I couldn't move. I was convinced that I was going to die. All
I could hear was his breathing up against my face and the screams of my
mother who was pleading with him to let me go. I managed to move my
right hand, then my arm and in a frantic move I made a grab for his hair
and yanked him backwards. His grip on my throat loosened and I felt a
rush of cool air fill my lungs. I was about to hit him as he fell, but instead I
allowed the pathetic man to fall topsy-turvy on to the floor like a rag doll.

Nothing more could be done with him. I was unexpectedly very
rational, my head was clear; perhaps it was the fresh oxygen pulsating
through me that calmed and settled my nerves. As I looked at him on the
floor, I put my hands to my neck band and knew that he had caused some
serious damage to me; my throat was hot, swollen and incredibly sore. But
all I could do was to tell him to get out, which he immediately did. I had
ordered my father to leave his house and he had done so like a lap dog. Just
raising my voice further injured my swollen larynx. I felt no exhilaration,
only distress and anguish – I had come home to this? This was in the days
before New Year's Day was a public holiday and after a quiet but painful
New Year's Eve with my nearest and dearest I hastened to the doctor tout
de suite.

I knew what his prognosis would be before I even stepped inside his
surgery; nothing Chris Flannery ever did was by accident. As I recall, it
went something like this:

Joseph, I'm sorry to tell you that I think your vocal chords have been
damaged. They were already weak, you have been giving them a good

old hiding over the past year, but this attack has caused considerable strain on your larynx. Your larynx holds together your vocal chords as well as allowing air to go through to the lungs. I'm afraid it has been rather badly impaired. The only thing I can suggest to you is to go home, take lots of rest and speak as little as possible. Maybe in a few months' time you might be able to sing a little, but I wouldn't hold your breath [he had a lovely way with words]. You cannot sing now, you obviously realise that? Well, it might be that way for a long time. In fact you may never be able to sing in the same way again. Once your larynx has repaired itself, it will configure in a different way. That might mean that your singing voice will alter.

He could see that I was absolutely devastated, but, in truth, he wasn't telling me anything I didn't already instinctively know. Ha! One way or another, my father always succeeded in having the last word; he was always able to injure me in some way, shape or form that was far in excess of what I could do to him. My immediate return to the Joe Loss Orchestra was simply impossible, and my long-term future as a singer looked grim. Thanks, father. I went for a quiet drink in town and wandered rather aimlessly around until I found myself sitting at the bar in the Magic Clock. There was a matinee and some of the performers from the Liverpool Playhouse and the Royal Court Theatre were there downing a few drinks, enjoying their careers, their bonhomie, their good luck; I was bitter, very bitter. I repeated over and over to myself: 'OK, so perhaps I would have been replaced by the incoming Ross MacManus, but by then I could have put the feelers out for another position. I was a professional, somebody would have wanted me … you know what mother always says: "one door closes, another one opens".' These thoughts swirled around my head all night as I drank. Like my father I drank myself into oblivion that night, but my throat was sore; the more I drank, the worse it got, but so what? It was all over wasn't it?

I awoke the next afternoon, 2 January 1956, with the mother of all hangovers. Somehow I had dragged myself back to my apartment at Princes Avenue. How, I still don't know, but there was Mrs Wydett, the madam of the household, holding a cold flannel to my forehead and a cup of hot coffee to my lips. The original 'tart with a heart', she was very sympathetic when I explained to her my predicament. After a few days I began to rationalise the situation a little more. I had to be honest with myself in order to carry on and, after sending a telegram to Joe Loss' offices in

Soho, I came to several salutary conclusions. My voice had already been damaged during the autumn and winter of 1955, of that there was no doubt. I would have been unable to resume my career after the Christmas break, of that there was also little doubt. If I was perfectly honest, I could only describe myself as a passable vocalist, of that there was equally little question. And if I was brutally frank, the last two months or so with the band had been utterly exhausting, and not just a little lonely and depressing. Exhausting because of the workload; lonely for obvious reasons; and depressing because I could see and hear new music coming up in the rearview mirror that was going to overtake big band singing at such a pace that the scene would be left reeling, and I knew I couldn't sing rock 'n' roll.

While I was down in London I had continued to scratch that musical itch that I had mentioned a while ago. Wandering around Soho in the mid-1950s could be an interesting affair, I can tell you. However, the nightlife for me paled into insignificance when I discovered a number of small pubs and cellar clubs in and around Wardour Street and Soho Square. In these places I came across some of the most amazing music I had ever heard. The likes of Ken Colyer, Chris Barber and Humphrey Lyttelton were all blowing up a storm without any of the showbiz pretensions that I had been used to. They stood there in their belts and braces and simply belted it out. Not only that, but when they went for a drink at half time, a few of the band would stay behind and play their way through some old African American spirituals and what sounded to me like the blues. They would play on a variety of different instruments, none of which I was used to in a band like Loss'. The guitar was centre stage, a washboard was being used, mouth organs and bass fiddles, banjos and clarinets were all used for solo work, not simply to accompany a band leader and the rest of the orchestra. It was all very illuminating to me and it also sounded rather like the stuff I had heard in the Duck House and on the Isle of Man, that rock 'n' roll that the press had been talking about so much: the stuff that was about to apparently deprave our children, at least according to the cultural critics of the day. I liked it!

I just knew that something was bound to happen with such a natural scene as this; I could feel it then, and I felt it again as I discovered that skiffle groups were forming all over the country, including Liverpool: change was in the air. The whole spectrum of popular music performance had been opened up, as far as I could see, by one recording: Lonnie Donegan's *Rock Island Line*. Not only were smaller combos now eminently possible, which laid waste to ideas about big band legitimacy, but skiffle was also breaching the theoretical barriers that had stood in my way before joining the Joe Loss Orchestra. No longer did kids have to learn to read music, as I had done in a hurry for Joe Loss. With a cheap guitar and knowledge of C, F and G, they could bypass the stereotypical path of the popular music mainstream. I remember picking up a copy of the *New Musical Express* which read something like: 'Never before has a musical craze been so easy to "do it yourself".' The journalists were right. Others had said that rock 'n' roll was only a passing fad. In truth, it might have been but for two important developments. First of all the legacy of easy access left by Lonnie Donegan, and secondly, the sexuality of Elvis Presley, who was to follow Donegan into the charts that May. Although Bill Haley had created a stir, he was far too old and sounded too much like a swing band in overdrive. As for Donegan, this was the music of the rank amateur and gloried in that fact. And Elvis, well, just ask my brother, Peter: for him Elvis was the king.

6

THE LIFE OF BRIAN PLUS TEENAGE REBELS AND FURTHER DETOURS

TOXTETH'S BUILT ENVIRONMENT certainly contributed to Liverpool's sense of self-identity (hubris, even) through the physical representation of wealth derived from the kind of trade I was growing to enjoy. But by at least the midpoint of the twentieth century it had also come to represent a lack of black Liverpudlian identity, as the very physicality of that environment came to represent contradictions of disappearance, neglect and rejection. When race is used as a stick to beat one's neighbours, how can the supposed identity of being 'Liverpudlian' serve as anything other than a pretentious synonym for self, reputation and social standing? I came to see that by at least the mid-1950s I was part of a 'district of otherness' full of ambiguity, ambivalence and indeed downright confusion, emerging at a time when not only Liverpool's post-Second World War decline was approaching its nadir, but also the post-colonial transformation of the UK was reaching its zenith. One significant minutiae inscribed into this tortuous process of twisted (yet unfolding) dialectics was that the ancient moniker of 'Toxteth' in real terms came to be superseded by its increasingly more evocative postal address of 'Liverpool 8'.

Mother would not deem a visit to my Princes Road residence a possibility. She thought that Liverpool 8 was far too transient and dangerous, and she was fully aware that Mrs Wydett was what she called a 'posh tart'. I always thought at the time that this was a bit matronly, as if she really wanted me back at City Road, but in retrospect I see now that she was probably worried about the growing black population in that part of town.

Our racist attitudes in those far-off 1950s were as much implicit as explicit. Few of us would ever like to be described as racist, but racism existed, even amongst one's own family, and even in this case from my dear mother. She was never a racist as such, but harboured such tendencies like most of us did then. Liverpool 8 was for the blacks, not her son. But I loved it; the sense of community was tangible. The name Liverpool 8 originally signified a designation for the postal district of Toxteth (e.g. Anfield was Liverpool 4, West Derby was Liverpool 12 and so on), but perhaps like all things British, such seemingly neutral names soon received cultural and geographical status. Certainly, the history of Toxteth is in itself a fascinating indicator of cultural distinctions, influences and (dis)continuities. Toxteth was Liverpool's early to mid-nineteenth-century Nob Hill, built by ship owners, cotton and corn traders and the like, and, as Margaret Simey once informed me, was utterly redolent of 'the Liverpool merchant tradition'. Like all districts of Liverpool, Toxteth was further subdivided into wards ostensibly for local government and political purposes. But such wards not only signified pragmatic political administrative borders, but were also bounded by issues of race and transience.

Originally built to exude wealth and opulence, little nineteenth-century expense was spared on the large, detached designer properties in both the Granby and Abercromby wards. For example, the house in which I rented my own comfortable accommodation was originally part of a one-off designer-built property commissioned in the mid to late nineteenth century. However, by at the very least the early 1950s many such properties were long past their sell-by date. Some had actually been abandoned by their owners during the Blitz and never reoccupied, others were literally falling down where they stood (2 Bentley Road, around the corner, was such an example), whereas still more were bearing the brunt of uncaring absentee landlords and the associated problems of multiple occupancies.

Such multiple occupancies were dilemmas developed partially as a consequence of a continuum of transience throughout the twentieth century, but three waves from the middle of the century onwards can be identified. Firstly, following the 1940 Blitz, black families who had been bombed out of their homes nearer the docks and the river in the hitherto 'traditional' black area around Pitt Street, came to be accommodated in the crumbling Victorian and Edwardian buildings of the L8 Abercromby ward. Secondly, L8's Granby ward also contained streets of smaller terraced housing such as those in the river streets, Eden, Cam, Exe and Thames, which housed predominantly white families. These were, by the mid to late 1950s, declared slum clearance streets. White families left and the houses were boarded up, ready for demolition. A few black families occupied these properties on an ad hoc basis. Thirdly (and perhaps from this historical distance most importantly), there came the post-war expansion of the University of Liverpool following the Robbins Report on Higher Education. The university was allowed to expand and acquired 80 acres of land in the Abercromby ward, systematically evicting the closely packed residents from streets adjoining Abercromby Square, such as Bedford Street and Myrtle Street.

Despite all of this trickery and back-sliding by Liverpool's elite, the shops on Lodge Lane and Kingsley Road were always full of happy, friendly faces. The clubs were full of fascinating music, ranging from US R&B to Caribbean and African rhythms. As I grappled to come to terms with a new life and a new job (I had started work at British Enka in Speke), I wouldn't have chosen anywhere else to live. Despite severe levels of deprivation, Liverpool 8 bred a self-supporting optimism and confidence in 1956. Another young man who enjoyed the rather bohemian atmosphere in Toxteth and spent a great deal of time at Victoria Terrace, 30 Princes Road during the first part of that year was a youthful Brian Epstein. Brian, you might remember, had outed himself to me prior to my sojourn with the Joe Loss Orchestra, and it was he, Albert Marrion and the rest of the crowd from the Magic Clock 'secret society' who really helped me through my dark days of depression after the incident with my father. I have mentioned the name of Albert Marrion once before and he is deserving of a small pen picture; he was a prominent Liverpool businessman and photographer and a member of the local Jewish community. He was a wise man and confidant to me and many others as well. He not only had to face issues concerning his own sexuality but also the hazards of local business conditions. He suffered from the blind and destructive forces of prejudice, while at the same time understood how patience could result not only in riches but also wisdom. I was amazed to discover, however, that Brian had yet to inform either Albert or his own family of his sexuality. Some twelve months or more after he had opened up his heart to me he was still leading a life of secrecy, a life of danger.

One evening I had just retired to bed at around midnight when there was a ringing of the bell on the main door of number 30. I knew that neither Mrs Wydett nor any of her girls were expecting gentlemen callers because they were all out, believe it or not, at a police ball. I immediately threw on my dressing gown and went downstairs in case it was an emergency. Well, it was, after a fashion. Brian was standing in the light of the doorway in a beautiful lounge suit, but with his shirt open to the waist and blood dripping from his face on to his expensive Van Heusen trubanised white shirt. 'For God's sake Brian, come in … what happened this time?' I demanded as I ushered him up the broad sweeping staircase of number 30. Brian was clearly traumatised and he mumbled something about Sefton Park, only ten minutes away from my apartment, then began to cry. I immediately grasped what had happened. One of Brian's bits of rough again, I thought; I felt like saying to him, 'Oh God Brian, when will you learn?' But how could I? He was not to blame: why condemn him for wanting to love somebody? I corrected myself: 'Actually Brian, just say nothing, at least for the moment … let's get you inside and cleaned up.'

I reached for my apartment door and bundled him towards the dining table with one hand, whilst searching for the Dettol and cotton wool with the other. Brian was in quite a mess but, although his face was badly swollen – his nose, upper lip and cheekbone – I was grateful that I could see nothing broken. In truth I thanked the heavens, for had anything been fractured a visit to Sefton General Hospital and questions would have surely ensued. I cleaned him up as best I could and poured him a brandy from a small bottle I kept in case of emergencies. After ten minutes or so of delicate dabbing, drying and drinking, Brian explained to me what had happened. From memory it went something like this:

Oh Joe, when will I learn? I met a chap in the Lisbon Pub; he seemed so nice. He said he worked on the docks and I bought him a few drinks. He was very strong, very muscular, but he said he liked me. At closing time I said I'd give him a lift and we ended up driving through Sefton Park. He seemed to want me as much as I wanted him … he was agreeable and he seemed really gentle. But when we'd finished he demanded my wallet. He said he'd kill me unless I gave him my wallet. So I gave it to him; Joe, it's got everything in, my address … everything. And then he hit me two, maybe three times in the face. I slumped to the pavement by my car and passed out. When I came around all I could think of was coming here. I couldn't go home looking like this, I just couldn't. You're my only real friend Joe, you know me. My family still doesn't really know. But Joe, they will if that bastard starts to look in my wallet. What am I going to do?

What was he going to do? That comment immediately took me back to the back room of my little shop in Walton a year or so previously. Just like then, there was precious little anyone could actually do. These were very difficult times for gay men. It sounded like Brian had met a prospective blackmailer – there were many stalking the gay community of Liverpool at this time. I remember asserting: 'Just try to relax Brian; it's no use getting in a state. All we can do at this stage is hope that you never hear from him again. If you do, then you'll be faced with a few important decisions, but let's not jump the gun, he was probably after a bit of quick sex and a few bob, that's the way a lot of them work.' My heart truly went out to him. He was always so vulnerable, especially, as I was to discover, when his promiscuous tendencies got the better of him on occasions such as these. The brandy had its effect and he eventually fell asleep on the couch, snivelling in his sleep like a small child sent to bed without any supper. Sleep, however, had deserted me. I sat in the bay window looking out over the broad expanse of Princes Boulevard and started to put together the pieces of my own rather curious jigsaw of a life. To paraphrase Pirsig, the bravery process occurs when one is quiet long enough to see, hear and feel the universe, not just one's own stale opinions about it.

I gradually came to realise in those early hours of twilight that I was a great deal more like Brian than I had previously realised. Brian's persecutor had also prompted me to search inside myself: search for a self that I could recognise, discover a reason for my father's hatred, perhaps; find an answer to those questions of my youth, why Auntie Winnie had remarked that I could never be a priest. In the half light of an early February morning in 1956, with a bruised and battered Brian Epstein fast asleep on my sofa, I suddenly realised that my father had hated me because he had seen in me something that I had hitherto not seen myself. I revolted him, I was effeminate; to him I was a 'puff'. Of course! How could I have been so stupid? Mother, father, Pat, Southampton, our friends at the Magic Clock – I finally acknowledged that Brian Epstein's characteristics were also those of my own. The sex, admittedly, was of little interest to me for it frightened me somewhat, but the rest of it: the community, the feeling of well-being I received from the crowd in Queen's Square, explained just about everything. I too was like Brian. The tag of 'untouchable' given to me by the chaps in Queen's Square was obviously some kind of 'holding' description. They, like my own father, knew something about me that I had not hitherto recognised – how stupid had I been? How naive, more like. And how so like me to shy away from the perhaps more incendiary aspects of real life. Life was not just about staring in the window of a newsagent's shop or lighting candles in churches on Scotland Road. As with my favourite films on the silver screen, there were always bound to be myriad subplots, undeniable confusions and multiple febrile pathways.

By 7.30 that morning Brian had been patched up, fed and watered and sent off to find his car, parked somewhere along Devonshire Road. I closed the door of number 30 behind him and prepared to get the bus to Speke for my daily start at 8.30 a.m. at British Enka. For the first time ever, I felt I knew exactly who I was. As I boarded the bus to work everything seemed to fall into place. I was a little frightened, of course; I was looking at people on the bus and wondering whether they too knew that I was not heterosexual – whether they had already worked it out while I was keeping myself in perfect ignorance and denial. Did I look any different? Of course, by the time I had got off the bus at the factory I was thinking rather more rationally. Such realisations did not necessarily change one's visage or out-wardly alter anything. I commenced work with some trepidation, but then ordered my tea and biscuits from the tea lady just as usual; she suspected nothing – it was just another day. The most important thing was that I felt like a weight had been lifted from my shoulders. There was one problem, however; while working at British Enka I was receiving a lot of attention from my supervisor. He had been giving me a vast amount of piece work, allowing me to earn extraordinary wages for the mid-1950s, and I had pre-viously not realised why. We had become friends during this period but it hadn't occurred to me that Kenny, my supervisor, actually fancied me. I had also seen him in the Queen's Square area but still hadn't realised that he too was gay – but I liked him: he seemed rather sad and vulnerable.

Kenny was a very down-at-heel character at this time, poorly dressed and rather underfed. I discovered that he was looking after his terminally ill father in what could only be described as a Walton slum, and it appeared to me that he was rather neglecting himself for the sake of his dad (but, of course, I was in no position to comment). We began to spend a little time together after work and, one evening after Kenny and I had been for a drink, I asked to see his father and we returned to his house. The house was utterly dilapidated and Kenny's father was also in a terrible state: riddled with cancer and in great pain; bedridden, incontinent and excru-ciatingly thin. All the more shocking for me was that he was in full control of his mental faculties and was able to judge his proximity to death. While Kenny was out of the room, his father told me that he would, indeed, be dead within the week. He could see that I was both visibly repelled by his condition (I couldn't help it) and viscerally disturbed by his candour. But he told me he had no time for dishonest optimism and asked me to take care of Kenny once he had expired. Kenny entered the room with medication for his father (morphine, I think; nothing else would do) and at that moment I looked at Kenny and agreed. A little later that evening I took Kenny back to City Road and asked mother if, once Kenny's father had died, he could stay in my old room. Mother, of course, agreed. That evening we spent some time together in my old room and Kenny made advances on me that I didn't resist. I felt whole now. I understood myself almost completely.

To save my mother's blushes, by the early spring Kenny had moved in to share my Princes Road apartment. Mrs Wydett had kindly given us a large flat in the house. My previous accommodation was really only a bedsit, and she gave us a beautiful suite on the second floor with two separate bedrooms. Kenny and I were earning good money, we had a great deal in common and we enjoyed each other's company. Brian was still coming round, however, for after his rather disastrous episode in Sefton Park he was indeed being blackmailed. He had also become somewhat infatuated with me, having discovered from Albert Marrion that I had elected to admit my own homosexuality. Brian could be a curious case. Having discovered that I was now officially 'available', he had decided that he wanted me. The fact that Kenny and I were basically a partnership had little bearing on the matter. If Brian wanted something he usually got it in one way or another. He frequented Alexander Terrace so much during the spring of 1956 that Mrs Wydett thought he had moved in, but his purpose for being there was well focused. He had to leave money at Princes Park's gates for his blackmailer and thought that he might as well attempt to bed me at the same time. I was very flattered, but he was unsuccessful.

Mother, in the meantime, was still having a rough time with father. She had promised me that she would abscond when Peter was able to leave school but that was still some months off and father's behaviour had sunk to an all-time low. I decided to house hunt for her in order to put gentle pressure on her to keep her promise and during that summer discovered that the Sefton Building Company were selling building plots in Aintree, not far from the famous racecourse. I placed a deposit on a plot without her knowledge and presented her with a fait accompli that September; when Peter was old enough, I declared, out she would move. Peter was heading to naval college the following year, and that was the time when she would also up sticks. I left British Enka that summer. Despite my rather inflated pay packets, I wasn't really happy working in a factory and had missed the relative freedom of self-employment. In July I had spotted a run-down lock-up shop in Marsh Lane, Bootle, and decided to stock it with fancy goods. It was a moderate success, nothing like my previous shop, but nevertheless at least equal to my wages from British Enka. I bought an old grey Vauxhall in order to transport my meagre stock to and from the shop and felt an incredible sense of freedom: self-assured, self-employed and mobile in the Liverpool of the 1950s. Life was good again – it could be good again, I thought: how did that happen? Could it last? Probably not, I fretted.

Despite Brian's lack of success in attempting to woo me into bed, Kenny became very jealous. It seemed that every time he returned home from work there would be Brian sitting in our apartment. I felt so sorry for Kenny but what could I do? After years of looking after his invalid father, the security that I offered him had most likely come as a revelation. Perhaps for the first time in his life he had people around him, both my family and our friends from Queen's Square, who cared about him. But this did little to assuage his jealousy, his insecurity; in fact, Kenny remained a thoroughly insecure person throughout his life. I should have stopped Brian from continually turning up on my doorstep. I knew what he wanted, and it wasn't simply my companionship. But he was my oldest friend; he was also like me and there was a genuine bond, but I would have to admit that I was very insensitive in allowing Brian to practically rule our leisure time and place a wedge between myself and Kenny. I was dilatory in tackling this tryst, but I was also very inexperienced in relationships. After all, it had only been a couple of months since I had worked out my own sexuality. I was about to challenge Brian on his infatuation one afternoon in August when he suddenly informed me that he was moving to London. I was shocked. 'What? When? Why?' I babbled, somewhat taken aback, and actually a little aggrieved. Brian explained:

> I've auditioned for RADA, Joe. You above anybody know how I feel about the theatres. I've been thinking about it for a while. If I can make something of myself in the arts I know I'll feel better about myself. I feel as if I'm drifting at the moment. London beckons Joe … at least for a while.

I couldn't argue with that. Brian had been drifting, and drifting badly. He was still prone to his little bits of rough, and I knew he was still being blackmailed, but he then announced proudly: 'I've told them who I am, Joe. I've told them at home, and they've been wonderful about it. Father and Clive were upset but they've handled it very well. Mother has been very sympathetic. Oh Joe it's such a weight off my mind, you couldn't possibly understand.'

'Brian,' I stated firmly but rather nervously. 'Of course I understand. We've both kept secrets from our families. I'm really proud of you. It's not something that I could ever come to talk about with my lot. I suppose that they know deep down, but I could never discuss it with them. You've been very brave, and also put paid to the blackmailer in one fell swoop. I hope everything goes well and that I'll be seeing you on the Playhouse soon.'

We embraced and he was left looking like the cat that got the cream. In truth, I was a little relieved, for sooner or later I thought he might have complicated my relationship with Kenny. I cared for him very much; one might even describe it as a love between us, and it would probably have only been a matter of time before my resolve might have weakened. Brian's departure saddened me and I would miss him, but it didn't half simplify matters, or so I thought.

All autumn, however, Kenny remained in a foul mood. After Brian's departure to London, never a day passed without Kenny attempting to remind me of some fictitious sexual transgression. His jealousy had become unbearable. I would return home from a successful day's work in my new shop in Marsh Lane only to be on the end of a tirade of abuse about Brian. 'Kenny,' I would exclaim, 'Brian's gone, and in any case, nothing happened!' But he wouldn't listen. Brian was inside his head and overshadowed a large part of Kenny's thoughts. I tried to rationalise, even ignore the situation, but matters grew worse; it seemed as if Kenny was out for some kind of curious, masochistic revenge. In his mind I had been unfaithful; there was absolutely nothing I could do to convince him otherwise, and so he was punishing himself and me, creating mythical scenarios of Brian and myself, imagining the two of us together behind his back. These powerful images grew darker and darker in his mind as the year came to an end. As a consequence I too was feeling rather despondent; after all, it's infectious isn't it? I'd promised his now deceased father that I would look after his youngest son, but the whole situation was becoming intolerable. By November we were unable to communicate; he was inconsolable, depressed and incredibly angry; and all for nothing.

One Wednesday afternoon I returned home early from the shop, it being half-day closing, to find an unknown bicycle in the hallway of number 30. I presumed, to begin with, that it was one of Mrs Wydett's less affluent customers, but on opening my apartment door I discovered that the visitor was with Kenny in his bedroom. I didn't make a scene, but closed the door behind me, got into my car and drove around Liverpool for a while. Disappointment rather than despair enveloped me. I felt that I'd been let down. Perhaps it was my own fault: Brian was too close for comfort as far as Kenny was concerned and presumably he had decided that something was going on. I should have been more sensitive to his jealousy, but it seemed to me that he should have taken my word for the fact that nothing was happening. I was strangely calm. 'Oh well, there's nothing like folk for letting you down,' I thought as I headed down Queen's Drive back to Toxteth to deal with the matter. I was determined to handle the situation as soon as possible and simply told Kenny that as far as I was concerned any close relationship we had previously enjoyed was now at an end. I suggested that we could stay together as flatmates, perhaps repairing our relationship as friends given time, but no more. I also suggested that he might like to take a little time away to think about it. I was aghast to discover that he had already applied for a job in London and was to start almost immediately. He called me a few names, never spoke to me for a week or so, and then left for the Nestlé chocolate factory in London.

By the end of an eventful but ultimately confusing year I had at least discovered my own sexuality, my real identity. This was a revelation, although I realised that for the rest of my life I had to be utterly circumspect about everything I was to do or say – still, it was a relief to know myself a little, and I suppose I had Brian Epstein to thank for that. I certainly rediscovered a freedom brought about by self-employment and the trust of good friends such as Brian; but I had also at least temporarily dismantled my dreams of showbiz and had experienced disloyalty, distrust and disrepute. I thought I had a partner in whom I could trust – well, one can't be right about everything. As I sat alongside Albert Marrion, the father I never really had, in the bar of the Stork Hotel the day before New Year's Eve 1956 and poured my heart out to that wonderful, ever-consoling gentleman, I wondered just what 1957 had in store for me.

By 1957 my youngest brother Peter was almost a man and, inspired by Elvis, Bill Haley, Buddy Holly and the rest of those rock 'n' roll and skiffle revolutionaries, together with the ever-present James Dean, he had started to make his first tentative steps into an industry that could have provided him with great fame and fortune. Via my own deft managerial touches, however, together with Peter's almost kamikaze approach to the music business, this was never to be, but a lot of fun lay ahead in the attempt.

Peter had unhappily returned from naval college after a brief period below the salt. The navy has always been a male refuge and, like me, he had been propositioned. Again like his elder brother, he had escaped home. But unlike me, Peter had not returned with his tail between his legs. He was angry, disgusted and ready for anything that happened to cross his path. He was a handsome, athletic youth who worked hard and played hard. He had no difficulty in getting girls or jobs – there were plenty of the latter in the late 1950s – and like many of his age Peter felt he had a point to prove.

His baptism into showbiz was modest enough. Illegally drinking alcohol in Everton goalkeeper Albert Dunlop's club in Spellow Lane one evening with his pals, he was eventually worn down by them to get up and sing a ten-to-ten song. Apparently they had long since discovered that he could belt out a fair Al Martino or Elvis impersonation, in the right key and with some feeling to boot. So after six months of refusals Peter finally capitulated and sang a number backed by the resident John McGhee trio. Not only did he knock everybody out that night, but he also fed off his own adrenal glands so much that he wouldn't get off the stage! By singing Peter had discovered how to address his own anger, frustration and ego in one fell swoop. He was only 17 at this time and shouldn't have really been in the club at all, being underage. However, being a Flannery, he was well known in the Everton area as a good lad who, although occasionally a bit lippy, was essentially as sound as a pound and so he and his mates were allowed to quietly mingle. Thoughts of our drunken father were normally enough to dissuade Peter from drinking alcohol at this stage, but a couple of lager and limes found their way inside him that night and his adrenalin was duly released via *Hound Dog* and *Heartbreak Hotel*.

His great hero at this time, just like almost every other young lad in Liverpool, was Elvis Presley. The impact of Elvis has been more than well documented elsewhere, but nobody has yet come remotely close to describing how Presley changed, wholesale, young Liverpudlian attitudes towards popular music and entertainment. My own brother Peter was a tough young man; he enjoyed music as a youth but, prior to the advent of rock, was less than impressed by the smooth crooners who assailed his ears with thirty-two-bar love songs about moon, June and spoon. He was always somewhat suspicious of them and thought they were rather effete, confining his heroes to the more obviously masculine ranks of Everton Football Club's first eleven. But Elvis was different. To Peter, Elvis was, if not quite a father figure, then certainly an errant but respected elder sibling. He looked good but could also handle himself. Dennis Lotis or

Dickie Valentine could never make such claims. Elvis was an incredibly strong image for lads such as Peter.

I'll never forget a youthful John Lennon rambling on, as was his wont in 1962, saying something like: 'without Elvis I'd have had no direction, nowhere to go, nobody to look up to; Elvis put a kind of perspective on everything.' John was speaking for a great deal of Liverpool's young male population, I suspect. Peter's performances of Elvis numbers were noted by a young group in the audience who were looking for a singer. Following being almost physically dragged off the stage ('enough! enough!'), he was approached by this group and asked to attend their practice session the following week. He didn't take much persuading and, following a success-ful audition, became at first an ad hoc and then a full-time member of a skiffle-cum-rock aggregation joyfully entitled the Teenage Rebels. On tea chest bass in this curious amalgam of apprentice dockers and decorators was a young Vince Earl, later of the Hurricanes, the TTs and, of course, TV's *Brookside*.

The band played both rock and skiffle, which by the end of 1957 had begun to occur in most bands with increasing regularity. The skiffle and rock movements were rather separate to begin with (skiffle being an off-shoot of the trad scene); however, once stripped down rock was very similar to skiffle and any acoustically based outfit could quite easily slip in a number of rock 'n' roll songs without too much trouble; Dickie Bishop's *No Other Baby* was a prime example of such slippage, though the trad jazzers mostly hated this rather irreverent behaviour, of course. They only allowed this music on to their territory, e.g. at the home of Liverpool jazz at this time, the Cavern Club, as a matter of sufferance. Chris Barber and Ken Colyer had essentially 'created' the genre and so it was, ipso facto, part of the scene. But it was considered rather low class and plebe-ian by some, attracting the 'wrong sort' to this exclusive musical scene. As I call it all to mind, from trad's perspective jazz was the Liverpool Institute for Boys and Blackburne House for Girls; skiffle was a bit sec-ondary modern. However, Lonnie Donegan, who had been a member of both Barber's and Colyer's bands, influenced in turn a younger audience who were unconcerned about skiffle's attachment to a rather older and sniffier scene, and they saw little difference between, say, *John Henry* or *Don't You Rock Me Daddy-o* and *Rip It Up* or *Shake, Rattle and Roll*. And, of course, they were right. Musically it was almost identical, being twelve-, eight- or sixteen-bar blues. It was just the rather antiquarian attitude of the trad jazzers that had declared some kind of separateness for skiffle –

it was not intrinsic within the music itself. By 1957 the skiffle boom was about to peak and trough: a younger generation picked up on the musical similarities and brought them together. Skiffle didn't really disappear at all, it simply mutated.

By the following year, most of those who had been attracted to the music business via this DIY music were performing either electrified rock or blues, and they saw no contradiction via the simultaneous presence of skiffle and rock. The trad jazzers felt differently, of course; skiffle was 'their music' after all. But nobody could ever profess to own a genre of music and claims of this sort simply reeked of snobbishness and pessimism. Cavern owners Alan Sytner and latterly Ray McFall were forced to own up and abandon their concepts of purism if they were to keep their club in business. Simply allowing their regulars to throw pennies at Rory Storm or ordering the Quarry Men to 'cut out the bloody rock' was not the answer. This is why the trad jazz scene, although intrinsic to the rise of the great British pop movements of the 1960s, can never be described as 'pop' as such. I thought the tradders too old, too antiquarian, and for me far too elitist; from 1957 to this day I have always steered clear of their rather stuffy attitude towards music, even though I love early jazz music. To my brother, skiffle and rock were simply new shoots from the same branch.

So Peter rather guardedly (after all, I was his older brother) came to me asking a little advice about how to stage the group and, quelling my own desires for singing again, I came to act as a kind of middleman for the Teenage Rebels. Initially I helped the band into a residency of sorts at the Railway Club in Aintree. This was a club that I had played many times before my vocal chords were impaired and I was well known as a reliable performer. The committee at the club decided to give them a 20-minute slot as long as I sang a few songs as well. My voice had recovered a little by this time, although it never returned to its previous strength, and I was pleased to accommodate them. The Railway Club wasn't really ready for the full force of the rather raw and anarchic Teenage Rebels, however, and at first the club committee thought they were dreadful (they were!) and asked me to reduce their 20 minutes by half. But once the word had got around that a skiffle-rock band was playing at the Railway, the members discovered, probably to their horror, that the queues to get into the club were right down the street. The Teenage Rebels were what was happening and, in a short space of time, there was standing room only and I stood in the wings. I remember they were paid about £8 most weeks and, to begin with, the money was shared between us all, but as they became more popular and my own slot receded, I handed over the £8, less a percentage, effectively making me their manager.

Although Peter was asked to join the Rebels, it soon became clear that he was becoming the focal point of the band. He was developing into a very attractive teenager and, for a time, physically resembled Elvis (this would unfortunately at least partially contribute to his undoing in the following decade as Elvis faded from view). So, by the end of 1957, the Teenage Rebels had mutated somewhat, with band members leaving and joining at a rate of knots, and the unit becoming fundamentally a backing band for Peter. I was able to get the group a couple of showcase slots at Ossie Wade's in Walton – the Sunday showcase that had helped Ken Dodd and me years earlier. Local agents religiously attended these performances, and although they were at first very resistant to skiffle and rock, they soon realised that there was money in them there hills, and booked us. When the Rebels were asked to audition for a club or venue I would always suggest that the club owner or promoter turn up at Wade's, because that was where we did our auditions. This meant that proprie-tor Ada Wade was very happy to put us on her Sunday bill, because of incoming business, and that we were not performing freebies at a venue to satisfy a tight-fisted promoter. You see, promoters would tell perhaps half a dozen bands to audition on one night, and then charge the kids a shilling to get in and not pay the bands because of the audition tag: mean and miserly, to say the least.

Being a good Catholic boy, I also advertised the band in the pages of the Catholic Pictorial. This weekly paper enjoyed a large circulation in the Merseyside area and, as many Catholic churches were receiving drinking and dancing licences for their parochial clubs during the latter months of the decade, I recognised a potential market for the band. Within a matter of weeks of placing the small advertisement, the Rebels' diary was full of bookings at Catholic church clubs and the group was even perform-ing early evening gigs for schoolchildren. One writer working on the Catholic Pictorial at that time was cub reporter Bob Azurdia, subsequently of BBC Radio Merseyside fame, and I invited him to our first gig. He sent in a glowing report to the editor, guaranteeing our future prospects on the Catholic parochial club circuit – the Big Time!

In any case, gigs were becoming plentiful right across Merseyside as small-time promoters opened up jive hives and rock 'n' roll dances to cater for new tastes. There were plenty of places to play but Liverpool was and remains a very territorial city. Therefore, despite this glut it was unusual for a north-end band to play the south end for fear of trouble from local teddy boys. In the north venues such as the Aintree Institute, the Litherland Town Hall, Blair Hall, the jive hive at St Luke's Hall in Crosby and more besides were open to rock 'n' roll fans during 1958–59. You see, live rock was in great demand, but national stars like Tommy Steele and Terry Dene (and the Joe Loss Orchestra, one might add) were unable to fully satiate that demand. There was a paucity of decent British rock and rollers and, by the closing years of the decade, young Liverpudlians were far more interested in the US sounds that one could hear on Radio Luxembourg each night rather than the mollified British copies purveyed by Lance Fortune, Marty Wilde and Cliff Richard. These were all useful performers, you understand, but appeared to some rather vapid and lightweight, unable to shrug off that light entertainment mantle that had dogged British music for years. If a local band could provide dancers with a sound closer to the likes of Buddy Holly, Little Richard and the Drifters, or even the Platters, then they would prove to be a success. So things began to stir in an attempt to execute that mandate, and alongside the Teenage Rebels a number of groups in other parts of the city formed and began to establish their own followings.

By the end of 1958 each district of Liverpool could boast at least one rock-cum-skiffle group. Kingsize Taylor and the Dominoes were to become the 'boss' group of the north end of the city, whereas the Texas (or occasionally Texans) Skiffle Group (later Rory Storm and the Hurricanes) and trad crossovers the Bluegenes had a few gigs in the city centre. Rock and skiffle bands such as the Deltones Skiffle Group, Bob Evans' Five Shillings and the Bobby Bell Rockers operated south of the city, whereas a great group called Dale Roberts and the Jaywalkers played at the Raven, Connah's Quay and on the Wirral. The Teenage Rebels came to share bills with most of the above and entered a variety of skiffle and rock competitions with outfits such as the Angels, the Gin Mill Skifflers, the Hy-Katz, the 95 Skiffle Group and the Eddie Clayton Skiffle Group, amongst probably many others that are now long lost or only partially flickering lantern slides in the annals of Liverpool music-making.

Jim Gretty from Hessey's Music Shop in Stanley Street, just off Whitechapel in Liverpool, was like an agent-cum-godfather to us. Jim was a regular performer in the Liverpool area in the late 1950s with good connections. His greatest love was country music, but he could see the similarities between rock, skiffle and country when many others didn't, and he allowed first the Teenage Rebels and then, a little later, Peter's next group, the Detours, to have a shop-window gig. In fact, Gretty had such a liking for Peter's act that he would often share the door receipts with us: a very equitable man. All of this activity was supplemented by two important sectors. Firstly, Peter was an avid record collector and the discs that I remember him buying (mostly releases on the Decca London-American label, the main outlet for US labels in this country in the late 1950s and early 1960s) provided him with a fantastic repertoire to supplement his fascination with Elvis Presley. Secondly, the more I look back, the more I feel the role of the US air force base at Burtonwood had an equally enormous impact on the education of Liverpool's musical youth of the 1950s, such as Peter. The US airmen were a visible attestation to the existence of black America: they colonised certain parts of the south end of the city after dark at weekends, they introduced black music to many in Liverpool via those aforementioned shebeens and tribal clubs in Toxteth, and both black and white Americans were very generous with gifts to Liverpool girls, often lavishing handfuls of 45s on them purchased back at the base. Those semi-mythologised Cunard Yanks were simply one earlier contributory factor to Liverpool's sound-scape. For me, the emergence of the sound of Merseybeat was more closely linked to the real Yanks at Burtonwood, together with the record deletion bins in Whitechapel (NEMS, Rushworth's Beaver Radio, Newmart Electronics); a lot of US music arrived in Liverpool via this back door, rather than the Pier Head.

There was very little money in it at this early stage and by the end of 1958 the Teenage Rebels were basically sponsored by yours truly, for outgoings were exceeding income. They had all but jettisoned most of their acoustic instrumentation and skiffle repertoire for a louder, 'beatier' brand of rock and R&B, and this had cost money. Basically, I had become by default, as much as anything else, their sponsor. I didn't begrudge it. Peter was very happy. He and I were freeing our egos somewhat, but we were also getting results, for the Rebels were becoming if not quite a top-line local draw, then something at least approaching a leading second division outfit (just like Liverpool FC at this time). In any case, I had the money to spare, for things were looking up on the business front. Following the rather slow death of my personal affairs the previous year, I had proceeded to throw myself into work and retail trading more and more.

At the beginning of the New Year my little shop in Bootle was compulsory purchased, which netted me a nice sum, and for a while I worked as a salesman for Gross cash registers – also a nice little earner. However, when my mother showed positive signs of being ready to finally leave my father during 1958, I encouraged her to purchase a shop and accommodation at Breeze Hill. My mother, as usual, had a real eye for a bargain and had spotted a rather run-down general store-cum-tobacconist in the north of the city. It was going for a song, could easily be built up again and was an ideal opportunity. I saw it as a great chance to get her to sever her dutiful obligation to my father, who had become even more drunken and depraved. The Breeze Hill shop was duly purchased and mother was set up, as I thought, for life. While the house in Aintree was being built, mother resided at the shop and I decided to join her.

She was delighted, of course. She had never liked my residing in Liverpool 8 and was glad of the company. Peter was at naval college in Gravesend while the deals were being struck by notorious Liverpool solicitor Rex Makin, but hitchhiked home soon afterwards after his lucky escape. He decided, probably correctly, not to live in Breeze Hill, or at City Road, but to shack up with a pal in Everton. This was a very tactful thing for a young teenager to do and I admired his diplomacy. He loved both his mother and father very much, and couldn't really understand why the marriage had failed. He merely regarded father as a man's man and saw little fault with his macho behaviour. He failed to realise, as a young child often does, that machismo can end up in tears, especially for the woman. He made up his mind to stay out of the way and in hindsight that was a good decision.

Mother restocked Breeze Hill and we refurbished the apartment above for the two of us. I bid a tearful farewell to Mrs Wydett at Alexander Terrace and drove to Breeze Hill in my newly acquired but rather ancient and rusting Vauxhall saloon. Within a very short space of time the shop began to turn a profit and we continued to restock, expanding into our usual lines of fancy goods and a little bric-a-brac. It was an early morning call seven days per week supplying the local workforce with papers and cigarettes, but they were very grateful. The previous owner had not been a good early riser, hence the low takings and enforced sale of the business, and they were all very relieved that a degree of professionalism had resurfaced. It was around this time that Peter and the Teenage Rebels amalgamated, and so it was also at this time that my future working hours were established: late finish, early start.

Although everything went well for the first few weeks at Breeze Hill, I could detect that mother was pining for my father. She had made the break, true, but in reality it wasn't working. She was depressed of an evening being alone (I was out with the Teenage Rebels three nights a week at times), and was also being pursued by father on her days off. It came as no surprise when he turned up at Breeze Hill one night during the summer of 1959, full of booze, forcefully demanding that she return. At one stage during the slanging match between the three of us, father saw how well the apartment had been furnished and, in a rage, immediately tore up the stair carpet. He threatened to finish off the job and, in order to stop any further violence, mother agreed to return to City Road that very night. She had missed him, as strange as that might sound, and once she had made that decision to return she couldn't get out of Breeze Hill quickly enough.

I must admit that I was deeply hurt by this action. But after some rumination I decided that it was her decision, and I was in no position to legislate. This was a personal matter between mother and my father. All was not lost, of course. The house in Aintree was being built and mother fully appreciated that it was for her and her alone. She realised very soon that another more permanent split would be inevitable, but for the time being she would rather live with the beast than be apart from him. It all seems rather odd, doesn't it? Actually wanting to be with a man you intend to leave in due course. But that was the way her mind worked and, after considerable thought, I felt she would fulfil her bargain in her own good time. This proved to be the case, for when the house in Aintree was finally finished she moved out and away from my father, never to return. She later referred to the Breeze Hill incident as a 'dry run' and I fully understood. But at that time she left me with a job, a band, a shop, stock and a 4 a.m. alarm call. Evidently a level of rationalisation was called for. As for the job, well, that was easy – I left!

Another familiar face had turned up at the Breeze Hill shop by late 1959. Kenny had returned from his sojourn in east London and had decided to look me up. In truth, he had nowhere to stay, looked terrible and was, of course, skint. Being a soft touch, and still caring for him, I allowed him to stay. We got on immediately, although I stated to him right away that there was to be no funny business, and after a couple of weeks he and I were effectively sharing our lives. I suppose I needed him. My life was very full and I wanted to share it with him. However, I was determined not to enter into any kind of sexual relationship, for I knew that I could never totally trust him again. The relationship remained purely platonic and this seemed to be OK as far as Kenny was concerned. He was able to get a job with the ambulance service, which he loved, and also began to help me with the Teenage Rebels, which he hated. Kenny was a real snob as far as music was concerned, and although he appreciated that rock 'n' roll was important for the kids, he thought that they would all eventually grow out of it and come to listen to proper, i.e. classical, music such as Brahms, Holst, Elgar and Wagner.

Nevertheless he had some great ideas about marketing the Teenage Rebels. It was at a gig at the Aintree Institute one night that Kenny decided that the Rebels needed a new name and image. He suggested that the group would be rather restricted by their moniker if rock was to continue (which he doubted), because 'Teenage Rebels' sounded rather pre-pubescent and a little 'skiffly' – and this genre was by that time yesterday's news. After their performance, the group were consulted and they immediately agreed, stating that they had also thought that it was time for a change. They hadn't thus far, however, come up with any suitable alternative. Driving back along Queen's Drive that night we were infuriatingly diverted by a series of road works in the Breeze Hill area (a flyover was being prepared which did not bode well for my shop), at which point Kenny promptly suggested the name 'Detours'. The band were delighted and instantly resolved to rename the Teenage Rebels on the spot. Thereafter, Kenny instigated a clever fly-posting and leafleting campaign around north Liverpool and Birkenhead (our regular gigging areas at that time) to inform fans that the Rebels had organically mutated into the Detours, and that the band would be 100 per cent rock 'n' roll in the future. It was a good move. Any element of a now rather dated skiffle sound could be utterly purged and the band's repertoire, which was becoming more adventurous all the time, would be reflected in a more appropriate name.

The renaming of the band proved to be an important watershed, for the almost symbiotic alignment of the name with the musical material immediately appealed to the small-time booking agents and the Detours began to play Blair Hall, Litherland Town Hall and Aintree Institute with greater regularity. Gigs improved and, likewise, so did the band; in fact, Peter was beginning to develop a strong Elvis-style voice, something that would prove both a help and a hindrance to him in years to come, and also a confident stage persona. Via both, he was also acquiring a personal following of some strength, made up for the most part of young females. Kenny's input into my embryonic management was invaluable, but it was part of a deeper process. He was punishing himself daily for his previous jealousy and transgressions and was never able to fully forgive himself. I was truly glad that he was back in my life but I never felt that we could become one, as we had previously done. My life, up to that point, had been one long series of immense disappointments, of which my experiences with Kenny were the nadir. Even though Kenny had decided to devote so much time to my interests despite a loathing for rock 'n' roll and a rather ambivalent attitude towards my brother (he would tell me on many occasions that Peter was using me), I had made my decision to become celibate.

Brian Epstein was also back on the scene, having returned from what proved to be an unsuccessful stab at training for the acting profession, and he and I would, whenever possible, continue our educational journey through theatre and show business. I would effectively go out with Brian for we enjoyed each other's company and would discuss the intricacies of performance in some detail. Brian still lusted after me, and on more than one occasion attempted to seduce me; however, there was really no point and by the advent of the new decade he had come to terms with the fact that I would remain his greatest ally, his oldest rock, but would never be his sexual partner. He seldom discussed his time at RADA. It struck me as an unhappy period in his life and I never really pursued the matter. Despite a persisting degree of jealousy which could never be fully extinguished, Kenny was far more philosophical about my social arrangements and slowly but surely came to terms with my desire for close and loving friendships without any additional complications. At this time, Brian did not articulate any real desire for direct artist management, as such, but he did express a passing interest in the whys and wherefores of my involvement with the Detours. In fact, he was rather dismissive of the whole procedure, suggesting that I had already overcommitted myself with the Breeze Hill business. It was business rather than music, during this period of his life, that seemed to be driving him. Although NEMS was an expanding and successful business, music was merely one facet. The 'white goods' (fridges and washing machines) together with radiograms and record players (in conjunction with the associated hire-purchase agreements) were making the Epsteins a seriously wealthy family. Brian's brother Clive was in control of these sales, however.

So Brian had finally thrown himself into the family business with a vengeance, perhaps in order to come to terms with his own artistic failings. He certainly seemed to have placed his own personal artistic desires to one side, for he somewhat schizophrenically separated his day-time and night-time existences with consummate clarity. He told me one night, after we were returning from a Halle performance in Manchester, that the arts were now no more than a source of entertainment to him, and that the real world was one of business. Nobody knows for sure whether Brian was kidding himself, for within a matter of twelve months he was once more hankering after the excitement of showbiz, but he did appear very satisfied with his lot as a respected local entrepreneur and, as we would talk on our evenings together, his frustrations, both artistic and sexual, rarely surfaced. I think of this stage of his life as his Chamber of Commerce period. Perhaps it was I, and my stories of the Detours' loud and brash music, dancers and excitement, who rekindled the spark, but who knows? One thing I do think occurred was an abyss in his life. He seemed to grasp the real but lean towards the conceptual. This weakened one persona while driving the other. The problem, in my opinion, was that it made him more, rather than less, vulnerable.

It was around this time, however, that after discussing the merits of Vivien Leigh one evening in the Magic Clock, we discovered, to our delight, that Ms Leigh was shortly to be visiting Liverpool in *A Streetcar Named Desire*. Brian and I immediately booked the front row of the Royal Court Theatre for the entire week's performances and, dressed up to the nines each evening, became permanent fixtures in front of the stage. Brian, of course, was always immaculate, wearing the finest clothes that Liverpool could offer in the late 1950s. I would always aim to equal him in style but never felt that I could hold a candle to his sheer elegance and deportment, for the most part courtesy of the renowned Liverpool tailor Beno Dorn. From Sunday to Thursday we were ever present, lapping up Vivien's extraordinary yet rather latent talent. On the Friday evening, however, Brian telephoned me to say that he couldn't make it to the theatre. It was Jewish Sabbath and the family were demanding his presence.

This was understandable but it didn't prevent me from going, so I ritualistically prepared myself for another performance of *Streetcar*. By the end of the evening Ms Leigh had given probably her finest performance of the week and was receiving tumultuous applause. As she took her bows she placed one foot gingerly on the footlights and dropped her eyes towards me, then towards Brian's empty seat, and then back to me again and, with a curious grin on her charming face, mouthed the question, 'where's your friend?' before flouncing off to her admirers backstage. I was, of course, unable to reply, but I sat in the theatre bar afterwards naturally thrilled that Ms Leigh (like Ms Hutton a few years previously) had picked me out of the audience. I realised, of course, that it was Brian not myself who had made an impression on the actress. He did have a presence of his own; so much, in fact, that he was able to significantly change the atmosphere of any room he entered. Brian was alive with charm and refinement.

Breeze Hill was a very profitable enterprise for me during the late 1950s. Not only via direct sales in the shop per se, but also through the innumerable agencies that I had established with the women in the locality. I had clubs for everything: from ladies' stockings and later tights to Christmas selection boxes. I handed out considerable commission, too, so everybody wanted a piece of the action. The area was booming as far as factory work was concerned and agents would operate for me in the many sites along the East Lancashire Road. We colonised the English Electric, Lucas' factories and many of the new units being built on the way out of Liverpool towards the new town of Kirkby. I watched this overspill area rapidly expand during 1958–59 and promised myself that I would do something about it from a business point of view. I had little trouble collecting money from the agents. They all appreciated the opportunity to make a little extra or purchase a few of the new consumer durables that had been made available to the working classes during this time. I also ran a catalogue for the Great Universal Stores and a great amount of agency commission went on items such as electric irons, radiograms, carpet cleaners and spin driers from the catalogue, thus increasing my own commission. The shop was amply providing my bread and butter, and the agents were supplying me with the cream. The shop always looked well stocked, adding to its appeal for browsers, and was open very long hours, well into the night, at least as the primordial bylaws would allow.

For the agency trade I relied heavily on two local women, Marjorie Chandler and Norah Daley. Norah was a wonderful woman who was not exactly enjoying domestic bliss at home, and so the shop's late hours were something of an escape route for her. She was already my best agent, but also began to spend a great deal of time looking after the shop when I was out with the Teenage Rebels/Detours. We also spent time together when I stayed on the premises, stock-taking and accounting. One evening, hearing a knock and expecting to see her cheery smile, I opened the side door to receive an enormous blow to the face. It was so brutal that I was propelled backwards about 10 feet. I was seeing stars as I picked myself up from the bottom of the staircase, blood dripping from my poor nose. I realised that it was Norah's husband: 'Where is she? I'll fucking kill her and you when I get my hands on her … I know what you've been up to … where is she?' I couldn't believe my ears. She was one of my best agents and we were the best of friends, but I had already decided that I didn't kick with that foot any longer. I staggered to my feet and, not really thinking, declared, 'You don't know what you're talking about … I'm probably more interested in you than her, you stupid fucking bastard.'

Here was a rather foul-mouthed Joe Flannery looking down at one of the area's real hard men, informing him in no uncertain terms that he was striking a 'queer'. What had I done? I flinched, and just as I thought I was about to receive another going over for that disclosure, the perpetrator looked at me in utter confusion, turned on his heels and left. He was faced with a complex strategic retort and couldn't cope with it. It was, indeed, a lucky escape. I never saw Norah again. Without the help from her my time was squeezed even further and, although the money was marvellous, I was beginning to look for fresh fields. Kenny was in total agreement for he was expressing some concerns about my health. I was looking tired, becoming irritable and had lost weight. All of this he put down to the exhausting timetable that I had set for myself. I took his observations on board. After all, he knew what he was talking about, having seen his own father waste away to nothing.

Breeze Hill went up for sale as a going concern, but not before I made my first prestige purchase. I was beginning to sift through cupboards and papers, sorting out my affairs, when I came across a brown manila envelope in the storeroom to the rear of the shop. On the envelope was written 'Wills' in my own handwriting, and upon opening the envelope I discovered £600. I had been making that much money that I had placed amounts of cash in two safe places in order to pay one bill, and had forgotten about one of them. Wills the tobacco manufacturers, with whom I dealt directly, had long since been paid. The £600 was promptly turned into a new (or near-new – I forget) Mediterranean-blue Vauxhall Wyvern and with that parked outside the shop it took no time at all to persuade any prospective purchasers that this truly was a gold mine (it was, but only with desperately hard work). I had also decided what to do next. I applied to Liverpool City Council for licences to trade in Kirkby New Town as a mobile shop proprietor. Kirkby Urban District was a local government district in Lancashire from 1958 to 1974. From 1949 onwards, the main settlement of the district was Kirkby New Town. A district council was created in 1958.

I had been watching the actions of one of my great heroes, Mrs Bessie Braddock, with great interest. She, as a local councillor and then a Member of Parliament, had been deeply involved in establishing this new housing scheme on the outskirts of Liverpool at Kirkby. A great amount of demolition followed the war damage in the Scotland Road area of the city, spoken of earlier. For those heritage buffs who would have us believe that Liverpool's inner city area was raped of its character in those post-war years, Mrs Braddock's motives and machinations serve as a salutary reminder of the terrible housing that Liverpudlians had to endure during the first half of the twentieth century. The properties, often owned by absentee Rachman-style landlords were partially flattened by the Luftwaffe (for which we remain truly thankful) and the job was finished by a Liverpool council with precious little money to spare. Locals were then offered what must have seemed like a dream come true: a property in the countryside, on greenbelt land, away from inner-city smog and pollution; splendid modern housing with every convenience, far removed from the collapsed drains, outside privvies and court dwellings that ordinary families had been so used to. It was an offer of paradise for those who had only known squalid conditions and disease-ridden streets, and was a brave and triumphant move for its day.

We have all been made aware of the attendant problems associated with these housing estates in later years – isolation, unemployment, vandalism, drugs – nevertheless, this ought not to detract from the pioneers who established these bold programmes. The problems of the 1950s were less structural, in any case. There was very little unemployment and vandalism was rare. Indeed, all that the new inhabitants of Kirkby had to worry about was buses and shopping. The latter of these two problems was particularly pressing for there were literally no shops. Entire families were moving out to Kirkby and were unable to buy a loaf of bread. This is where I came in, for, while the shops remained to be built, there was obviously great potential for mobile trading. There had already been a few traders working the Westvale, Northwood and Southdene estates in Kirkby, but they had come in for some heavy criticism owning to the unsanitary conditions of their vehicles. I determined to inform the authorities that I would have a mobile shop purpose built if they would grant me a licence. The council absolutely loved the idea and so, after receiving my new Wyvern, together with a very generous offer for Breeze Hill, I ordered an Austin chassis from a dealer in Bootle, and a hand-built mobile shop to cover it.

I refused any suggestions of skimping, for I knew that the more money I spent, the higher the likelihood that I would be offered first refusal on any shop units that might subsequently become available. The mobile shop had everything – beautiful display windows, two sinks, electric fittings – and I was cleared to trade as a grocer and greengrocer in Kirkby. It meant that those early morning rises were to continue, but I was well used to that by this time. So within a matter of months the mobile was ready, the Breeze Hill shop was disposed of and Kenny and I were ready to move – but where to?

I decided to rent a lovely apartment in the Stoneycroft area of Liverpool, sort of halfway between the city and the East Lancashire Road: an address that was to become one of the most important meeting places for all the luminaries on the burgeoning Merseybeat scene; an address that probably remains imprinted on the mind of Sir Paul McCartney to this very day: 10 Gardner Road.

7

JACK GOOD, LEE CURTIS AND EVEN MORE DETOURS

MY NEW ADDRESS on the borders of Stoneycroft and Tuebrook was a large Victorian house that had previously belonged to one large family; however, they had moved to the more suburban Childwall area of Liverpool and rather than sell up, had decided to create three separate apartments for rent. I was the first tenant and was delighted to discover that the former occupants were extremely engaging and house proud. So much so, in fact, that they gave me an allowance for carpets and wallpaper to facilitate my move. I thought that this was a wonderful suggestion: they were actually asking me to decorate the apartment up to a standard rather than on the cheap. I thanked them for their generosity and suggested that I add to their allowance in order to purchase the finest carpeting and wall covering that I could afford. They were delighted and from that moment on they left their beautiful house in my capable hands. Two further tenants were brought in later that month and they were also given leave to decorate to the highest possible standards. It really was the most splendid flat one could imagine, with all mod cons for the late 1950s such as water heaters, back boilers behind the roaring coal fires and well-appointed separate bathrooms (most flats at this time shared communal facilities). Kenny and I were very happy as we moved in during the summer of 1959. It was also at this time that Peter officially became 'Lee Curtis'. This was another of Kenny's bright ideas. Throughout 1959 the Detours had continued to rise in popularity, but it was Peter who had really begun to attract most of the attention. Kenny suggested that, like the famous Larry Parnes artists of the day such as Marty Wilde, Billy Fury and Dickie Pride, Peter should undergo a dominant-sounding name change so that the band could go out as 'somebody and the Detours'. This was, of course, all the rage by this time; however, after the success of the Beatles in 1962, stylistic pop noms de plumes became rather dated, a change which also perhaps contributed a little to Peter's inability to establish a top-line singing career in the UK.

As for that name, well, by this time Peter had taken to researching his art with a scrupulous dedication and was aware of innumerable black R&B performers from all over the States, many of whom meant next to nothing to the average pop fan in the UK. Like many music lovers on Merseyside, he was fully aware, perhaps before many other people in the country, of the most happening people and sounds in the States at this time. A couple of songs entitled *Upstairs at Daddy G's* and *Pretty Little Angel Eyes* had attracted some attention in the States. The latter of the two had even become a sizeable hit in the UK, and both had been recorded by an excellent black singer named Curtis Lee. Reversed, the name seemed perfect – Lee Curtis – and so one night, at a parochial club in north Liverpool in 1959, Peter Flannery, lead singer with the Detours, became Lee Curtis. The band was never officially renamed 'Lee Curtis and the Detours' for fear of further in-fighting via bruised egos, but they became known as such organically by their fans due to Peter's extraordinary stage presence and backstage reputation with the girls. In fact, soon it became quite clear to Kenny and I that fans were flocking simply to see Lee Curtis. It was around this time that I first met one of the great instigators of television rock in the UK, Mr Jack Good. Kenny had quite correctly stated that if Lee was to stand any chance at all of making it in the show-business world of 1959–60, then a TV appearance was an absolute must.

Although I previously described an underground scene existing on Merseyside in almost antithesis to London concepts about rock, Kenny and I could see that any over-ground success in British rock 'n' roll was still largely dependent upon TV and touring, for the two had been intrinsically linked since the days of the BBC's pioneering *Six-Five Special* back in 1957. This had been produced by the amazing Jack Good, together with a BBC hack by the name of Jo Douglas. Jack Good was a television pioneer par excellence and aside from *Six-Five Special* for the BBC, went on to produce *Oh Boy!*, *Wham!* and *Boy Meets Girl* for the Independent TV network. These were effectively the first British TV teen-based music programmes. Jack Good's programmes introduced a number of the UK's first rock-based pop stars such as Tommy Steele, Marty Wilde, Billy Fury,

Jess Conrad, and Cliff Richard, and he probably did more than most to expand rock 'n' roll music in the 1950s. I recall he also later worked with the Beatles, when Brian Epstein commissioned him to produce *Around the Beatles*, one of the first major TV showcases for the group.

Good was determined to go against the BBC bosses' wishes to emphasise the magazine format of the *Six-Five Special*. He wanted music and lots of movement. To get his way at the BBC he had sets built, but shortly before the show started they were wheeled out of the way and he filled the space with the milling audience and performers – a nice touch! Apparently the show's running order was sketched out on Friday morning and the only complete run-through happened immediately before transmission. Most such TV productions in the 1950s were broadcast live, so once the programme had started there was no going back and Good achieved his goals; he later told me he was a firm believer in the maxim 'whatever works for you, works: don't over-complicate things'. The show even launched the hand jive in the UK and Good wrote (or had ghost-written) an instruction book, *Hand Jive at Six-Five*. Sadly not one episode of the *Six-Five Special* shows was taped, so they are lost forever, although a low-budget film based on the show survives, but it's absolute rubbish. Although Jack had given the BBC a show that was attracting 12 million viewers, he was being paid only £18 a week – scandalous!

Good suitably left the BBC for Independent Television and launched *Oh Boy!* during September 1958. After trial broadcasts in the Midlands, it went national, in direct competition with *Six-Five Special* on Saturday evenings. *Six-Five Special* stuck to its mix of rock, jazz, skiffle, crooners, and bad gags, but rock 'n' roll was at the heart of *Oh Boy!* The programmes were broadcast from the Hackney Empire, London and made a star of Cliff Richard, as well as showcasing Billy Fury. For me, *Oh Boy!* was Jack Good at his very best. Each show was 26 minutes long and no song lasted more than a minute. When ITV replaced the show on 12 September 1959 with the more slushy and stereotyped *Boy Meets Girl* a short era had evidently ended and the press wondered whether Jack had lost his touch. Jack later claimed his wife persuaded him that rock 'n' roll was on the way out and to adopt a more middle-of-the-road approach, but when we met he confessed that he was under pressure from ITV and they, in turn, from their advertisers to conform.

So, the Jack Good formula was (at least to begin with) quite amazing but was undoubtedly beginning to wear a little thin by 1960. Yet it was still he, and characters such as Larry Parnes and John Barry, who called the shots as far as the teenage pop process was concerned. All this was to change in a short period of time, of course, precisely because of parochial scenes in Liverpool, Manchester, Birmingham and Newcastle, but as an aspiring manager I had no template to work from apart from that of Larry Parnes and to a lesser extent Adam Faith's manager the recalcitrant Eve Taylor. The success of Larry Parnes' artists on Jack Good's TV shows and then all around the UK on what seemed to me to be rather randomly constructed package tours (Plymouth one day, Great Yarmouth the next?) seemed to be the only real marker; after all it was so new and exciting. So, although Kenny and I could witness a marvellous local scene developing, we were still at a loss as to precisely what we should do about it. Surely, we reasoned, TV programmes such as *Boy Meets Girl* and *Drumbeat* and those such as Larry Parnes and Jack Good were the only avenues open to us.

With this in mind, we contacted Jack Good and asked him to audition Lee. After sending a few of Bob Azurdia's rave reviews from the Catholic Pictorial we were granted that audition and during the first month of 1960 Lee, Kenny and I visited the 2i's Coffee Bar in Soho and met Good to see if he could advance what we saw as Lee's promising career. The band stayed at home, which was probably a big mistake. Although Good only really wanted to audition Lee as a solo artist we probably should have been bold and insisted that he sing with his own unit. After all, they were as tight as a drum by this time, having played so many gigs, and Good was renowned for appreciating good musicians – Joe Brown, for example. My decision to allow Lee to travel without the Detours can be seen in hindsight as one of my crucial errors. I wanted success for him because he was my own flesh and blood, but this masked the fact that I was rather ignorant of the potential created by those other musicians around him; they also helped to make him rather special. I presumed that he exuded charm and stage presence because he was a Flannery. It is obvious to me now that Lee Curtis was good because his many line-ups were also exceptional. All of this would have been far less apparent to me at that time, for I was interested in Lee alone. This continued to be regrettable for me: on many occasions I naively placed his interests ahead of not only my own, but also those of his willing musical associates; I admit I was ultimately misguided. For example, I remember much later (in 1964) my good friend Johnny Kidd approaching me after a particularly fraught evening with my brother in the Star Club in Hamburg, and begging me to 'fuck him off and manage me'. But how could I?

So the audition didn't go as well as we'd hoped. We met Adam Faith at the 2i's to begin with. Adam was just breaking at this time and was very affable, interested in what had been going on in Liverpool and quite an intellectual, but he also sowed some seeds of doubt in Lee's mind, I think, by suggesting that the London scene liked good-looking guys such as my brother. Adam's tone was decidedly ironic. Lee, at this time, was something of a homophobe and Faith's comments utterly freaked him out. By the time we were in Jack Good's auditions the next morning Lee was in no mood for singing and was looking at practically everybody sideways. Nevertheless, he did sing for Jack, and Good in turn was very gracious about Lee's abilities. But Jack Good I think detected a heated intransigence in Lee, brought on no doubt by Adam Faith's suggestive elucidations the previous day, and suggested that we return to Liverpool to develop an Elvis-like stage personality. Whether this was down to Lee's proximity to Elvis or his general antagonism, I shall never really know. Probably it was a combination of the two.

Whatever the motivations, it turned out to be very good advice. Despite being at the heart of the Elvis lookalike scene and promoting the likes of Marty Wilde and Vince Eager, Good quietly informed me that he could see that he was beginning to flog a rather decrepit and dying horse. By the time Jess Conrad, Craig Douglas and Mark Wynter arrived on the scene later that year, the impact of rock as a rebellious soundtrack had been diminished and, by telling us to return to Liverpool, Good was effectively suggesting that we prepare ourselves for something new. Certainly a man like Good, who appeared to have an innate ability to sniff out the next big thing, would have detected whether a scene was promising or not. I remember his words to me quite clearly. They were somewhat patronising but nonetheless perceptive; it went something like this:

This can't go on forever, you know, Mr Flannery, and I do detect things stirring in the provinces; go home and build up a scene in your home city. It's the only way forward and the only way to stop the music press simply demanding that we reproduce the same kind of singer year in year out. For me it is becoming tiresome. Take my word for it – we need a change.

Jack Good was soon to bail out himself to work in US television; he helped create the teen monster that was *Shindig!*

By 1963, even Larry Parnes was to inform me that he was 'moving into larger promotions' and had accepted that his days as a rock svengali-like figure had been overtaken by the provincial rock 'n' roll scene suggested by Good. Of course, Lee's ego was at least temporarily dented but that was no bad thing and Kenny and I came away from London far more upbeat than my young brother. Good's words lingered in our minds as we made our way home: 'stay away from something in its death throes' were actually his final comments as we stepped into the taxi to take us back to Euston station. That failed audition proved to be something of a turning point, for myself, Kenny, Lee and, actually, Brian Epstein. Over dinner one evening shortly afterwards in Manchester I related the Jack Good affair to a highly interested Brian. While he maintained, at least through starters and main course, that Cliff Richard, the Shadows and Adam Faith were selling by the lorry load at NEMS and that he could see no justification in Jack Good's asides, by dessert he was being gently persuaded by yours truly that something of not a little magnitude might be possible in Liverpool and other urban centres around the country.

So despite remaining somewhat sceptical, during our return drive to Liverpool he suggested that I availed myself of his own growing knowledge of the record industry by allowing him to make available his A&R contacts in the record business to me, on Lee's behalf. I was delighted but declined, suggesting that if Jack Good didn't think Lee Curtis was ready for TV, then perhaps he wasn't altogether ready for the world of recording either. Brian could see that the Jack Good incident had galvanised me. Now, I told him, my principal function was to discharge my duties as manager in a much more professional way and I would keep Lee and the group to their roots in Liverpool while hopefully a scene grew around them.

I did accept Brian's generous offer of using him as a way of obtaining new releases and hard-to-find singles. After all I was still steeped in the big band sounds of my youth. I soon built up a massive 7in record collection in the process. All of it was American R&B, country music and rock 'n' roll; most of it was released on Decca's black-and-silver London-American imprint. Soon Lee, via his own record collecting, together with my assiduous attention to little-promoted US numbers, had one of the finest repertoires in Liverpool (although he took a great deal of persuading not to use so much Presley material) and the Detours began obtaining gigs in the central and southern parts of Liverpool, the Wirral, north-east Wales, Widnes and Runcorn. During the early part of 1961 Kenny and I even promoted our own rock 'n' roll night at the Co-operative Society's Blair Hall. This proved to be an enormous success and led to more self-styled promotions with Kenny's increasingly wacky ideas taking the fore.

Kenny's flyers and advertising campaigns were really ahead of their time. He would leave sort of esoteric messages on posters around the areas that Lee was booked to play. They might inform the punter of the venue, but not the date; they might just say 'guess who's on at …?' or 'Lee is coming'. Kenny would have made a great anarchist, I think. Of course, years later the anarchic punk publicists used similar tactics to advertise their bands and scenes. Yes, Kenny was a good advertising man all right, even though he hated both rock 'n' roll and the music business. As a result of Kenny's promotion and Lee's undoubted talent, I was even beginning to recoup some of my outgoings and was able to dress the band in some marvellous stage attire: beautiful mohair suits, Chelsea boots and so on.

Money wasn't really a problem for us at this stage, for shortly after the mobile shop business started to profit I was given the opportunity by Liverpool City Council to tender for two shops in Kirkby. Because of my growing business reputation on the estates in Kirkby, I found that I could easily beat off the competition from Waterworths, the famous Liverpool-based chain of fruit and vegetable stores, and was duly handed the keys to the empty shops in June 1961. I was naturally delighted and cash registers rang before my eyes. A captive market of thousands of people, over 10 miles away from Liverpool city centre, with me as sole proprietor of both outlets. They were to be fruit and vegetable and wet fish stores, selling the best quality at the cheapest prices. We were also allowed to sell a few cooked chickens and I installed rotisseries in both shops, amazing pieces of futuristic equipment for the locals of Kirkby in 1961. They would queue for what seemed like hours waiting for the spit-roasted chickens to come off the rotisseries. I placed my now husbandless mother in one shop and employed local staff in the other. My old friend Ken Dodd was hired for the grand opening which duly stopped the traffic in and around the Kirkby estates of Westvale and Northwood for the best part of the day. By this time Ken was a very big star indeed. In point of fact, I received a severe written reprimand from the Lancashire Education Department owing to the vast amount of school absenteeism that day. All the kids (and their parents) wanted to see 'Doddy' and had duly sagged off school: I can't say that I blamed them.

Within a short time I was able to suggest to Kenny that he give up his job as an ambulance driver and operate the mobile shop for me in the more remote parts of Kirkby. This he did and so, by the autumn of 1961, I had three very lucrative enterprises in this new town. The fame of the area was also beginning to spread nationally by this time, for the *Z Cars*

TV series had been launched on the BBC. The producers of this gritty piece of northern realism had picked Kirkby under the fictional name of Newtown for the site of their weekly piece of kitchen-sink police drama, and a kind of celebrity through infamy had brought the entire development to the public's attention – probably for all the wrong reasons! *Z Cars* proved to be another of those stereotypes into which the good people of Merseyside were dropped by the time of the Beatles' advent. Films such as *Violent Playground* and *These Dangerous Years* (both set in Liverpool) had already portrayed the city as an aggressive and hazardous place and *Z Cars* merely added to this typecasting. Nevertheless I suppose any publicity was good publicity for what was by this time something of a provincial backwater, even though, to my knowledge, the producers of *Z Cars* never actually went anywhere near the town of Kirkby.

After a long and hard day's work, Kenny and I would return to Gardner Road exhausted but usually in a happy frame of mind. Our relationship remained as close as it could be, but forever platonic. We both understood, I think, that there could be no going back and both of us had to live with the consequences of our earlier actions and decisions. Actually, the status of our relationship grew as we came to understand each other's shortcomings, weaknesses and dreams without thinking of them as at all threatening. Kenny, on the one hand, understood my vicarious craving for success via my brother, although he often described it as 'bordering on masochism'. I, on the other hand, tried to respect his flaws – including (like John Lennon) his morbid interest in the Third Reich. He felt that an attempt to trace the genealogy of our post-fascist world could be found via a close examination of fascism. It's not that I didn't agree; I recall telling him that Harry Epstein had once told me that emergent within fascism (or indeed Marxism, for that matter) were diverse discourses that eventually put paid to the ideology itself. But I simply thought we had to move on: this new age of the 1960s was full of excitement and overly dwelling on that previous era filled me with dread.

We never threw out our ashes at Gardner Road, but would bank up the fires on the cold winter's nights before and after gigs. This cosy netherworld began to attract young musicians. Other bands began to assemble and muster at Gardner Road alongside the Detours and, within a short space of time, the apartment became a real haven for musos. Not only were the Detours constantly at the flat, waiting for their instructions, but other performers, having heard of the salubrious environment and warm welcome, began to arrive on the doorstep. It became open house. There was, however, an additional attraction; by the Christmas of 1961 Kenny and I had become so busy by day and night that we employed a housekeeper, the wonderful and resilient Anne, and Anne's catering and attention to detail, not to mention her beautiful young daughter, far outstripped her rather caustic tongue. She was very welcoming to young band members who mostly saw beyond her authoritarian facade.

Shortly after the opening of the second shop in Kirkby, mother had recognised Anne from years previously as an old and trusted friend from Scotland Road. After the war Anne had married a Norwegian seaman and had settled in Norway for many years, but she had returned to Merseyside in 1958 to nurse an ageing relative and was housed in Northwood, Kirkby. At first, her daughter Girda was still at school in Norway while Anne was making a home for her, but once her mother had settled the daughter followed. However, Anne's financial position was always a little precarious and, after discovering this, mother asked her whether she would be interested in helping me keep Gardner Road up to the meticulous standards that I was used to, despite the presence of 1,001 musicians. She agreed and soon I had the best housekeeper anyone could wish for.

Anne travelled from Kirkby to Tuebrook (no mean distance) at least three times each week. Her catering was second to none and her variations on Scandinavian foods were particularly exciting. This was at a time when to the average Liverpudlian egg and chips was about as exotic as one could get, but Anne introduced us to the verities of smorgasbord, which was loved by all, and soon she handled almost all of the catering for our ever-increasing numbers of guests and dinner parties. Indeed, on the few occasions when she was unavailable, Kenny and I would have to bring in renowned Liverpool outside caterers Sampson and Barlow's, such was her reputation. She was especially nifty when catering for what she described as 'big nobs'. She would be referring to stars such as Russ Conway, with whom I had struck up a friendship after one of his many appearances at the Liverpool Empire. Russ' Bentley was often seen parked outside the Gardner Road apartment, and I'm sure that he would turn up when in the north-west of England specifically to taste Anne's cuisine.

While we tucked into one of Anne's delicacies I would gently tease out information and advice from Russ about that minefield known as the music business. He was always very gracious with his advice even though he realised from an early stage that he was providing me with information that was to contribute to his own downturn in popularity. What I mean by this is that Russ realised that he was an entertainer of the old school. He was essentially an, albeit very talented, hangover from variety performance, and variety had become less and less attractive to the younger generation in the post-war era. It was too stagey, too organised and too perfect. Furthermore, after skiffle literally anything appeared to be possible. Certainly, one no longer needed Russ' mastery of an instrument (in his case the piano) in order to make it. Russ, however, realised that the music scene in Liverpool included attitude and I remember his warning about this 'once the balloon had burst' as he put it: 'You'll have to deal with a lot of bullshit, Joe, but not simply from the business end … and God knows that's full of it.' I recall his words to this day (in fact, I remember writing them down after he had gone) for he went on to say:

> What I mean is that one of the things that is going to ensure success for some of these groups is their attitude. Egos. But this could also prove their downfall. The problem with one's ego is that, in the first instance, it makes you very focused. But after the success, the energy and the intelligence just seems to lose out to the ego altogether. I fear this for a lot of the local bands *because* of their resilience: Lee in particular.

Russ was starring in the Liverpool Empire in panto at that time, and even held auditions for young Liverpudlian groups to discover what this local talent was actually like (he had been talent spotted himself). The Detours were too busy or too frightened to attend, but others such as Mike Byrne's early band the Thunderbirds did. Mike much later told me, in describing his own efforts, that Russ' genuine enthusiasm did not actually stretch to admiring the Thunderbirds' rank amateurism. But Mike and I agree that Russ Conway should be acknowledged as one of the first London-based professionals actually to acknowledge the existence of a local scene in Liverpool.

So Anne and by 1960 her daughter Girda, coupled with the variety of musicians coming and going at the flat, provided a wonderful if rather frenetic atmosphere most of the time, while the good citizens of Kirkby unwittingly provided the financial wherewithal. Soon Girda had a job and so Anne, no longer tied by any semblance of family life, spent even more hours at Gardner Road. She never actually stayed, but just gave that all-pervading impression that she was always somewhere about the place. After my early morning calls to deliver fresh produce from Liverpool Market to my shops I would return home at about 11 a.m. Anne would always have breakfast ready for me, or even a dinner (she was noted for her excellent gravy). At Christmas she would prepare all the meals and would bring items of traditional Norwegian life to decorate the apartment. Her Scandinavian embroidery always fascinated me for it was so intricate and delicate. She was also a real DIY expert on the quiet. I would return home to find previously sticking doors opening freely, stiff window latches oiled, sashes operating smoothly and small repairs and improvements to furniture. She was an amazing woman (and Kenny and I were useless at such things). And then the beautiful Girda would join us too, and she would be thrilled by all of the comings and goings. Not only would she be able to talk to and be chased by some important national rock and rollers like Johnny Kidd, Heinz, Eden Kane and Shane Fenton, but she was also privy to the birth of a musical revolution. By 1962 the Beatles had joined the legions of rockers at Gardner Road and Paul McCartney, especially, developed something of a crush on Girda for quite some time (always liked blondes, did Paul). Girda was so incredibly shy, however, that she would run into the kitchen when Paul even looked at her. Various Manchester artists would also use Gardner Road as a stopover. That excellent and desperately underrated Mancunian vocalist Pete MacLaine was present on a number of occasions, as were various members of the Hollies. It was truly a home from home for the waifs and strays of the early sixties music scene.

Everyone was treated alike by Anne, however. She was totally unaffected by egos, stardom and petulance. She was like a surrogate mother to the groups and would chastise them if they were late or hadn't ironed their stage clothes. There would be occasions when I would return home to find three or four young musicians semi-clothed, only to find that Anne had got them to strip off their shirts because they needed 'a good ironing'. She had me worried at times, but she knew that even though I was earning my crust via retail, my heart was totally with the music, and so she acted as both their conscience and my guardian angel, constantly reminding them of their duties to me as professionals. Anne could be very caustic with my brother and was at times highly critical of him, disliking his inflated ego while appreciating his obvious talent. She would tell him to his face that I deserved better from him, that his band deserved better too, but Lee would laugh it all off – unlike the attentive John Lennon and Paul McCartney who seemed to pay a great deal of attention to Anne's salutary remarks. Anne, sadly, died in 1997 but shortly before her death we spoke and she reminded me of the times that she spent at Gardner Road 'helping tidy up the Beatles' rather scruffy image'. By 1962, of course, Brian Epstein had the Beatles under his control; however, that control was actually shared to a great degree, at least while at Gardner Road, with yours truly and my housekeeper. It was Anne, as she reminded me shortly before her death, who suggested to Brian that the Beatles should be put into the best quality suits that he could afford. It was also Anne who ridiculed Brian one evening for turning up in an all-leather outfit … it was never seen again.

Although pop history loves to dwell on myth, often attributing seminal moments to specific characters, suggesting genius and inspired thought and inspirational moments, the real flashes of history actually revolve around stinging remarks, little asides and offhand suggestions. A great deal of popular music history finds this a little too complicated and rather difficult to record, for it appears better to suggest gleams of impulse rather than ridicule, satire and irony. But Anne's place in the Beatles story is a valid one. It was she who was a catalyst for all visitors to Gardner Road; it was she who fed them, pressed their shirts, lampooned them and deflated their egos. It was even she who suggested that Brian Epstein should 'act his age' and remove the aforementioned and utterly ridiculous one-piece leather suit (it had made us all laugh so much, however, including his charges the Beatles). Some musos might even stay the night, deliberately saving on board and lodgings; others would simply fall asleep, being so whacked after a couple of gigs; but many others arrived simply because the vibe and food was good, the conversations excellent and Anne's daughter Girda stunningly beautiful. By 1961 this small unadopted road on the borders of Stoneycroft and Tuebrook had become a hidden haunt for many local and national rock stars, without the neighbours having even the slightest idea.

8

THE BEATLES AT GARDNER ROAD, BRIAN EPSTEIN AND MERSEYBEAT

WHEN I FIRST came to manage Lee's various rock bands, my previous experiences with the likes of Joe Loss came in very handy. Not only from a personal point of view in that I was able to deal with agents, venue managers and 'sharks' with a reasonable amount of alacrity, but also because I became something of a guru for the young people who came around to see Kenny and I at the apartment. I often thought that I was being somewhat miscast in the role of a music pedagogue; after all, despite my local solo career, I was only on the road with Loss for less than twelve months. However, I continued to relate anecdotes about my experiences of the music business, if so asked. Before too long, as I have previously stated, I was holding court to myriad young musicians and would-be rock 'n' roll singers, usually after Lee had informed them of his older brother's exploits with Loss and around the various flea pits, pubs and clubs in the Liverpool area. I felt that they needed to know who could be trusted and who could not. Although I was always as diplomatic as I could possibly be, I felt it only right to warn them off some of the more rogueish small-time operators in and around Liverpool. Many groups were already smarting after having suffered financially at the hands of battle of the bands merchants and I felt a degree of responsibility to them.

Who would pay? Who would try to argue their way out of paying? Who had PA equipment? Who tried to pinch yours? Which halls had dressing rooms? Which just had toilets? Merseybeat aficionados will recognise names such as Ted Knibbs, Bob Wooler, Alan Williams, Sam Leach,

Ray McFall and Sam Kelly. All of them, and more besides, regularly came under the microscope, as did I in one way or another. It could be incredibly competitive; for example, a little later, probably post-1963, even Brian was taken to a few dirty tricks in order to push his artists forward. On one occasion he booked Lee Curtis and the All Stars into a venue as far away as Kent but then rang the venue, cancelled Lee Curtis saying he was ill and sent Billy J. Kramer in his place. As good as Billy J. could be, his voice was not substantial (most of his recordings were double-tracked) and Brian evidently saw an opportunity to test Kramer in front of a non-partisan audience. One might describe Brian under these circumstances as a bit of a twat! However, I shall leave it up to you, dear reader, to ascertain which categories fitted which character. As for the Detours, we were still ploughing our way through our list of Catholic parochial clubs and were less reliant on local promoters than many. The Catholic church was, by and large, a very good payer!

Early in 1961 the names Lennon and McCartney started to drop into conversations at band meetings. I'd never previously heard of them, but learnt that these two belonged to a rather nebulous outfit who had been around for a number of years (apparently mostly without a drummer), that they were also as thick as thieves and had recently returned from a short season in Hamburg a changed band. 'Why Hamburg?' I enquired. One member of the Detours, I forget who, told me something like: 'Of all the people who I never expected to make a decent sound, it was Lennon's lot.' The comment continued: 'They weren't very reliable, let people down and used to turn up without a drummer half the time, but now they're back from Germany they sound totally different.' Those at the apartment on that rainy night in, I believe, January 1961 thought little more of it as the conversation ebbed and flowed for a few hours more; however, that Hamburg trip greatly interested me, and I made a mental note to check out this group at the first available opportunity. If a trip to Hamburg had produced such apparently dramatic effects on this band's sound, then it ought to be investigated for Lee Curtis' sake. Why on earth had they gone to Hamburg, in any case? Lennon and McCartney's group was called the Beatles, a most bizarre yet memorable moniker for a rock group in the early 1960s. I thought they were probably students or beatniks (or both) with an uncommercial name like that.

Their name came up again, some weeks later. I was informed that they were returning to Hamburg 'by demand' and I was not a little jealous. I still hadn't learnt anything concrete about this German connection and still hadn't come across the band at first hand. My informant also told me, however, that they were tied to a cafe proprietor by the name of Alan Williams, and it was he who had organised the trip to Germany. I knew Alan by reputation. He had organised the Merseyside leg of the ill-fated Eddie Cochran and Gene Vincent tour the previous year and ran a cafe in Slater Street called the Jacaranda. This was a hang-out for art school beatniks and tramps as far as I was aware. However, together with his wife Beryl, Alan had also started opening the cellar of the cafe up at night for live music. This was a radical thing to do in those days. As far as I was aware, his cafe wasn't licensed for alcohol, and so he had the vagaries of the Liverpool police to contend with; the Jacaranda was also in the city centre and so Alan, I presumed, had the protection racketeers to deal with as well. So I most certainly didn't envy him, especially after being informed that the Beatles were something of a handful too. The main attraction of the Jacaranda had been a West Indian steel band; I was also informed that it was this band of Caribbean musicians that had made the initial contact with the clubs in Hamburg. They were soon followed by Derry and the Seniors (one of Liverpool's top rock bands and another outfit in whom Williams had more than a passing interest); 'curiouser and curiouser,' I thought. As it turned out, the information I had received early in 1961 was both a little old and inaccurate. Alan Williams had already fallen out not only with his young protégés the Beatles before they had returned to Liverpool at the end of 1960, but also the Hamburg pioneers Derry and the Seniors. So, by the time I came to be discussing the group with my old friend Brian Epstein, I discovered that they were conspicuously managerless, but effectively being managed by drummer Pete Best's mother, Mona.

I hadn't seen Brian Epstein for several months. As previously stated, Kenny and I were, if not quite an item, certainly stable and Brian, being Brian, had done one of his usual disappearing acts. In truth, I just thought NEMS was taking up most of his time. This branch of Epstein's had actually outgrown the furniture stores so much that the Epstein dynasty had opened up another store in Liverpool city centre to corner the ever-growing market for audio and televisual sales. But when our paths did cross again that July of 1961, I could see that far from being a young man maturing into a business environment, he was actually once again very restless. We had organised a trip to the theatre in Manchester and Brian had come to meet me at Gardner Road. Brian brought with him a copy of a broadsheet that had just been circulated entitled *Mersey Beat* and he was very animated about how the paper was discussing the local scene in which my own

Lee Curtis continued to prosper. He was highly charged that night and was envious that I was not only managing a band on this thriving scene, but had acted on Jack Good's recommendation to help cultivate something provincial. I detected that evening as we travelled to Manchester down the East Lancashire Road in his little car, that he was incredibly excited. In fact, I vividly remember Brian parking on Oxford Road outside the theatre and being so excited that he damaged both the car in front and the car behind as he pulled in to park. 'That's what bumpers are for, Joe,' he exclaimed as I hid my face in my hands. It would never have occurred to me at that time, but Brian may have been rather high on some prescriptive drug or other. Certainly, in retrospect, his actions seemed to indicate as much. Giving him the benefit of the doubt, I suppose it could have easily been excitement, so I will simply put it down to that.

Following a wonderful evening of banter over an excellent dinner and show, that copy of *Mersey Beat* came up in conversation once again on the journey back to Liverpool along the East Lancashire Road. I hadn't seen it before that evening, even though I had already been informed that it had been available since the beginning of the month. I was quite impressed. For a broadsheet to be published in Liverpool, dealing almost exclusively with musical activity on Merseyside, seemed to indicate something very important was either happening or about to happen. It also became obvious to me that Brian had seen something that had galvanised his ostensibly successful but in fact drifting business and personal life. The cover of that first edition mentioned the Beatles and Brian informed me that he had discovered that they were without a manager. He said no more that evening, but it was evident that the prospect of group management now interested him. He was rather disappointed to discover that I had no opinion to offer on the young group. I told him I had heard of them, but that the Detours had not shared a bill with them up until that time. Brian thought that this was rather unusual, but I informed him that Lee's circuit was still very north Liverpool and North Wales-based, whereas the Beatles, I had been informed, were something of a south Liverpool-based group. All I could tell him was that I had heard that they had been something of a handful, but that this was only rather third-hand news, and that their names had cropped up in conversations in Gardner Road amongst other musicians because of their musical excellence. Brian was evidently smitten.

By issue number two of *Mersey Beat* (it was bi-monthly), the editor Bill Harry had (rather generously, I might add) noted that the Beatles had secured a recording contract with Polydor Records in West Germany;

a touch of speculative journalism, this, but nevertheless great copy for a local music journal. Brian rang to tell me, agitatedly, that he had ordered a large amount of copies for his two NEMS stores and that they had sold out in a matter of forty-eight hours. He stated, quite categorically, that once he had a moment of spare time he would investigate this group personally. He had been informed by punters at NEMS that the Beatles played at the Cavern Club, literally within 2 minutes' walking distance from his office in Whitechapel. Lee Curtis hadn't officially played this venue at this stage. I informed him, however, that the Beatles were once again bound for Germany, and he would have to wait. I have to admit that at least mentally I laughed off his enthusiasm, in any case. Brian was always thinking of projects in order to bolster what he saw as his rather mundane existence at NEMS. History informed me that they seldom ever came to fruition, and at first this seemed to be just another one of those projects.

However, by August 1961, Brian was interested in *Mersey Beat* enough to be reviewing the latest record releases in the paper. I remember him being very proud of that small contribution, although I had to keep reminding him that his own by then rather middle-of-the-road tastes and those of the *Mersey Beat*-buying public were actually a million miles apart. In fact, if one takes a look at some of Brian's reviews from that era, they seem incongruous, to say the least. However, at least from my perspective it was that important contact with Bill Harry and *Mersey Beat*, together with my own direct involvement in the local scene, that finally prompted Brian to visit the Cavern. I had learnt that Bill Harry, editor of the paper, was a good friend of John Lennon of the Beatles and looking again at the paper it all made perfect sense. I've often wondered whether the Beatles would have received the local publicity that they did in those early days had John not been a member of the group, despite their obvious talent. Nevertheless, *Mersey Beat* and Bill and Virginia Harry have a significant part to play in this incredible story. Harry recognised, as only a few of us did, at a very early stage that a synchronic historical moment was taking place in Liverpool. He remarked to me once that he thought Liverpool was rather like what he imagined New Orleans to have been like at the turn of the century. And who would argue with that inestimable value judgement?

I do feel that *Mersey Beat*'s contribution cannot be over-exaggerated. Certainly it was a vital conduit, of that there can be no doubt. As far as journalism is concerned it was hardly *Rolling Stone*, but that style of rock journalism which came to regard itself very seriously indeed some years later was born out of trailblazers like *Mersey Beat*. In fact, for me one of the best articles written about the Beatles during the 1960s actually came from the pages of *Mersey Beat* as far back as 1961. It was not written by Bill Harry, however, but came from the pen of Bob Wooler. In fact, the myth about 'Norman Jones', or whatever his name was, coming into NEMS asking Brian for a copy of *My Bonnie* and thus introducing Brian to the work of the Beatles is exploded by the fact that *Mersey Beat* would have been sitting on Brian's counter well before that time. I distinctly recall issue one had been published on 6 July 1961 precisely because NEMS had ordered those first few copies and Brian had shown me his copy on our trip to Manchester. By the way, regarding the Raymond Jones saga, I swear that Brian initially did not use the name 'Raymond' and that this entire episode was almost entirely the creation of Derek Taylor. Brian later informed me that when *A Cellarful of Noise* was being worked up, he was so busy that he simply told Taylor something like 'you write it, I'll check it', and that he hadn't actually checked it. Brian had a vague recollection that someone had been in for the *My Bonnie* 45 at some stage or other, but his recall was understandably very vague. However, because the record had been ordered from him, he had taken down the person's name and remembered, at least to me, 'Norman' and not 'Raymond' Jones. There was perhaps a grain of truth to it all, but from his perspective the story was pretty much a fake from start to finish.

So important was *Mersey Beat* to the Liverpool and national music scene (it mutated into *Disc and Music Echo*, but more of that in a little while) that it inspired a few imitators. Kenny, for example, involved himself in a short-lived competitor entitled *Combo*. This music paper was published in the north end of Merseyside and championed the causes of my own Carlton Brooke artists, together with bands from Crosby, Bootle and Southport. *Combo* was a lively little paper but was destined to fail. It ran from 1963–64, by which time even *Mersey Beat* was struggling for copy, and finally closed its doors in late 1964, reflecting, I think, the slowing down of interest in the 'Liverpool Sound' across the country. Quite simply, the music had been oversold while remaining relatively static. By 1965, *Mersey Beat* had been reduced to a column on the back page of *Disc and Music Echo* and was rather old hat.

But back to 1961. The decision to actually visit the Cavern would have been an enormous one for Brian. Make no mistake he would have been very nervous about being seen in such a venue. Although he was enthusiastic about this Liverpool music scene, his enthusiasm was from the relative distance of the middle-class Jewish bourgeoisie. Alan Sytner, the Cavern Club's original owner, did mention here and there (see Brocken, *Other Voices*, 2010) that Brian had spent his 21st birthday in the Cavern, but I am not sure that this was the case. Brian was born in 1934 and therefore this birthday would have fallen in 1955, which was well before the Mathew Street cellar was colonised by jazz lovers. So my feelings have always been, with great respect to the late Alan Sytner, that this was a club Brian might not have previously entered. Perhaps Sytner got it both right and wrong – Brian might have been in the Cavern Jazz Club to celebrate another family event, but at another time. Either way, the club had by 1962 changed dramatically and for me Brian was always out of touch with the teenage goings on there – at least to begin with.

I suppose this is where I stepped in, at least to a small degree, for by the autumn of 1961 we were once again seeing a great deal of each other. Each of us was enjoying the other's company in our little business brunches; Brian's life was revolving more and more around his retail business, plus he was getting increasingly interested in management as a potential diversion. However, it must be stressed that he had not made up his mind about managing anyone at this stage. So he asked me to go into the Cavern on his behalf. This I did during the late morning of 26 October 1961, whereupon I sat on the steps leading down into the main basement and listened to the Beatles rehearse prior to their lunchtime session. I did not meet them but merely listened in and made a mental note to report back to my friend. I duly reported my visit the following day to Brian with the simple message: 'If you don't get them someone else will.' Brian looked at me: 'Such as yourself?' I did not answer. Before his first visit to the Cavern he paid me another, more casual, call one Wednesday afternoon, whereupon we discussed the Detours' finances, my brother's appeal, PR, bookings and publicity, and took a trip to my font of all wisdom – The Musical Box on Rocky Lane – for a few records that NEMS did not have in stock. By early November he had asked Bill Harry to arrange a meeting with the Beatles and on 9 November, accompanied by his NEMS colleague Alistair Taylor, he met the group. By 10 December Brian was ensconced as manager of the Beatles and during December I once more saw very little of him. The Detours were working solidly in North Wales and Birkenhead whereas the Beatles continued their residency at the Cavern, while also expanding their fan base to hitherto uncharted waters such as Widnes, Runcorn and Ellesmere Port. Brian and I eventually met up once again in town at the beginning of 1962 at the Liverpool (Storyville) Jazz Society, when finally the Beatles and the Detours shared the same bill, promoted as I recall, by Sam Leach.

The Detours were checking the equipment prior to the gig when they discovered that one of the amps had blown. This was a severe setback. The Detours' sound at that time was very loud with a lot of bass and great emphasis on beat and twang. Although I claimed to be roadie as well as manager, I could barely change a fuse and so when that alternative proved fruitless, I decided that I would just have to try to borrow an amp from another band. I turned away from the stage area to discover Brian standing in the shadows watching the Detours warm up. Initially I asked him whether he had come to see the show, forgetting that he had now also entered the managerial merry-go-round, but he was quick to remind me that he was now in charge of the Beatles, who were also on the bill that evening. At last our musical paths had crossed! Seizing my chance, I asked Brian about the amp. He replied in his usual rather affected but debonair manner: 'Well of course it is fine with me Joe, but you had better ask the band … they're upstairs in the band room.'

I negotiated the winding staircase in the decaying warehouse to what were laughingly described as the dressing rooms to see what I could scrounge, whereupon I came across the Beatles. Their local profile had risen greatly in the intervening couple of months and they were now sharing the top spot with Lee Curtis and the Detours. But they were still extremely friendly and complimentary about Lee, albeit with a discernible sense of irony and a competitive edge. Brian had followed me up the staircase and promptly introduced me to his boys; they, in turn, having found out that I was an old friend of Brian's, greeted me with a genuine warmth that I shall never forget. Even in the short time that Brian had been with them, he had obviously made a great impression. They loved him, and when it was suggested that the Detours borrow an amp from them I was delighted to hear John (it appeared to me that he was the spokesperson for the band) say: 'Yeah sure, the show must go on; but take care of it, OK?'

This was the beginning of my friendship with the Beatles. After the gig, which was a roaring success except for the fact that, as usual, we had to chase Sam Leach all over the place to get paid, we sat around chewing the cud. Brian informed the Beatles that I was an ex-performer and professional manager, and that my apartment in Gardner Road was open house to all musicians. They did not appear at Gardner Road immediately, but after learning from the eminent Bob Wooler, DJ at the Cavern, that my address was behind the recently opened Granada Bowling Alley on Green Lane, they soon began turning up for tea, toast and advice in between games of ten-pin bowling. During the month of March 1962, they seemed to me to spend almost all of their spare time at Gardner Road. As stated previously, I think Girda was a big attraction for Paul, but they all loved the ambience, particularly John Lennon who would often fall asleep in the chair in front of the fire after endlessly doodling on scraps of paper. I got the impression that there was little at home to inspire him and that he preferred the warmth (in more ways than one) of Gardner Road. John would generally sleep through until late in the morning, when he would be awoken by the arriving Anne pulling out the ashes from the extinguished fire and lighting the new blaze with the assistance of his doodle-ridden scraps of paper.

Even at this early stage, it was becoming quite evident to Kenny and me that something simply had to happen for the Beatles. The more I saw of them, the more they impressed me, not simply as musicians but as people. They were very professional for such young men: they rehearsed a good deal; they wrote some of their own songs, which was a highly unusual kind of folksy/beatnik-type thing to do in the Liverpool of the early 1960s. What's more, the songs, although perhaps a little derivative, were not half bad. They were also kind, thoughtful, yet acerbic and funny; they could already play well (I was very impressed by George's abilities on the guitar) but wanted to improve, hence their professional status and lack of day-time 'real' jobs. All in all they were most impressive young men and were quite unlike any young rock 'n' rollers I had previously met – even the famous ones. They were highly focused individually and collectively; or at least three of them were. As for Pete Best, I'm not so sure. But it was difficult for him because the other three were so bloody close. It could at times be very difficult to talk to any of them seriously, when all three were together. One could only do this when they were on their own. For me this would usually be in the early hours of the morning when I would occasionally run one or the other of them home in my car. Then I would feel I could get to know the real John, Paul or George. Even though Lee Curtis was my own protégé and I was involved in all of this because of my perceptions of his talent, I could not fail to see that Brian had been very lucky. He had come across four very talented young musicians who needed him just as much as he needed them. I never really received the same kind of vibe from Lee. He often made me feel uncomfortable, that I was freeloading, whereas the Beatles made me feel proud of my actions in this emerging scene.

1 Agnes Flannery – Joe's mum. (Author's collection)

2 Joe Flannery aged 4. (Author's collection)

3 The Beatles. (Author's collection)

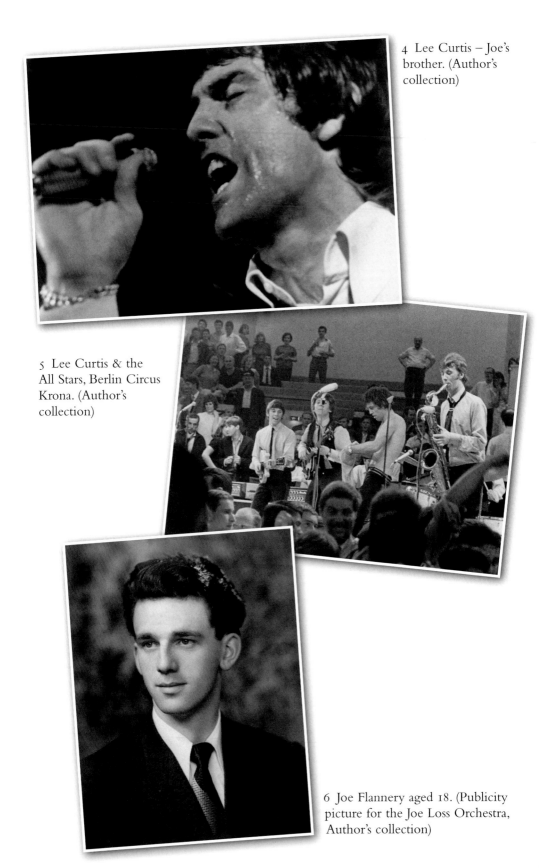

4 Lee Curtis – Joe's brother. (Author's collection)

5 Lee Curtis & the All Stars, Berlin Circus Krona. (Author's collection)

6 Joe Flannery aged 18. (Publicity picture for the Joe Loss Orchestra, Author's collection)

7 Brian Epstein and Joe Flannery, 'The Untouchables'. (Author's collection)

8 Brian Epstein dressed for Ascot, 1963. (Author's collection)

9 Kenny and Joe at St George's Hall, Liverpool, for the Liverpool Student Union concert 1961. (Author's collection)

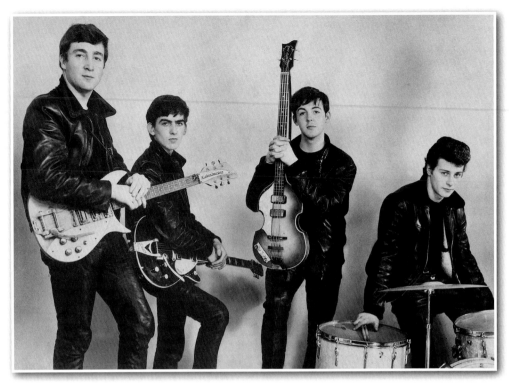

10 The Beatles: John Lennon, George Harrison, Paul McCartney and Pete Best.
(© Albert Marian)

11 The Beatles: George Harrison, Pete Best, Paul McCartney and John Lennon. (Author's
collection)

12 Cilla Black, 1960s. (© NEMS Enterprises)

13 Beryl Marsden, 1960s. (Author's collection)

14 Joe Flannery at the Mobile Shop in Kirkby with the car George Harrison learnt to drive in. (Author's collection)

15 Joe Flannery, Lee Curtis and their brother Gerard arriving at Decca Studios, London, 1961. (Author's collection)

16 Brian Epstein, 1960s. (Epstein family collection)

17 Joe Flannery and Simon Hind, guitarist of the All Stars, in the dressing room at the Star Club. (Author's collection)

18 The Star Club stage, Hamburg. (Author's collection)

19 Joe Flannery's membership card to the Star Club (note number Joe 90). (Author's collection)

20 The entrance to the Star Club, Hamburg. (Author's collection)

21 Jimi Hendrix Experience appearing at the Star Club. (Author's collection)

22 The Beatles. (Author's collection)

23 The Star Club bar with Lee Curtis, Pam Birch, Freddie Starr and members of the All Stars. (Author's collection)

25 Cynthia and John Lennon on their wedding day. (Author's collection)

24 Linda McCartney on the farm at Mull of Kintyre. (Author's collection)

26 Paul McCartney and son James on the Mull of Kintyre. (Author's collection)

27 Agnes Flannery (Joe's mum) with children and grandchildren. (Author's collection)

28 Lee Curtis and Pete Best, Hamburg Beatles Convection, late 1970s. (Author's collection)

29 Joe Flannery and Clive Epstein in their office at Allerton Road, Liverpool, with their new signing, the band Light and Phil Boardman. (Author's collection)

30 Ringo Starr and Joe Flannery at the New Star Club, Hamburg. (Author's collection)

31 Ringo Starr, Horst Fascher, Lee Curtis and Joe Flannery at the New Star Club, Hamburg. (Author's collection)

32 George Harrison – with his psychedelic mini. (Author's collection)

33 John Lennon leaving Savile Row, London. (Author's collection)

34 Joe Flannery with Cynthia Lennon and James Last 7 guitarist. (Author's collection)

35 Joe Flannery at Electric Lady Studios, NYC. (Author's collection)

36 Joe Flannery, Bill Harry and staff at Carling Music, London. (Author's collection)

37 Joe Flannery and friend Horst Fascher. (Author's collection)

38 Joe Flannery at Liverpool Promenade. (Author's collection)

39 Paul McGann and Joe Flannery at the Beatles Convention, Adelphi Hotel, Liverpool. (Author's collection)

40 Terence Trent D'Arby and Joe Flannery at the Apollo, Manchester. (Author's collection)

41 Joe Flannery and Paul McCartney, *Liverpool Oratorio* opening of LIPA. (Author's collection)

42 Roy Edwards, Ken Dodd and Joe Flannery. (Author's collection)

43 Sgt. Pepper Live poster, Liverpool Empire. (Author's collection)

44 Julie Goodyear and Joe Flannery receiving Culture Ambassadorships of Liverpool. (Author's collection)

45 Joe Flannery and David Essex outside St George's Hall, Liverpool. (Author's collection)

46 Paul McCartney and Joe Flannery, Liverpool Echo Arena. (Author's collection)

Brian's life took on a new turn. Always immaculate, he now also had an aura of exhilaration. I recognised a different Brian from the one that I had known so well; he was vicariously living his life through his young charges. Occasionally he would try to impress them with the appearance of a cool, calm businessman. At other times, he would try to make an impression on them by dressing in a similar manner to them, such as the previously discussed all-leather suit which on Brian looked a little weird – as we all told him. Actually, that leather outfit brought me into direct contact with his family for the first time in years. The thoughts of Brian wearing leather actually summoned up thoughts of Nazis to Harry and Queenie Epstein and, together with Brian discussing visits to Germany, his parents, as orthodox Jews, were briefly a little disturbed. Clive and Harry Epstein even visited me one afternoon at the flat to discuss what they translated as disturbing fascist or sado-masochistic inclinations in Brian. I was able to persuade them that there was no need to worry: it was a musical thing, not politics, and they were unlikely to see the offending leathers again. Sure enough, Brian had indeed taken the hint and the offending suit was consigned to a charity shop.

John Lennon would frequently see through Brian's innate insecurity – he recognised it, of course. In fact, John would often play upon it, which was cruel but typically John. Brian would usually get over any Lennon jibe, particularly those about his 'ambiguous' sexuality or Jewishness, by visiting me privately and pouring his heart out, almost like therapy, I suppose. Sexual matters were not generally discussed, you understand (don't forget that these were still the days when love between men was considered an act of gross indecency), but he was aware that we shared many insecurities, many common interests and, of course, a great and guarded friendship. One occasion when I wasn't able to intervene and help Brian overcome some very cutting remarks about his sexuality led him, I believe, to an act of revenge that was very unfortunate and quite beneath him. It is a perspective on a little-known piece of Merseybeat history that I believe has hitherto not been fully revealed.

It was September 1964 and I, as you will later discover, was enjoying life in West Germany. Kenny had returned home to talent spot groups and informed me that Bill Harry had instigated what he thought was a slur campaign against Brian. I never saw or heard of any evidence to support this whatsoever and nothing was ever printed, but according to Kenny, Brian Epstein's homosexuality had become an issue. He was apparently deeply hurt but could not come to me about it, for he was in London and

I was in Hamburg. Had we spoken at that time, I would certainly have advised him to forget it. I would have also presumed that he would have settled back into his usual pattern of erecting his sophisticated façade; this time, however, it seems that he didn't let the matter lie. On this particular day in 1964, according to Kenny, Bill Harry could be found standing in his own office watching Brian Epstein emptying out Virginia Harry's desk. So much had the remark touched a raw nerve that Brian Epstein had purchased *Mersey Beat* outright from Ray McFall, right under the nose of the editors. Apparently Brian had informed Bill that he was perfectly willing to let him stay on under his ownership, but that Virginia would not be allowed near the place.

All of this information came to me second hand and I have no way of verifying any of it. However, I must say that if it were authentic, while applauding Brian's tenacity in standing up for himself, I found his tactics to be more than a little awry and rather futile. The matter of his sexuality would never go away by simply purchasing a now declining parochial music paper. Brian, I felt, had to face facts sooner or later that wandering around both Liverpool and London with his secretary on his arm fooled nobody. It all had to be faced out at some stage. I know times were different then – God knows, I realise that – but nevertheless, one can only live a lie for so long. Brian's purchase of *Mersey Beat* was his attempt at a short-term solution, an attempt to silence the gossip at a crucial time in the Beatles' career by, literally, buying out the source. Of course, it was financially a bad move and although Brian was by this time a very wealthy man and could afford a loss leader or two, it was still somewhat reckless. *Mersey Beat*, whilst being perhaps the most important conduit and flagship for the Liverpool scene prior to 1963, had never really made any money and, in fact, lost a packet (hence McFall's quiescence in regard to the sale); post-1963 it was both circulated and imitated across the country making its previously assured and unique qualities recede considerably. Brian eventually did a deal, converting *Mersey Beat* into *Music Echo* and then combining that publication with one of the lesser music weeklies, *Disc* – a rather pallid and puerile newsgatherer if ever there was one. On each occasion Brian reduced the editor's clout in line with the genre's thinning influence. I knew that he was determined to display to those that know what he was up to just how serious he could be; he was prepared to silence perhaps the most important historical feature of the Liverpool beat scene, except of course the music itself.

All of this was, as I have stated, not to my liking. I have never been one of those who subscribed to the axiom that revenge is sweet and, believe me, I have been placed in several positions where revenge could have been exacted on numerous occasions. Furthermore, I felt (and still feel) that his decision was too drastic; it smacked of a man not listening to the advice of others. My own opinion was that, had he listened to those close to him, he would have discovered that *Mersey Beat* would have financially shot itself in the foot in good time anyway. As previously suggested, by 1964 it was already an anachronism, especially since most of the fat cats from London had moved in and the best of our musicians had moved out. In fact, for many of our exiled musicians, whose bands would sadly break up during 1965 and 1966, the back pages of *Melody Maker* and the enduring contacts with myself and the Star Club in Hamburg would prove to be of far more benefit than *Mersey Beat*, especially if one didn't want to return to Liverpool – and, let's face it, who did? The money for live bands was reducing, not increasing, precisely because there were so many third-rate bands appearing on the streets. So, from 1963 onward until its effective closure via its merger with *Disc*, *Mersey Beat* was in terminal decline.

There has been a great deal written about this periodical in its heyday, but little about its decline. I believe that, despite the antagonism, Brian acted erroneously in facilitating this descent. It has often been stated to me that Ray McFall had invited Brian's financial interest because of the faltering finances at the Cavern. This, of course, is probably correct, but I believe it to be only part of the story. According to Kenny, and through my later conversations with Brian in London and on the telephone, I am utterly convinced that he purchased *Mersey Beat* in order to ruin it. By late 1964 he was regarding money as something of a plaything and, to counter homophobia, I felt that he used that money to accelerate that publica-tion's decline. I feel that Bill Harry, in particular, was ultimately very badly treated and let down by Brian Epstein.

I think that Bill Harry would have emerged as one of this country's leading music journalists, but this was sadly not to be after the somewhat dubious decline of the *Mersey Beat* newspaper. Although he remains per-haps the best-respected Beatles historian, I do feel that this is only one string to his bow. By the mid-1960s there was a plethora of publications covering the new pop scene. *Music Echo* was never placed in a strong enough position by Brian to compete, remaining in the north-west. An editor from London, Brian Harvey, was brought in to strip the remain-ing local colour from its pages. Brian Epstein later remarked to me in

NEMS ENTERPRISES LTD

DIRECTORS: B. AND C. J. EPSTEIN

12-14 WHITECHAPEL, LIVERPOOL, 1 · TELEPHONE ROYAL 7895

BE/BA:

24th September 1962

Dear Manfred,

Just a note to confirm that GERRY & THE PACEMAKERS
will arrive at Hamburg airport at 1955 hours on
Sunday next 30th September. As they have not
obtained working permits would you please arrange
for someone from the Star Club to meet the group
at the airport in order to avoid complications.

I would be grateful if you will please arrange
for the following monies to be sent to me:

To 4 single air flights Liverpool/Hamburg
(as per contract) at £19. 7. - each   £77. 8. -

To nominal commission (as arranged)
9 weeks @ 50 marks per week   450 marks.

Incidentally, you will be interested to know that
THE BEATLES first record is being issued in this
country on Friday October 5th and it is really a
wonderful disc. As soon as I have a copy I will
send you one. In the meantime I am sending some
new 'literature' and I will soon be sending you
some more photographs.

With best wishes.

Yours sincerely,
Brian Epstein.

Manfred Weisleder,
Star-Club,
HAMBURG-Altona,
Grosse Freiheit 39, Germany

P.S. Photographs of THE BEATLES and BIG THREE
will be sent as soon as they are ready.

A letter from Brian Epstein to Manfred Weissleder in Hamburg informing him
of Gerry and the Pacemakers travel plans. (Author's collection)

London one evening, on one of my visits back to Britain, that 'revenge did happen to have a sweet taste'. While he remained unspecific about the subject matter as we sat in the back of a Rolls-Royce on the way to a West End theatre, my mind connected *Mersey Beat* with a certain toy coronation coach.

Names that I would get to know extremely well over the subsequent years either by accident or design were coined by the Beatles in 1962 at Gardner Road, while they ate me out of house and home and were being chased out of the way by Anne. It was during the March of that year that I first heard the name of Stuart Sutcliffe. The boys explained to me that he was their former bassist. I remember John telling me one evening after a gig that Stuart was still in Hamburg and studying painting. In his words, he was 'Me best mate, actually … I miss him not being around, even though he was rubbish on the bass'. Sadly, I was never to meet Stuart for little did any of us realise that he was already terminally ill and the very day before they were to return to the Reeperbahn, Stuart had already died in Astrid Kirchherr's arms. The Beatles played the newly opened Star Club in Hamburg that April. This was an extremely well-paid gig, for the club had been opened by Manfred Weissleder in order (as he later informed me) to put all of the other Reeperbahn clubs out of business and he was prepared to pay the best money in order to do just that. The Star Club had a massive capacity, seating well over 1,000 punters and Brian and I had already viewed the new club at close quarters – but more of that in a little while.

It was at this time that I became even closer involved with Brian Epstein in a more formal business capacity. Even as the Beatles were off to the Star Club (13 April–31 May 1962) I was ringing around many booking agencies and, on behalf of the Beatles and Lee Curtis, was being approached by many more, all of whom wanted to know about this Liverpool thing. Brian was by this time also showing signs of empire-building and had his eye firmly on one or two other artistes regularly appearing at the Cavern that spring. He enlightened me one evening over dinner that he admired a Larry Parnes style of artist management, and suggested that a stable of Liverpudlians might be possible, with all the best local acts under the joint managerial umbrella of NEMS and my newly named agency of Carlton Brooke. Brian then asked whether a legal combination of NEMS with Carlton Brooke might be possible. I was a little wary, not because I held any misgivings about Brian's integrity, but because I still thought of him as something of a fantasist who was using NEMS's finances to fund his dreams.

Whereas the hard-earned money from the people of Kirkby had unintentionally helped to develop a music scene in Liverpool via my own business profits going into funding Lee Curtis and the Detours, Brian was using a bottomless pit of old Epstein money mixed with his NEMS profits to support his fantasies. I did not begrudge him this and wished him well throughout; I simply thought that in my world such finances were a little more difficult to come by. Furthermore, I did consider that if he, like Parnes, had a number of artistes under his mantle, some (like Dickie Pride, who for me was Parnes' finest artist) would suffer at the expense of others. I was to later discover this to be true with my own artistes. I also continually reminded myself of Jack Good's words to me. For Good, Parnes' style of management seemed steeped in the past, and who was I to argue? So I rather reluctantly declined Brian's offer to amalgamate formally: a mistake? Perhaps.

I had, by this time, given my management role the working title of Carlton Brooke because it was a practicable thing to do. Lee Curtis' popularity was growing locally and Kenny had suggested that Lee needed an official title behind him in order to increase the professional visage surrounding him. I agreed and took the name of the cinema on the corner of Green Lane and Tuebrook (Carlton) and merged it with the last syllable of this busy shopping area on the border of Stoneycroft; our agency was thus 'Carlton Brooke'. I added an 'e' for sophistication! Upon reading the business notices section in the *Liverpool Daily Post* and *Echo* at one of our business brunches that spring, Brian admitted to be green with jealousy; his immediate comment was: 'You always seem to come up with the best names and titles, Joe. Even the Lee Curtis ideas – where on earth do those ideas come from?' 'To be honest, Brian,' I reminded him, 'most of those ideas were Kenny's.' This observation was not entirely true; however, I continually felt the need to remind Brian that I was not available, and by prodding him about Kenny's continued presence I felt that Brian was ever so gently informed that another was standing in the wings. Shortly afterwards – perhaps a month or two later – NEMS Enterprises was registered as a theatrical, concert and booking agency, just like Carlton Brooke. There were no staff to speak of at NEMS but Clive Epstein was appointed Brian's company secretary on the advice of their father Harry, who was, I think, ever mindful of Brian's short concentration span.

So, now that NEMS was officially an agency by the early summer of 1962, Brian had begun to express opinions about signing other artists. He was showing particular interest in the Remo Four, originally the Remo Quartet, who had been playing the Cavern since rock 'n' roll had been allowed through those hallowed jazz portals. They had their own residency at the Cavern for a while and then became the backing group for Johnny Sandon, former lead singer with the Searchers. They were a very professional if, in my opinion, a rather unremarkable group and went through a number of personnel changes over the years, eventually being George Harrison's studio band on *Wonderwall* and then having a hit record in 1970 as Ashton, Gardner and Dyke; *Resurrection Shuffle* was ostensibly a piss-take on the sock-it-to-me soul of the day, but proved to be a very successful and enduring song.

Brian initially hired the Remo Four to back one of his starlets, Tommy Quickly, in 1963, and during this time they also backed Liverpool's finest vocal group, the Chants, in addition to appearing on the Beatles' autumn tour of 1964. I think he saw them as Liverpool's version of Sounds Incorporated. However, he lost interest in them after a few failed singles for Pye and it was left to yours truly to help pick up the pieces by booking them into the Star Club later that year. NEMS also showed an interest in the Four Jays, the Big Three, the aforementioned Chants and Gerry and the Pacemakers. Gerry Marsden, leader of the Pacemakers, was an incredibly likeable guy and was also very popular with the Beatles. In fact, the two bands had played a gig together in 1961 as an octet. Brian already knew Gerry a little, I think, via the NEMS shop on Whitechapel. Gerry was quite a record collector and was forever in and out of NEMS. Brian, however, was also very impressed with Gerry's all-round professionalism and greatly admired the band for persisting with a stand-up piano. He remarked to me on a number of occasions that their dedication to humping a piano around knew few bounds (these were the days immediately preceding those smaller and lighter Farfisa and Vox organs). I particularly recall one gig they played via Carlton Brooke at Chester fire station where the piano had to be hauled up from Northgate Street via a block and tackle into the concert room above the engine house – how they did it, I'll never know.

Bill Harry has suggested that Brian Epstein's tactics for signing acts were based around earmarking those *Mersey Beat* poll-winners who were not already committed to management. This is mostly true; however, he was also very interested in managing Lee Curtis. In fact, I still believe that one of his main reasons for wishing to combine our operations was to get Lee on his books. To have the top two acts in Liverpool signed to NEMS would have assuaged his ego considerably. So, for a second time during that important summer of 1962, Brian mooted whether we might officially combine our interests. This second offer came on the back of a small coup that I had made, i.e. getting the Beatles into Herefordshire, Shropshire and North Wales. Lee Curtis had already made some breakthroughs on the north-east Wales coast and into the Welsh Marches. Towns such as Connah's Quay, Flint and Shotton were good for the Detours, but by spring of 1962 one could also add Hereford, Malvern, Ludlow and Whitchurch. Having agreed to take over responsibility for bookings away from Liverpool on behalf of NEMS, I managed to get a deal with a variety agency we called Cana (but actually read 'CVA' on their billheads), who handled many dance-hall venues in the Hereford, Stroud, Worcester and Gloucester areas. I was also able to persuade the operators of a small club in Rhyl, quaintly entitled the Regent Dansette, to take the Beatles during July that summer. The Beatles' status had by this time undoubtedly grown: they'd been broadcasting on regional BBC radio, for a start; but to be honest, these gigs were obtained via Lee Curtis' reputation as a live performer. Brian, however, was suitably impressed: he thought that this was really travelling.

'As far away as Stroud and Rhyl?' he enquired.

'Yes, Brian, as far away as Stroud and Rhyl,' I ironically reiterated.

'I think we're on our way, Joseph! By the way, where's Stroud?'

The Beatles were also supported on these two prestigious occasions by groups I would have a great deal of contact with over the coming years in Germany. At Stroud there was the Rebel Rousers, who would perform for me many times during my stay in Hamburg, and at Rhyl, a group recommended to me by Bob Wooler, the Strangers. They never really made it as such but were a tight little group, at least as far as I recall. The lead singer of the Strangers was Joe Fagin, who in the 1980s enjoyed a couple of hits with *That's Livin' Alright* and *Back With the Boys Again*, both TV show themes by Ian La Frenais and Dick Clement.

I must admit that I was very tempted to combine formally with Brian after this achievement, but in the end I held out for two reasons. Firstly, I had to remind myself that the only reason I had taken this crazy job on in the first place was to assist my brother. At this time I had no other acts formally signed with Carlton Brooke (although I too was looking) and the entire purpose of my late nights and early mornings was to help Lee gain an outlet for his obvious talent. Of course, my loyalty to this aim, I realise now, was somewhat misguided. Brian could have done far more for Lee than I in the long run, but this would not have appeared clear at the time. After all, Brian Epstein appeared to be the interloper. I had been managing

Lee since 1959, whereas he had only come on to the scene in late 1961. His experiences were limited to retail and wholesale, whereas I had been at something approaching the sharp end for three years.

Secondly, even if I had agreed to the coalition, my brother would not have gone near Brian, I'm afraid to say. He knew that Brian was gay and Lee, being something of a homophobe back then (not that either of those expressions were in currency at that time), could never have envisaged any kind of deal with Epstein. Brian even illegally approached Lee that summer but was immediately spurned. Lee suspected that Brian's motives were not exactly honourable. I've always wondered about this. I can easily imagine Brian being attracted to my younger brother; after all, he was attracted to me. However, I don't really feel that he would have put his entire NEMS operation into overdrive via an infatuation for Lee Curtis. Some have said that he certainly did this for Tommy Quickly and that Brian simply wanted to bed the young Tommy, but I have always felt that the myth of Brian's homosexuality has outgrown the reality. Primarily Brian wanted success. He was unable to gain artistic success directly for himself and so his plan B was to acquire it vicariously through his artistes. Even though he might have fancied not only myself, but also Lee and Tommy Quickly, perhaps even John Lennon (although I have always doubted this), I don't believe that he would have compromised his artistic goal for one single second. Lee, however, has never agreed with this analysis. For him, Brian was always after something else and, despite my arguments to the contrary over many years, he still believes this to be true.

The Beatles might have been mostly away from Merseyside that spring and early summer of 1962 but it was by that stage pandemonium. While Brian was rapidly running out of record company contacts hawking their rather weak demo tape from company to company, I was handling a massive increase in enquiries for our two groups. Brian and I met every week at our Gardner Road or Whitechapel addresses – sometimes even at the Epstein family home on Queen's Drive. Invariably Brian was for accepting practically every offer if the price appeared to be right. Both Kenny and I had to keep reminding him, however, that now that bookings were sometimes six or even nine months in advance, provisos and riders had to be written into contracts demanding payment reviews and get-out clauses in case our groups' fees or work commitments had expanded so much that contracts were placed in jeopardy.

Brian didn't even know what I was talking about at first and I had to explain to him that the Beatles were going to be bigger than any of us had imagined. Brian wanted this as a dream but his grasp on reality could sometimes be rather tenuous. Many other local groups were also going to be successful and to place his group at rates which seemed equitable in, say, May 1962 for a booking in January 1963 would not be serving the boys' or indeed NEMS' best interests. Whereas Brian could still be drawn into the seemingly equitable handshake, Kenny and I had to remind him that contracts spoke volumes about professionalism. We suggested that if he did not consider these points urgently he ran the risk of being taken to the cleaners and regarded as a bit of a soft touch by promoters. I felt that he still used NEMS' retail money a little too easily, and suggested to him that the two NEMS operations needed to be separated as soon as possible. He knew that this should be the case but was still, I feel, rather reluctant to deny himself access to the NEMS cheque book. His reluctance occasionally gave me the impression that he was playing with these four young men's lives a little. Although he had been astute enough from late 1961 to raise the asking price locally for the band, Brian tended to flounder when big money needed to be negotiated for advance bookings. It was at this stage that he suggested that if Carlton Brooke and NEMS were not to join forces, then the former should handle all bookings out of Liverpool on behalf of the latter for an agreed percentage. At this stage Brian, I think, was a superb visionary but not a great organiser. He felt the need to delegate responsibility to me, so that he could think a little more long term, especially if he was to make his boys any real money and not fund NEMS Enterprises from the shop takings.

One occasion illustrates this point well. By late 1962 all hell was about to break loose and the Beatles were about to become the national flavour of 1963. As the proprietor of Carlton Brooke and booking representative for NEMS, I had personally approached the Prestatyn Royal Lido in August 1962 to regularly book Merseyside groups into the venue; I began the arrangement by offering them the Beatles. The gigs were well paid (£30 per group) and very well organised (all the groups were even offered a sit-down meal prior to the evening's entertainment), and the Beatles first played there under Carlton Brooke/NEMS auspices on 24 November 1962, just as *Love Me Do* was tickling the charts. It was quite evident to everybody by this time that the Beatles in particular, and Liverpool groups generally, were in the ascendancy. So, back in August, I had made an agreement with the Royal Lido which stated that if the Beatles had expanded their popularity base by the time of the gig (November) with a chart placing being evidenced, then rather than re-negotiate their fee, the Lido should agree to take further Carlton Brooke and NEMS acts over the following weeks as a sign of goodwill.

This they resolved so to do. My reasoning was, I feel, quite pragmatic. If the Beatles were to be the success that Brian, Kenny and I expected, the chances of them ever being able to play the Lido again were very slim. Therefore, rather than hiking up the Beatles fee (which Brian would have done) and instantly losing our goodwill with the ballroom, this extra gentleman's agreement would ensure more work for other Carlton Brooke and NEMS bands over the course of 1963. Because of this one deal, Carlton Brooke and NEMs were able to place as many groups as we wanted into the Royal Lido, thus making more money for ourselves, creating more work for our bands and keeping the management of the Royal Lido happy (even though the Beatles never played there again). The Royal Lido proved to be a happy hunting ground for most of our local bands over the next twelve months or so.

On another occasion, in that insane New Year of 1963, the Beatles had been booked to play ATV's *Thank Your Lucky Stars* the same weekend as a long-term pre-arranged local gig and Brian wanted to cancel. He approached me to enquire whether there was a get-out clause in the contract (there was – I'd inserted it) and he asked me to pull the gig. This was not something I ever did, unless circumstances were well beyond our control. However, Brian was unaware that the ATV programme, which was indeed broadcast on the Saturday of the gig, was pre-recorded by a full week. Little did he also appreciate that our scheduled live show was to follow the broadcast by less than one hour, and that I had also written into the contract a door percentage fee. Of course, the live show went ahead after the Beatles had appeared on national TV and was a roaring success with hundreds of new fans milling around the streets outside the packed theatre. On this occasion Brian would have pulled the concert thinking that the Beatles were unavailable and the money too modest. Basically, he would have had the band sitting on their arses watching themselves on TV. Instead they were able to revel in their TV success in front of a baying audience and subsequently I was also able to arrange a further three bookings for Lee Curtis on the strength of that one Beatles gig in January 1963. To his credit, Brian did appreciate that he had to learn, and learn fast. He had developed business acumen of sorts, but he was used to selling things that people already wanted (records, record players and the like), whereas my trade involved trying to sell items to people that they already had (food).

AN AGREEMENT made this 29th, day of August, 1962, between
J. Flannery, hereinafter called the Management of the one part
and Brian Epstein Esq., hereinafter called the Artiste of the
other part.

WITNESSETH that the Management hereby engages the Artiste and
the Artiste accepts the engagement to present the act known as
"THE BEATLES" at the Ballroom and from the dates for the periods
and at the salaries stated in the schedule herto upon and subject
to the terms and conditions of Schedule 1 of the ordinary form of
Contract contained in the award of Mr A.J. Ashton, K. dated
22nd September 1919.

S C H E D U L E

The Artiste agrees to appear at one evening performance at a
salary of £30-0-0d. (Thirty pounds) on Saturday, November 24th
1962. At the Royal Lido, Prestatyn, N.h. Wales, commencing at
8-0pm.

The Artistes will not be required to play for more than a total
of 2½ Hours in two seperate sessions.

ADDITIONAL CLAUSES

1. The said Artistes will not appear within a ten mile radius 10
   weeks prior to the engagement.

We the undersigned have read and
understood the above Schedule and
additional clauses and agree to adher
to same in detail.

Signature..........................

Address....Nems Enterprises Limited.

12-14, Whitechapel, Liverpool 1

The contract between Joe Flannery, Brian Epstein and the Prestatyn Royal Lido
that saw the Beatles playing the venue on 24 November 1962 for £30. (Author's
collection)

Once he had begun building up his artist roster he encouraged those artists to visit me for at least an alternative point of view and one which was backed up by a longer period of time in the local music industry as an agent. Brian and I also continued our regular working breakfasts during 1962, constantly hypothesising about our next moves; at times I felt like his supervisor. On a personal basis I would occasionally detect that Brian was checking me out regarding my current status with Kenny; at other times it was strictly business. He would still be experiencing extreme peaks and troughs of emotion brought on, I feel, by his deep-seated loneliness and almost clinical depression. He was filling his life up as one might fill up an empty vessel, which was good, I suppose, but without the correct contents it could be a rather shallow affair. Brian was in constant fear that he was merely filling himself up with people. He would say to me that he was 'boring' and that he 'bored people' – he never appeared to realise that his charisma was quite amazing; instead he felt that eventually people would find his company wearisome, leaving only the emptiness that he always felt. I still don't accept that he was infatuated with some of his artists (John Lennon, Tommy Quickly, Michael Haslam, etc.) but I do think that from this very early stage he could envisage a time when they had no further use for him, and this frightened him more than words could say. His professionalism did grow, however, and in a very short space of time he was not just acting a managerial role, but actually being professional and, after consultation with me and visitors to Liverpool (and Gardner Road) such as Joe Meek, Lionel Bart and Russ Conway, he began to appreciate and then make professional decisions.

For example, one area that troubled him was that the Beatles used to enjoy a drink in between sets wherever they would play. This was fine up to a point, but they had also grown accustomed to coming out of the band room or dressing room and mixing with the punters. It was often a good opportunity to speak either to existing girlfriends or tap off with new ones. Now, in the old days 1960–62, this was good local PR; it was also a matter of necessity, for many of the dressing rooms at various venues were little more than toilets (some actually were toilets) and it was wise to mingle. However, by 1962, as their appeal grew, this mixing with the crowd looked decidedly unprofessional. Apparently there had already been the odd skirmish in the past when a member of the Beatles had attempted to eye up a girl in the audience, only to find during the break that she was attached to a rather grizzly looking gang member bent on destruction. There had also been the usual problems at the Liscard Grosvenor

Ballroom when a word said in the wrong place could lead to mayhem. I had also witnessed this with Lee Curtis on several occasions.

So Brian and I decreed that for all artists being promoted or handled by NEMS and Carlton Brooke this would have to stop. There was enormous resistance to begin with, but I suggested to Brian that it might be a good idea to send drinks into band rooms, accompanied, if necessary, by said girlfriends and a few sandwiches, thus effectively turning the band room into what is described in the business as a greenroom. While this would cut down on group movements, via the alcohol, food and whiff of the opposite sex, they would perhaps be placated. There were two distinct advantages to this tactic as far as I could see. Firstly, the unprofessional wanderings and the possibilities of potential hammerings would cease. Secondly, and more importantly, an aura of unavailability and distance would be built around any group performing under the Carlton Brooke/NEMS banner, thus hopefully increasing their esteem and prestige. It all seems rather obvious in the twenty-first century, and did so to the bigger stars in the early 1960s, but the Liverpool scene did have its element of accessibility and amateurism which was productive to begin with though not something that could be maintained if appeal was to broaden.

It was at the Queen's Hall, Widnes, in one of my out-of-town gigs, that this plan was first put into practice. Under the auspices of NEMS Enterprises, Brian and I promoted a string of Monday night gigs in Widnes, 12 miles outside of Liverpool. It was quite a gamble, for the Queen's Hall was a sizeable venue. On, I think, 3 and 10 or 11 September the Beatles played the Queen's Hall and were supported by Rory Storm and the Hurricanes. By this time the Beatles had Ringo Starr on drums, Rory's former drummer. Both bands were kept in their dressing rooms and drinks were sent in. Rory enjoyed this, as I remember, because he told me it made him feel like a star, but the rest of the band were not very impressed. The Beatles went along with it without much comment, but were perhaps a little rattled. Brian and I then eased off the policy for a few days but insisted that when the Beatles played there again the following week they remained, once again, in the dressing rooms. This time it worked a treat. The band was sent in drinks (and sandwiches courtesy of housekeeper Anne) and the boys were made to feel very special. Brian and I then undertook several promotions at the Queen's Hall throughout October, this time with Lee Curtis and his new band the All Stars, who by then had their new drummer Pete Best (but more of that later), the Fourmost and the Merseybeats, and all went extremely well. The groups responded well to this concept of look but don't touch, especially when, by the end of the evening, a posse of young fans had congregated outside the stage door, just as they would to see a national star. We had created an aura around the bands.

I suppose it could be argued that something may have been lost by doing this; that the innate democracy of the Merseyside scene was overturned by this new show-business attitude. I disagree. There were still ample opportunities for musicians to socialise afterwards and even jam during gigs. I had argued with Lee at the time that if one wanted to declare a democratic musical state then there was always the folk scene. The show-business veneer that we placed over groups made them more professional and there were immediate results. Subsequently bands arriving at Gardner Road came prepared mentally and appearance-wise, far more so than they had done previously. They would be less raucous before gigs and more responsible as musicians during it. As for the Beatles, Paul McCartney led the way there. He took this new approach very seriously, which meant on occasions he would drag the others kicking and screaming into this higher professional gear. But, in truth, the Beatles were very quick to realise that they simply had to distance themselves from their growing multitude of fans if they were to progress. Being a Beatle could no longer simply be a musical experience and a bit of a laugh. It became an educational process and perhaps more than any other Liverpool group of that era, the Beatles were the best at learning on the hoof.

The ABC Bowling Alley on Green Lane, Liverpool 13, did tremendous business as groups of all shapes, sizes and talent waited to get into Gardner Road to receive gig information or advice. I vividly remember bowling matches between the Beatles and Lee Curtis and the All Stars as they waited for Brian Epstein to arrive. Lee was a very good ten-pin bowler, if my memory serves me correctly. This interaction between these two groups is another seldom-told story, of course, for one is always given the impression that after the Pete Best affair (which I shall portray from my perspective very soon) the two groups did not speak – Bill Harry even alludes to this. However, this was simply not the case. The two groups often shared gigs after Brian and I joined forces and they got on well most of the time. John thought Lee was a poser, which he was; Lee thought John was a beatnik, which he was.

It would be fair to suggest that at this stage Epstein and Flannery was a unique and formidable pair with, of course, the redoubtable Kenny Meek ever present in the background. Both of us were bright and hungry for success, even though virtual opposites in class, temperament and approaches. As a facilitator I felt I was able to demonstrate the possibilities available in unfolding situations: figuring things out, if you will. Brian, on the other hand, was a romantic but he was gradually becoming a disciplined individual, at least in business terms. His attention to detail came to be second to none as he discovered that if all possibilities were covered to the best of one's ability then a situation would quickly gain its own momentum. One evening during that early summer of 1962 (in June, I think) exemplified this partnership well. I decided to hold a kind of interrogation session. Brian had been travelling to and from London in an attempt to get the Beatles a recording contract and had finally been successful with EMI's smallest imprint. I had yet to make any enquiries on behalf of Lee Curtis and I didn't know whether to be impressed or not. I felt that if Brian, with his connections, couldn't get a decent contract for his lot, then I stood even less of a chance. I tried to remain as immutable as possible, but the Beatles were an impatient lot. They could see that Brian was working as hard as he could for them, but they were desperate to try their hand at recording in the UK. Their previous experiences in Germany sounded a little Mickey Mouse to me, but they were constantly discussing it: how they might have changed things; how they would love another chance; and, of course, how they would like to try out their own songs in the studio.

They were including more and more of their own material into their act by this time, although I distinctly remember John going mad about including some Arthur Alexander songs that he had heard on Radio Luxembourg (*Anna*, *Soldier of Love* and *A Shot of Rhythm and Blues*, amongst others), and they were bursting with enthusiasm about trying them out in a studio. We decided, therefore, one free evening to hold an interrogation session, giving Brian the third degree in the middle of the floor, under spotlights, to explain what the record deal meant, where the band was going and how successful Brian felt we could all be. The boys (John, Paul, George and Pete) were very happy with Brian. As I have previously stated, it seemed to me that there was something quite synergetic about their meeting. But they were also rather agitated and in need of a clear future projection. I think they had realised, even by mid-1962, that they had all but conquered Liverpool and that their long-term careers lay away from Merseyside. After all, in those days there were no real recording facilities in the regions; there were no local big-time entrepreneurs, and the major labels were all exclusively London-based. So they needed assurances from Brian that he too felt this way and that he had pursued every available avenue towards their imminent deal with one of the big four's (EMI, Pye, Decca and Philips) smallest labels.

The evening, therefore, consisted of Brian Epstein, on a very uncomfortable dining chair, in the middle of the floor, with as many table and reading lamps as Anne and I could muster trained directly on his face. The cross-examination that followed from the Beatles was, in the main, absolutely serious, only broken by John's occasional comedic Germanic interludes of 'Ve have vays ov making you talk, Schweinhund!' By the end of the session, the Beatles and I had no doubts that Brian's heart was most decidedly in the right place. Kenny and I could tell that he worshipped them and would do or try anything in order to make them into very big stars. Towards the end of the session, half laughing, half crying, Brian emotionally promised faithfully – and I believe he kept his promise – that he would never let them down, financially. I was used as the star witness for the defence in regard to this assurance; Brian stated that if ever they thought he had dealt them a bad card or that he was not playing by their rules, then the group was to come directly to me, Joe Flannery – or, as John was to call me, 'Flo Jannery'.

It was very heartening for all of us to hear. The only problem as far as I was concerned was that, to me, it sounded rather rhetorical. I knew that Brian was already beginning to move in elevated company, well away from Merseyside, and that my advice and indeed company was beginning to appear rather parochial and perhaps even a little plebeian to him. London in those days seemed like a million miles away from Liverpool and Brian was finding his sojourns to the smoke very attractive (in more ways than one). I knew that if the band were to be the success that we all craved, then it would probably only be a matter of time before Brian upped and moved NEMS to the big city. Because of this, and although I felt privileged to be part of his declaration of fealty to his boys, I did feel that my first priority would be to remain with Lee Curtis. Knowing Brian as I did, it just seemed a little bit safer that way.

Of course, Brian had achieved the great step of securing a recording contract for his group with Parlophone a few weeks earlier; he was already seeking advice elsewhere. In fact, that pioneering contract with Parlophone during May 1962 caused discord between us. Brian and I had dinner to celebrate the contract and, while agreeing with him that it was a real breakthrough for any Liverpool group at that time to obtain a record deal (only Derry and the Seniors had been successful prior to this, with Pye), I informed him that I felt he could have been tougher with his negotiations. I remember telling him: 'Brian, this contract is actually a very poor offer. One penny per disc is terrible. The lads won't really be earning anything. At least try and get a penny per side.' But Brian wouldn't hear of it, saying something like: 'Joe, the deal's done and I don't want to ruin their chances. I was beginning to despair of any offer. In any case, I'm not a market-trader like you … I can't haggle.' I was quite hurt by this 'market-trader' comment and he could see it. I had tried to temper his self-satisfaction, I suppose not very tactfully, and his riposte was typically stinging, to say the least.

That evening I also informed him that I felt he had made a very poor deal with publishers Ardmore and Beechwood. I reminded him that Russ Conway had advised us never to go with the publishing company associated with the record company, and to always stick with independents. The independent publishers, I prodded him, were always better at promotion than the 'ancillary cogs within a big machine', as Russ had described the larger publishers. Russ had advised that independents were hungrier and more zealous. Brian looked rather ashen and admitted that he hadn't really listened at the time and he didn't know the first thing about music publishing. 'I don't really come across it at NEMS, to be honest, Joe,' he'd replied. 'In any case, I just want the boys to get on to a different level. I want them to be the only group from Liverpool to have a record and publishing deal, even if it's a poor one.'

I was astonished. His motivations were honourable enough, but his concept of getting a leg-up, of parochial one-upmanship, left me baffled. He was prepared, it seemed to me, to enter into any deal, with any recording company or publishing house, merely to elevate his boys above the local competition. Only time would tell whether this was a wise move but at that moment I was highly critical and Brian didn't like it. I later came to understand that Parlophone producer George Martin had also advised Brian not to pursue his deal with Ardmore and Beechwood, and had recommended that he visit the maverick music publisher Dick James. Apparently George shared my own misgivings about linked publishing and recording houses. Brian duly accepted George's advice, but even then did not strike a favourable deal. In fact, I do believe that James saw Brian coming, so to speak. I wish I had been there. This is not to suggest that James was an inequitable man. Far from it, in fact, for I believe that he is very unfairly treated by history following his sale of Northern to Lew Grade and the later fall-out with Elton John and John Reid. No, in my experiences, Dick was a very honourable man. It's just that music publishing, which ultimately by the mid-1960s became a business bread-and-butter issue about rights rather than sheet music sales, is a dog-eat-dog business. There's no other way of describing it, I'm afraid!

Six months previously Brian would have barely made a move without consultation with his father, Clive or myself, but now he considered himself very independent. This would have been a good thing were he truly independent but, in actual fact, he was being romanced by the London professionals: the 'men in suits' as John might have said. Thinking he was striking acceptable contracts, Brian was actually being cornered and forced to accept putative payments. He was regarded as a provincial by the London music elite and he didn't quite realise this. While he felt that he was moving amongst the decision makers and they were taking notice of him, he was actually subjecting himself to a degree of contempt by the moguls and he discovered that his contacts were mostly less than useless, and his NEMS credentials did not fully open doors. My own contacts in London (Conway, Parnes, Bart, etc.) were informing me that Brian was regarded by some as a rather 'snotty' and precocious 'northern' retailer trying to breach their southern-based cartel. The magnates were not prepared to co-operate. The truth of his connections was that they had led him to the smallest and most vulnerable of EMI's labels and to two terrible deals with music publishers. But all that concerned Brian was returning to Liverpool triumphant, waving contracts around and showing his boys that he was, indeed, the big wheel that he had claimed to be. I couldn't blame him for this, I suppose. He had placed himself under immense pressure and during that evening Brian had promised faithfully to deliver the Beatles into the 'industry proper', as he called it – and, of course, he did. However, perhaps because of this pressure, coupled with Brian's quick-fix agreements, they were never able to obtain the rights for their own songs and only became wealthy via the immense quantity of sales bearing their names as songwriters and performers. Despite the magnificent quality of their work, and the fact that they all became millionaires very quickly, they actually received very poor remuneration.

9

THE BEGINNING OF THE PARTING OF THE WAYS AND THE PETE BEST AFFAIR

BRIAN EPSTEIN AND I were sitting in the living room of my apartment in Gardner Road. A disc was revolving on the deck of the new Decca teak-effect radiogram in the corner of the room. The disc was an EMI acetate 45rpm, upon which somebody had scrawled 'Love Me Do'. Brian was frowning, his hands cupped in front of his face, his forefingers touching his top lip, as if deep in prayer. The record player's reject system clicked loudly and the turntable braked to a stop. Brian spoke: 'Joe, I don't like it. Something must be wrong with your radiogram. It doesn't sound like them at all … the drumming … oh, it's your record player … play it again, play it again.' I played it again. 'No, it's awful. There's something wrong with your record player. There has to be, it's terrible.' 'Listen Brian,' I exclaimed impatiently, 'if there's something wrong with this radiogram, blame your brother Clive, because I bought it from him at NEMS a couple of weeks ago … maybe I should complain!' I put another single on the deck, this time *Well I Ask You* by Eden Kane. There was nothing wrong with the radiogram. I put the acetate back on the deck and placed the arm on the disc. A harmonica wailed. Brian moved not a muscle. He was incredibly tense and discontented. The record was a bitter disappointment to him, being far too raw, too unconventional – too uncommercial. He was all for the Beatles writing their own material, but, as an expert retailer, he found *Love Me Do* far too primitive, I suppose. As usual I tried to encourage him: 'Get plenty of stock in at NEMS, Brian. It will sell really well in Liverpool.'

However, Brian remained unmoved. To be honest, my own feelings about the record were a little mixed as well. For a lover of, say, Nat King Cole such as me, this sounded extraordinarily spartan, pared down even. I remember thinking that it sounded almost a bit folk-like in places; perhaps it was the harmonica. But I did warm to it after a few plays and felt that it was an unusual, interesting and catchy song. In truth, although I didn't tell him at the time, it reminded me a little of the Vipers' *No Other Baby*, but if I'd have told him it would have made things worse. Even better, for me at least, was the B side *PS I Love You* which I had heard the group perform before. Curiously, I could not remember having heard the Beatles play *Love Me Do* previously, but as I became familiar with the melody, the unusual harmonica phrasing reminded me a little of Bruce Chanel's recent hit *Hey Baby* and Frank Ifield's *I Remember You*. *Hey Baby* was actually one of the first songs that I heard the Beatles play at the Cavern. They were rehearsing at the time and their rendition had been so good it had stopped me dead on the stairs. In time, Brian grew to accept *Love Me Do*; however, I don't think he ever liked it as such. My image of him sitting with his head in his hands remains with me even to this day, for the pressure he was feeling that evening was extraordinary. Even at that early stage the strain seemed to be bothering him – and that comment about the drumming?

By October 1962 Carlton Brooke was also becoming an important agency in its own right. The NEMS link up was still viable and being used more and more as the Beatles played out of town, therefore the money was good; but I think Brian felt that he had served his apprenticeship and wanted to run things his own way, even if that meant absorbing anxiety like blotting paper. My late friend Bob Wooler declared that this was the period in which his influence began to diminish, and I can sympathise. In any case, as far as Carlton Brooke was concerned, Lee Curtis and his new band, the All Stars, had become a major draw. I shall discuss this transition from Detours to All Stars a little later, but it is safe to say at this point that our promotions had been highly successful and a link up with Bill Marsden at the Top Rank Organisation had proved very lucrative. Bill ran both the Birkenhead Majestic and the Crewe Top Rank and our dual promotions of the Let's Go shows (named after the Routers song of the same name) became extraordinarily popular. Lee was revelling in this parochial success.

I was also very keen to take the group to Hamburg and was pulling out as many stops as I could to make that possible. So, together with my daytime commitments, life was pulling me away from the NEMS tandem.

However, I do feel that the most important reason why NEMS and Carlton Brooke began operating exclusively and my life began to diverge from Brian's was that I knew him too well. As Brian began to see a way forward on a national scale for his artists, I do believe it dawned on him that I had an intimate knowledge of his past. I had been very close and had shared some of his most intimate thoughts. I was someone to whom Brian had openly confessed his homosexuality. These details could prove something of an embarrassment to Brian: a skeleton in his closet, as it were. And so Brian proceeded to distance himself from me (and others such as Bob Wooler) in order to continue, on the one hand, his façade of courting his secretary and, on the other, delving into new experiences – particularly in London, one suspects.

Nothing would ever have induced me to kiss and tell, of course. As readers will appreciate, our relationship, in any case, was platonic. Despite Brian having his little crushes on me I was strictly not available; but I knew too much. It was during the autumn of 1962 that I decided not to discuss Beatles matters with anybody other than Brian, employees of NEMS or the Epstein family, and that's the way it has remained – until this moment, naturally. Even when I spoke to Philip Norman many years later, I informed him that under no circumstances would I contribute to a piece of work that would scrape the bottom of the barrel. He duly obliged. I feel this loyalty to Brian to this very day; it will never leave me. He need not have worried, nevertheless he did and furthermore he found it very difficult to detach himself from me quite as easily as he had previously thought. Therefore on another two occasions before I also burned my bridges and went to Hamburg, Brian invited me to get on what was becoming the NEMS gravy train.

Pete Best

Prior to our divergence, and historically of most interest to Beatles scholars, was the dismissal of Pete Best from the Beatles. I was directly involved in that stratagem and I would like to explain why he was dismissed, at least from my perspective. When Brian took over management of the Beatles he not only discussed matters with me, but also with Pete Best and his mother Mona. As far as I knew, the relationship between Pete and Brian was amicable enough, but as we became embroiled in the whole Beatles saga during 1962, it was clear to both Kenny and I that Brian's relationship

THE SUNDAY TIMES

P.O. Box 7 200 Gray's Inn Road London WC1X 8EZ *Telephone* 01-837 1234 *Telex* 22269

April 19 1979

Dear Pat,

Many thanks for your kindness and
great help in my project. It was very
pleasant to talk to you when I was in
Liverpool last week; and please accept,
once again, my assurance that I do not
intend to be gratuitously hurtful to
anyone, least of all the Epstein family.
My aim is to tell a story honestly, but
with sympathy.

I hope we shall meet again when I return
to the NW. Meantime, the best of luck with
your projects, and the house.

Sincerely

Philip

Philip **Norman**

TIMES NEWSPAPERS LIMITED
Reg. Office P.O. Box 7 New Printing House Square Gray's Inn Road London WC1X 8EZ
Reg. No. 894646 England

A letter from author Philip Norman to Joe Flannery following their meeting in
April 1979. (Author's collection)

with Mona was less than genial. You see, what most people tend not to realise about the post-Williams and pre-Epstein Beatles is that they were effectively managed by Mona Best as a vehicle for her good-looking son, Peter. Of that there is little doubt. Now there were further complications because of this relationship.

Back in August 1959, the Quarrymen had played the Casbah's first night after the Les Stewart Quartet had lost the gig. The Casbah was a coffee bar in Hayman's Green, West Derby, which had been opened by Mona Best; in fact, it was in the cellar of her residential property. The Quarrymen only really got the gig because of a guy by the name of Ken Brown, who, along with George Harrison, had left the previously booked Les Stewart and joined up with the practically defunct Quarrymen. Brown's tenure with the Quarrymen didn't last long, however, for six weeks later, after a disagreement over money with John Lennon, he was sacked and promptly formed a group with Mona's son Peter. This group became known as the Blackjacks. Importantly, Mona Best banned the Quarrymen from the Casbah for a period of time in support of Ken Brown. Relationships would always be strained between Mona and the group, even as the Beatles and even when Peter was invited to join them. You see, for the Beatles, the option of Peter was effectively Hobson's choice. The gig in Hamburg had been organised without a drummer, and Pete was only really invited to join because he could play as well as any and had a new drum kit. As far as my sources tell me – I was not part of the enclave at that time – Pete's mother did not approve of his joining the Beatles. She had little time for Lennon and still bore a grudge about the dismissal of Ken Brown. So during 1961, although Pete and his mother assumed the managerial role for the group, arranging gigs and negotiating fees etc., the Quarrymen element were not well pleased. John later told me that he thought Mona was 'very bossy, like Mimi' and was only using the Beatles for her 'darling son'.

This last comment was quite revealing as far as I was concerned. One couldn't blame Mona for doing this. She was presumably an ambitious lady, at least for her son, and Pete was shy. He did have a certain presence on stage which actually assisted the group at times, but although a lovely guy he wasn't exactly Mr Personality off the stage. He was quiet and rather brooding. In any case, it was rather difficult for him to break into the Beatles' thought processes. Those remaining three were so close it was practically impossible to separate them at times. So the oft-touted jealousy theory (i.e. that the three were jealous of the appeal and good looks of the one) simply doesn't go anywhere near the complications of Pete's membership of the group. Just because Pete might have appeared to have had a posse of girls hanging around him does not necessarily create jealousy. Let's face it, Paul had a regular girlfriend, as did John (Cynthia Powell) and there were enough girls to go around. From my recollections, George was always a little more reserved and more into playing his instrument. No, jealousy did not come into it at all, I feel.

For me, Pete's mother Mona was at the nexus of the crisis, even after Brian had become the group's manager. To begin with, at least from what John, Paul and George had told me during 1962, they had felt rather swamped by Mona during 1961. She had arranged a lot of bookings for them and was the initial impetus behind them getting their residency at the Cavern. I discovered that it had also been Mona, via her son Pete, who had contacted Peter Eckhorn and fixed them up with their Top Ten Club session in 1961. Neil Aspinall, their first roadie and close confidant, was a lodger at Hayman's Green and was romantically involved with Mona at the time (a baby resulted: Rogue). Mona had tried to get Granada Television interested in the band. However, all of these apparent plus points actually counted against her. John told me that she had tried to dominate proceedings and she presumed that the group was merely a vehicle for her son, as at times it might have seemed. So, for John, Paul and George, Brian's taking over the reins was a blessed release. Brian had no intention of removing Pete, but made things very clear to everybody concerned that he and nobody else was now responsible for not only their welfare, but their way of life. And why shouldn't he? Brian had been searching for such an experience as this and he wasn't going to let it slip through his fingers. He held a very important coffee morning during 1962, to which I was privy. He invited all of the female companions and relatives of the artists, which by this time also included Gerry and the Pacemakers, expressly to inform them that he was in control and that he would always look after his protégés, as he called them.

The vast majority of those present were absolutely delighted that Brian had both involved them and laid down the law. They now knew exactly where they and their loved ones stood. Not so Mona Best, however, who was fuming. She felt that control had been wrested away from her and for the next few days she made Brian's life a misery, constantly ringing him on the phone, decreeing that she be more closely involved in the group's affairs. Brian informed me that he felt that Mona was looking for some kind of ulterior motive for the meeting, that she thought it masked some kind of evil conspiracy; but the meeting was simply held to set the record straight. He gloomily told me at one stage that he was sorry he held it, but I countered this by stating that the coffee morning had been very effective and that Mona simply had to back off: 'This is now a professional operation, Brian. It can't stand input from loose cannon such as Mona Best.' So one can see that, from my perspective, Brian actually had no intentions of sacking Pete. He told me that he was just going to have to put up with Mona 'from time to time … as the mood takes her'. He voiced his opinion that 'In a perfect world, Joe, everybody would be on your side, but this isn't a perfect world, is it?' In fact, his resolution satisfied me at this stage for I was in something of an invidious position, being gladly received at 8 Hayman's Green, the Bests' home. It was only a short drive away from Gardner Road and I was frequently made very welcome, most notably by the Bests' dog (either a Great Dane or an Irish Wolf Hound, I can't remember exactly which) who enjoyed tossing itself off against my leg. I did think, however, that Mona didn't see me as such a threat as she did Brian. She was probably right.

I had spoken to John Lennon shortly after the coffee morning, however, and he had expressed a more than typically caustic response to the Mona affair, stating to me that he was pleased that Brian had laid down the law because he'd just about had enough of her. John and I had become very close at this stage. We would frequently drive down to the Pier Head in my Vauxhall (as, indeed, Brian and I would do) and stand at the railings, eating one of those terrible meat pies that they used to sell there and looking out over the narrow expanse of the River Mersey and the vaster margins of the Irish Sea. John was forever dreaming of America. It was as if his spiritual home was across the Atlantic; he ached to play in the USA, the great source of his inspiration. On this occasion he told me that he was not going to let Mona Best get in the way:

> I want to be over there; I can almost taste it now, Joe. Brian's going to be good for us. It works. He might be a bit of a snob and all that, but we click. With Mona around it'll always stay just a dream. With Brian it feels like it might just happen.

Giving me the distinct impression that he immediately intended to do something about it, he told me he would speak to the 'other two'. I drove John home, but not before he had informed me that the Beatles were going to 'help sort this thing out for Brian'. Not only did Brian sign the

Beatles but, effectively, they also signed him. I speak of that inner sanctum, the almost impenetrable triumvirate of John, Paul and George. I could understand John's reaction. Following the new regime of Brian (and myself, to a small degree) the relief expressed by the three Beatles was palpable. They were only young men, let us not forget, and Brian was far from being a tyrant or selective; in other words, he was interested in the Beatles as a group, not as a conveyance for one member which, in the world of early 1960s British popular music, was a revolutionary concept in its own right. This is an important point, I feel.

John's reaction also proved to me that the relationship between the three and Pete was rather tenuous and my impressions of Pete being 'suffered' by the rest were amplified at this time. Subsequently I have even wondered whether, had the Beatles possessed more time to look for a drummer prior to going to Hamburg, they would have considered involving themselves with the Bests once again. Possibly, but to my mind at least those encounters during 1962 gave me the impression that they considered Pete to be a jobbing drummer. For example, the barriers between the three and Pete had already commenced as early as the Decca recording sessions of New Year's 1962. When the news finally came through in March that Decca had unceremoniously turned down the group, to my knowledge nobody informed Pete. Similarly, when the Parlophone deal went through, nobody bothered to let him know. This suggests to me that Pete was less popular with the remaining members of the band (in my view, because of his mother). Although he has stated that there were no problems during his stint with the group, one man's view of a working relationship can be entirely from those of another.

So from that particular perspective, it was indeed the Beatles who took the decision to dismiss Pete Best from the group, and the reason? Well, Pete's mother, Mona. The response from Mona herself after Pete was dismissed from the group was very revealing. She immediately phoned everybody, not including myself for I was then attempting to handle Pete's next career move, in a mad panic. It was as if she had finally realised that the group was no longer her personal plaything. Not only was she poking her nose into the running of the band, but she had just had Neil Aspinall's baby. Brian was already concerned about keeping Cynthia's pregnancy out of the news (that was the way it had to be done in those days) and he told me that Mona's liaison with Neil was 'very indiscreet – the last straw'; that was something, coming from a man who could be very indiscreet himself at times. Pete therefore was removed, but not sacked as such, for Brian had a plan.

It was at this crucial stage that I stepped in. Pete was naturally very hurt and despondent. After unsuccessfully trying to place Pete with a group briefly under his managerial scope at that time (the Merseybeats), Brian approached me to consider placing Pete with Lee Curtis and the All Stars, who were then probably Liverpool's second most popular group after the Beatles. I was in a rather difficult position. The All Stars had been assembled around Lee earlier that year from the pick of the local musicians. They were a class act and to remove any one of them would be a great pity, especially at the whim of another manager. However, on the credit side, Pete was very popular in Liverpool and had quite a large personal following. Any group who picked up on the now redundant drummer would also attract his fan base, but as a consequence face the probability of disruption. In addition, NEMS and Carlton Brooke were in cahoots at the time and I felt pressure from Brian to work as closely as possible with him.

I approached Pete about joining the All Stars and, after a little thought, he readily agreed. Lee and Pete already got on very well and he didn't require any coaxing. It only appears in retrospect that Pete was the forgotten man because the Beatles were unique and became all conquering; however, this was absolutely not the case at the time. We were all aware, by the summer of 1962, that given a fair crack of the whip Liverpool groups could make something of a splash and that the industry was in need of a change, but that was about it. Nobody could have predicted what was to happen. And so, from my perspective in 1962, Pete Best joining Lee Curtis and the All Stars was a reasonably sound move to make.

Another reason that Pete made the move was that he trusted me. I was considered to be one of the few competent managers around Liverpool at that time. He could see that he was joining a good band which was well managed and earning good money. And, significantly, a recording deal was beginning to take shape with Decca for the All Stars. Let us not forget, Decca was then one of the leading British labels (far larger than Parlophone) and had turned down the Beatles, whereas the same company was showing interest in and eventually signed Lee Curtis and the All Stars. To be a member of a band in the process of signing to Decca in 1962 (Tornadoes, Cruisers, Heinz) appeared to be far superior to being in one signing to Parlophone (Pinky and Perky, Adam Faith) – George Martin would be the first to admit this. In hindsight, this might appear ridiculous, for Decca played the fool with so many young musicians' careers in the 1960s, but this would not have been crystalline at that stage. In the simplest of terms, Dick Rowe had turned down the group that Pete had left, but had accepted the one that he was joining, so what more evidence did one need? It's all very well being wise after the event, as most Beatles historians content themselves with being, but one needs to get a feel for this localised activity before making value judgements about, say, the merits of George Martin's production values or some spurious London-centric call that Pete was not a good enough drummer to play on sessions.

Pete remains a more than adequate percussionist and almost every producer I have ever known would have used a session drummer on the first recording sessions of a young group – especially at EMI's Abbey Road and for a label that was under the cosh from its parent company. Martin, it seems to me, would have hired drummer Andy White for most if not all young, untried beat groups at that time – he was just playing it safe. Brian was very sad about the whole affair and spent sleepless nights worrying about it. He absorbed guilt on to the aforementioned pressure which made him unwell and even more dependent on his prescription drugs. But I reiterate that it was the Beatles' decision, not Brian's, and that Pete really was the fall guy for his mother's encumbrance. The irony attached to the entire Pete Best affair, which was lamentable whichever way we look at it, was that it happened very early in Brian's management and was not essentially of his making. However, clearly the whole scenario suited him well because it effectively removed a major thorn in his side, that of Mona Best. Because of this it was not something that could be openly debated. There was a furore in Liverpool over the sacking and hundreds of letters were sent into the local press (*Mersey Beat*, *Liverpool Echo*, *Liverpool Weekly News*, etc.). Pete, I feel, has always kept quiet about the matter simply out of loyalty and embarrassment. His career as a Beatle ended because of his mother; it's as simple and poignant as that.

When the Beatles were due to appear at the Cavern with new drummer Ringo Starr on Sunday 19 August 1962, the Best fans were out in force. Luckily for us Lee Curtis and the All Stars were not present, having been booked to play there the following Friday with the Big Three, but Brian rang me on the Monday following the Beatles gig and was very piqued about the actions of the 'cave-dwellers'. He informed me in a most disgruntled way that he had to have a bodyguard, George had ended up with a black eye and there were shouts of 'we want Pete' from the audience all night, in front of those Granada Television cameras to boot ('bloody hell' he lamented).

One other point: during late August and September I continued to assuage Pete's battered ego in preparation for his first gig with Lee Curtis.

He was a little down, of that there was no doubt, but it was all quite harmonious and Pete never really discussed the issue with me or any members of the band. He realised, I think, that, despite his departure from a band with a recording contract, he had made a reasonably good transfer; his stance was remarkably conservative. Meanwhile, I now had Mona Best to contend with. It seemed like she never allowed Kenny and I one minute's peace and, by September, her phone calls were driving me insane. The All Stars were due to play with Pete at the end of August but because I wanted the transition to be smooth for Bernie Rogers, the outgoing drummer, I scheduled the first date to be 10 September at one of our favourite haunts, the Top Rank Majestic in Birkenhead. This didn't suit Mona: she wanted her boy to be thrown in immediately ('for his fans'). I had to explain to her that I had accommodated Pete in Lee Curtis' band and a home had to be found for the displaced drummer, Bernie Rogers. Sadly, Mona couldn't have cared less about Bernie and just wanted her boy back on the boards as soon as possible. What had I let myself in for?

The All Stars

You're probably wondering where the 'All Stars' moniker came from. When last we more fully discussed Lee Curtis, he was a member of a group called the Detours. Well, the transition from Detours to All Stars in June 1962 was the result of our growing conviction that Lee was destined to be a front man and ultimately a soloist. The Detours had been gathering a strong following during the first year or so of the decade, but we knew that it was Lee Curtis who was the real attraction. Lee, Kenny and I also felt that the rest of the Detours were a little raw and inexperienced as musicians. They were a good band on the whole, but I was constantly thinking of ways to launch a career for Lee and Lee alone, and I wanted the best. By 1962 I was insisting that Lee consider performing as a front man with a better backing group. In hindsight this idea might have been rather misplaced. As writer and broadcaster Spencer Leigh has correctly stated on a number of occasions, Lee was a little late for Elvis and a little early for Tom Jones (Tom not only came to our shows in Wales and Hereford, but his band the Squires also supported us here and there). However, it's all very well to show wisdom after the event. Looking back, my concept of one good-looking guy at the front of a band could be seen as old hat by 1963, but who was to know in 1962? And, at the end of the day, even Decca records felt the same as yours truly that year, signing Brian Poole and the Tremeloes rather than the Beatles.

Additionally, as early as mid-1961 Lee had been receiving a few bookings in Manchester and I was very influenced by this equally interesting but sadly underestimated scene at the other end of the East Lancashire Road. I was dealing with Danny Betesh at the Oasis Club and practically all of the acts playing there were led by front men: for example, Pete Maclaine and the Dakotas; Wayne Fontana and the Mindbenders; Freddie and the Dreamers; and Herman and the Hermits (as the latter were then still known). This all led me to believe that such a group format was still viable and entertaining. The notion of the All Stars then came about because Lee, Kenny and I had decided that Lee needed a backing group of the highest possible quality in order to develop his growing appeal and status. So, Wayne Bickerton, Tony Waddington, Frank Bowen and Bernie Rogers, all excellent musicians in their own right, were recruited as the All Stars, the 'official' backing band for Lee Curtis. Percussionist Bernie was the only one to have performed previously with the Detours.

Our connections with Bill Marsden at the Top Rank Majestic in Birkenhead had led to gigs further afield and they were coming in thick and fast. Block bookings for Top Ranks included Crewe, Hull, Sheffield, Blackpool and Preston; it was at Preston that I made good friends with Dave Berry and helped bring him to Liverpool. We were also dealing with Kennedy Street Enterprises from Manchester, who had some incomparably well-paid gigs in Greater Manchester and Cheshire. I had contact with a promoter by the name of Dick James (not the publisher) who had what seemed like hundreds of pubs and jive hives wishing to book rock groups with good-looking singers in the north of England, such as the Twist and Jive in Urmston. I also made an acquaintance with Arthur Holmes, a larger concert promoter who handled a smattering of smaller venues as well. So life was good and promised to be better for Lee Curtis and Carlton Brooke. By spring 1962 Lee was basically a full-time professional. He was, in fact, in great demand in Liverpool and yet our appearances in the city were actually reducing owing to our popularity away from home – but that's the way we planned it.

I would have to admit that Lee and I also thought, even at this precocious stage, that a few of the Liverpool groups were losing their individuality somewhat, and we intended to exploit this. I suppose this hypothesis later proved to be accurate for, after 1964, the Liverpool scene was rather like stale beer – damp and rather flat – and one could hardly get a gig in London with a Liverpool accent. But, even as early as mid-1962, it seemed to us that everybody was trying to emulate everybody else. By forming the All Stars around Lee, I was attempting relatively successfully, despite my retrospective misgivings, to give him a degree of musical autonomy – an identity, I suppose. That's what using the aforementioned obscure source material was all about, as well as my attempts to discourage Lee from singing too much in an Elvis style. Therefore, the concept of sourcing the cream of Liverpool's young musicians to back him was an attempt to separate Lee from the growing crowd of, at times rather average groups manifesting on Merseyside.

I remember discussing this matter of similarity some years later with John Schroeder, the man who produced those two famous *This is Merseybeat* compilation albums, and he informed me that although he was very pleased with the first effort (recorded live at the Rialto on Upper Parliament Street in Liverpool), he was amazed at the similarity of groups the second time he came to Liverpool to record. He further stated to me that as he left the city following those second recordings, he was more than a little discontented, feeling that whatever specialness had existed in Liverpool for that first album may have deserted the city by the second. For me the constant anxiety about the 'Liverpool Sound' was the threat of, inevitably, reaching the bottom of the cover versions barrel. During my later return visits to Liverpool, talent spotting for the Star Club, it seemed to me that the Liverpool bands were becoming virtuosos at performing other people's clichés. Kenny found this to be so when he auditioned many bands in my absence at our Slater Street offices. The only way that one could transcend that sameness was to write one's own material, which was something that the Beatles but few others realised; perhaps they composed their way out of Liverpool?

There has been a great deal stated over the years about Merseybeat signalling a death knell for front men; however, I consider this to be an over-exaggerated simplification. With the notable exception of the Beatles, few of the Merseybeat groups that I came across considered this new line-up issue to be of any great significance. In fact, in retrospect it appears to me that most groups actually did sport a front man; for example: Earl Preston and the TTs (and the Realms); Gus Travis and the Midnighters; Rory Storm and the Hurricanes; Earl Royce and the Olympics; Vic and the Spidermen; Vince Earl and the Talismen; Derry Wilkie and the Seniors (and the Pressmen); Denny Seyton and the Sabres; Mark Peters and the Silhouettes, etc. This hardly seems to be strong evidence for the decline of the front man.

In addition, those groups who happened to find themselves without a front man at one stage or another simply carried on regardless. They did not essentially make music policy decisions but kept their line-ups stable as matters of expediency, for example the Searchers, Remo Four (Johnny Sandon) and the Coasters (Billy J.). Of course, it remains true to state that when a front man did leave a group it usually meant that the remaining three or four were not necessarily drawn towards playing with another prima donna. So, what I'm suggesting is that the oft-narrated fable of the Beatles and Merseybeat putting to the sword all concepts of rock singer plus backing band is something of a myth, at least locally. Certainly, the very concept of bringing together four or five talented musicians in order to play behind a star figure was not the apparent disaster that some rock historians have retrospectively suggested. In fact, one might suggest that in some small way, the '… and the …' line-up expressed the unpretentious appeal of early rock.

Nevertheless, the concept did have its problems and Kenny and I experienced several of them almost immediately. Principally there were several issues surrounding Russ Conway's earlier point about egos. To begin with the primary difficulties were between Wayne Bickerton and Lee but, as previously stated, following the recruitment of Pete Best, his mother Mona was also a severe thorn in our side. Wayne and Lee didn't really get on, I think. Both had rather inflated egos, which was great for the music but bad news for peace and harmony in the group. Wayne also knew, however, that the All Stars were good enough as a group without Lee. Tony Waddington agreed with this and soon became a close ally of Wayne Bickerton, further dividing the group. They worked very well together, arranging most of Lee's numbers – not that Lee ever really took much notice of such musicological matters. So, by autumn 1962, although our great master plan to promote Lee Curtis ahead of the pack by cherry-picking the All Stars appeared to be working on the surface, internally there were cliques forming within the group. When one adds my own desires for Lee to become a solo star, together with my premeditated resistance to stand-up rows, it quickly became apparent to both Kenny and myself that it would only be a matter of time before the group imploded. Our abiding subtext became one of attempting to hold the band together for long enough to complete gigs and further Lee's career. I was forced to take the classically conservative position of gatekeeper, thereby moderating my ambition with extreme caution. All this was further complicated by October 1962 as I signed Carlton Brooke's second artist, a 15-year-old bundle of dynamite by the name of Beryl Hogg.

Beryl Marsden

Carlton Brooke's link with NEMS was not exactly common knowledge but a few musicians, i.e. those who benefitted, had become aware of it. By the closing months of 1962 I was personally being approached by a number of groups and solo singers wishing to sign with the agency. I was very circumspect, however, and had not thus far done so. This was for two basic reasons. Firstly, there was my aforementioned opinion that many of Liverpool's groups were beginning to sound decidedly similar and I determined that it would have to be a rather special artiste to persuade me to further complicate my already tangled life. Secondly, I did not wish to sign a group who would challenge the pre-eminence of Lee Curtis. I realise that this was a very selfish motive, but he was my prime mover.

However, I had been aware that a young girl had been featuring as part of the Undertakers' set for a few weeks during the summer of 1962. She was very young, but the guys from the Undertakers had realised that she was a remarkable vocalist and, as occasionally happened in those days, had allowed her up on stage to belt out a few songs with the band. This sort of familiarity had its grounding in pub singing in and around Liverpool in which I was so immersed as a youth. There would always be somebody in the crowd who could knock out a song and it had become de rigueur in Liverpool to bring people up on to the stage.

Beryl had become a feature of the Undertakers almost by accident. However, I think the band had become a little disconcerted by it all. They were quite a macho outfit and, although appreciating this younger performer's obvious talents, were not altogether happy with her following them around in order to use them as a backing group for her own set; it didn't really soothe their psyches, I think! Beryl told me: 'They thought they were really cool and it was decidedly uncool to have a little 15-year-old girl hanging on to their leather jeans.' In addition to this, the Undertakers had been invited to Germany and Beryl had presumed that she would go too. However, she was underage and was devastated to discover that the band was leaving without her. When the Undertakers returned from their stint on the Reeperbahn, much to her chagrin, Beryl further discovered that they had changed their sound to cater for the German audiences ('… so I was out,' she recalled). Therefore, young Beryl Hogg approached me at the Pier Head one fine evening that autumn as we were organising a van load of musos to travel to a gig, and asked to sing with Lee Curtis and the All Stars.

I wasn't very happy about it, to be honest. I was quite aware of her talents, but could envisage problems. Firstly, she was not only very young, but also young looking. Even allowing a juvenile female the opportunity to step into a vehicle full of young men in those far-off days was tantamount to scandal. Secondly, in my naiveté I was concerned that her family should have allowed her out at such late hours. 'What kind of family would allow something like that?' I thought. Thirdly, there was the possibility of even further friction with our star Lee Curtis, and this simply had to be avoided at all costs. As it turned out, however, Beryl was very compelling, persuading me that her family was in agreement with her desires to sing. Lee also thought that it was a good idea because, according to what he'd heard, we'd nabbed 'the best thing about the Undertakers'. Thus, with my fear of the prospect of imminent arrest for baby snatching in the recesses of my mind, I agreed to give her a go. I was also in the process of putting a Let's Go show together at the Majestic in Birkenhead and was rather short of acts, so Beryl, I thought, could prove useful. As it turned out, she was far more than useful, emerging as Liverpool's best female vocalist of the 1960s.

Our venue that evening was the Tower Ballroom in New Brighton and Beryl was invited to sing a couple of numbers with Lee halfway through the performance. As I expected, she went down very well indeed, her powerful, charming voice ringing like a bell throughout the boundless expanses of the venue. Lee enjoyed it all immensely; he felt that Beryl added a little something to the evening's entertainments and so it was decided by all that Beryl should accompany Lee Curtis and the All Stars to a few more engagements as part of the entourage. Owing to her age, however, together with her limited repertoire, it was decided that she should not be overused and so she was described as 'Lee Curtis' Special Guest, Beryl'. Pete Best had just joined the All Stars when Beryl began her stint in the Let's Go shows. The band was almost like a local super-group at the time: Lee, Pete, Beryl and the rest of the band, and although Beryl never really enjoyed the Let's Go gigs – she thought they were terrible, actually – those gigs and that band turned her into a consummate professional in a very short space of time. Practically instantaneously MCs began making comparisons between Beryl and the original Little Miss Dynamite, Brenda Lee. Beryl had certainly studied Brenda's vocal characteristics, of that there can be little doubt, but it was rather unfair to compare the two. Beryl's voice was, if anything, somewhat raunchier than Brenda's. Nevertheless, I found myself with two independent artistes on my books, both of whom were being favourably compared to two of America's biggest rock stars, namely Elvis Presley and Brenda Lee. At first it was rather encouraging and not a little flattering. However, as Merseybeat began to be perceived as a movement which was laying waste to all of the popular music stars of the past, those comparisons began to haunt both the artistes and myself.

I was working hand-in-glove with the wonderfully inspirational Bill Marsden, manager of the Birkenhead Majestic at this time. The Majestic was my kind of venue. It was almost baronial in comparison to the cellar clubs and people's halls of Liverpool and had a touch of class both in architectural style and atmosphere. It was Bill's inspirational input into Lee Curtis' career that prompted me to suggest to Beryl that 'Hogg' was not necessarily the most theatrical of names for stepping on to the stage with Lee Curtis, and that perhaps a name change was in order. We were performing for Bill one evening in Crewe, supporting Shane Fenton (later Alvin Stardust) and the Fentones. After a particularly arduous night, I returned to Gardner Road with Lee and the band, Beryl, Shane Fenton and Bill Marsden all in tow. During the after-gig post-mortem it occurred to me that 'Marsden' rolled off the tongue quite easily and was a 'nicer' name than Hogg. I was aware also that Gerry Marsden was leader of the Pacemakers and there would be, albeit incorrect, associations made: any publicity was, of course, good publicity. And so, with not only the young lady's approval, but that of all those mentioned above, Beryl Hogg became Beryl Marsden in Gardner Road one evening in 1962.

'Liverpool's own Brenda Lee', as Bob Wooler announced her (actually I thought she was better than that), made great headway over the next three months or so. With the help of Bill Marsden, who wanted to see Birkenhead (Liverpool's cousin 'over the water') blossom as a market, I was able to get the Carlton Brooke stable some very timely bookings. Kenny and I were still not really sure what the hell we were doing. To be honest, most of the time it was just happening to us. However, we were able to give off our usual air of self-confidence and our Let's Go gigs at the Top Rank Birkenhead Majestic were an overwhelming success, particularly those featuring Beryl – even though she continued to hate them! By the beginning of 1963 Beryl had already attracted the attentions of Decca Records' A&R staff. She served her apprenticeship with Lee over a couple of months and, as her voice strengthened, she was given her own solo spot with the All Stars backing her. Beryl had left school by this time and was technically working as a full-time professional singer (although I think she was signing on at the Labour Exchange). Beryl has described to me many times how she thought herself to be a real rebel in those days.

She certainly became a real handful! Although there were plenty of gigs for her, she was never happy with the kind of shows that I would promote. If one excludes Cilla Black's occasional ad hoc sojourns with the Dominoes and the Big Three, there were no local female beat singers with male bands at that time, and I presumed that the scene that she was playing was the one she wanted to play. But I couldn't have been more wrong, for Beryl was the archetypal prototype hippie: an R&B beatnik who hated all things commercial.

It was partly my fault that she was unhappy. To begin with I certainly failed to realise that not only was Beryl two generations or so younger than myself, but she was also a distance from the Lee Curtis (and the rest of Liverpool's rock 'n' roll bands) age band. Whereas most group members appearing in Liverpool might regard her as a Billie Davis-cum-Brenda Lee type, Beryl saw herself as more of an R&B type singer in the Etta James mould. The fact was that she had more in common with the generation of music makers following the Merseybeat generation, such as the Spencer Davis Group, the Who, the Action and the Small Faces, rather than those who had established the Liverpool scene. Indeed I now look back and wonder why I didn't introduce her to, say, the Roadrunners, Almost Blues or even the Hideaways, for these bands played the music that she truly loved; Beryl was far less interested in, say, Brenda Lee's back catalogue. So, while Beryl took an interest in and understood mod ideas and ideals, I was still catching up with three guitars and a set of drums. The upshot of this disparity was that I was rather too keen to see a ready-made market for a British Brenda Lee, while Beryl, having initially used Brenda as an inspirational role model, wished to move on to something far more musically diverse. I was looking at the type of female performers that were making it at that moment in time and styled Beryl's appearance accordingly. Therefore my role models for Beryl included the likes of Susan Maughan, Dusty Springfield and Helen Shapiro. While I was insisting that she wear party frocks and a tiara, she really wanted to rough it with the boys in jeans and T-shirts.

I found it impossible to be strict with her and, bless her, she exploited this to the full. The more I tried to call the tune, the less Beryl would dance to that tune. Eventually my management with her became based around the legendary Mexican stand-off. It became something of a ritual: we would exploit the other's weakness up to but not including the juncture at which our breaking point would be reached. This would then be followed by a cooling-off period when things would return to relative normality, only succeeded by another climb to the point of self-inflicted conflict and misery. The trouble was that she wanted to sing but she wasn't really interested in stardom (at least not in the same way that I was). She also wanted to have a good time and, at 16 years of age, who could blame her? My packaging was evidently misdirected. Nevertheless, despite my misplaced preoccupation with pretty dresses and Susan Maughan looka-likes, Beryl's ability rose above the stereotyping and important people in London and West Germany were alerted. She was talented enough to earn plaudits and, in retrospect, I can see that she was able to progress into the music business almost in spite of my marketing techniques. After a couple of rave reviews in *Mersey Beat* the Germans wanted Beryl in Hamburg. I shall be discussing my growing relationships with Germany very shortly; however, at this point a little narration of Beryl in Hamburg would greatly assist this recounting of our relationship.

By the opening months of 1963 Beryl had obtained a recording deal with Decca. She was only 16 years of age and I had finally relented and promised to take her to Germany. However, her tender years still dictated that she could not go as an adult, and she was duly making my life a misery. I steadfastly refused to take her with me on our first excursion but on my return discussed her professional desires with her parents and informed them that unless I took her to Germany she would probably attempt to get there under her own steam. This would have broken both British and West German law and she certainly wouldn't have been allowed back to work. So, I had hatched a plan. If I became her legal guardian for the dura-tion of the trip, Beryl could go to Hamburg under my wing, as it were; but I needed her parents' approval. This was not a problem; in fact, they were so delighted (her mum was lovely) I was attempting to guarantee their daughter's welfare that I was rather shocked – they understood so well what their daughter's aspirations were all about. I recall thinking: 'perhaps she's that much trouble they want her out of the house as soon as possible', but it wasn't like that.

I left the Hogg household in Wavertree and immediately caught the train from Liverpool Lime Street to Euston, and then took a cab to Bow Street in London. I was armed with their written approval and I obtained a special licence to become Beryl Hogg's legal guardian. Everything was set and I was mightily pleased that the London magistrates considered me respectable enough to act as Beryl's father; little did I know what I was letting myself in for. There was also one important overriding condition: West German law dictated that I had to personally guarantee that Beryl would be out of any night club in which she performed and back in the Hotel Pacific (our more salubrious digs after the brothel of the first visit) by 10 p.m. You see, every night at ten minutes to ten, all teenagers had to be off the streets. A curfew still reigned and the call of alles raus could be heard at that time over the length and breadth of the Reeperbahn. Now, as one can imagine, this was problematic. Firstly, how was I to get such a feisty young thing to obey this dictat? Beryl yearned to be in Hamburg not simply to sing, but to be where the action was. Secondly, how was I going to get her noticed anywhere on the Reeperbahn when she had to be off the streets two hours before many groups even began playing? I couldn't really solve the first problem but, as for the second, I realised that Beryl was ideal for the younger teenage market, and if she had to be supposedly tucked up in bed at 10 p.m., then so presumably did they. What we actually had was a captive market.

I gently broke it to Lee Curtis and the All Stars that I had arranged for them to perform an extra two sets earlier in the evening for the teenagers in addition to their own two sets, which were scheduled for midnight. I realised that I was asking a great deal from them, but Beryl was still being billed as their guest, so it would have been unprofessional to have arranged for another band to back her (at least, that's what I kept telling them). In any case, the All Stars loved Beryl, and of course they soon realised that by playing for a much younger audience they also had the potential to increase their own fan base beyond the young adults, sailors and prostitutes within the Star Club. In fact, one consequence of this ploy was that they experienced far greater longevity in West Germany than practically any other Liverpool band. By playing behind Beryl to those curfew-bound teenagers they attracted something approaching mass appeal while becoming musically very tight. Even now, the statistics will show that Lee Curtis played the Star Club more times than any other act. This was not only due to his immense popularity, but also the practicality of playing four gigs per night.

Predictably, all hell broke loose when Beryl reached Hamburg. There were umpteen embarrassing occasions. Picture me dragging Beryl kicking and screaming along the Reeperbahn back to the Hotel Pacific from the Top Ten Club (no one batted an eyelid: it could only happen in Hamburg). Then there was the time when she slipped through my cordon to see Jerry Lee Lewis at the Star Club and I found her literally under Jerry's piano. There was even the occasion when I found her in a transvestite bar trying to chat up the men – ah, the innocence of children. There were countless incidents involving Beryl's indiscipline and she naturally became very popular amongst the bands on the Reeperbahn circuit. I know for a fact, for example, that Beryl became very friendly with Tony Sheridan, Mick Green of the Pirates and all of the Rolling Stones; up until now she has believed that I was blissfully unaware of this latter association. But she was also a great trouper and I grew to love her very much. These days I know Beryl is grateful that I at least endeavoured to look after her welfare. Without my watchful eye she might have totally deserted the straight and narrow rather than just deviating from it occasionally. Her first visit to Germany, bolted in to the month given us by Manfred Weissleder after our first visit in March 1963, was very well received in more ways than one. Her second visit, however, became even more incident packed, because Beryl had failed to tell anybody that she was pregnant.

Manfred Weissleder was in the process of franchising the Star Club name right across West Germany when Beryl returned with Lee Curtis, the band and myself to Germany a little later that summer. We discovered that we had been booked into a wide variety of different and differing Star Clubs the length and breadth of the country. It became a very tiring and enduring stint for all of us and we all managed to lose a considerable amount of sleep and weight as the tour continued. All of us, that is, except Beryl. She would claim that she was eating well and enjoying life on the road and, like idiots, we believed her – after all, she appeared to be blooming! Beryl's subterfuge lasted until the day the landlady at our digs in Flensburg rather tersely informed me that 'the young fraulein ought to go home'. I was rather taken aback at the landlady's comments and asked, rather wearily, why she thought that this should be the case, thinking that Beryl had been revelling in her waywardness once again. 'You must realise, Herr Flannery, she is carrying a child!' she retorted. I was, to use another colloquialism, gobsmacked and somewhat mortified. I was supposed to be this all-seeing, all-pervading manager, au fait with the ways of the world, and yet I hadn't detected that Beryl's bump was not growing in direct proportion to her intake of sauerkraut and Black Forest gateau. I confronted Beryl and, in floods of tears, she admitted to me that she was indeed about five months pregnant. She was naturally rather distraught about the whole affair. So was I, but for very different reasons.

Prior to leaving again for Germany, Beryl had recorded her first single for Decca. I had high hopes for it. It was a cover of the Barbara George number *I Know*, and Beryl had given her all during the recording. It was a damn good song, she liked its provenance and had done it full justice. It had been released during August in the UK and had been selling rather well, being played on Radio Luxembourg and, believe it or not, the BBC on several occasions. It was also chalking up brisk sales in London, where growing legions of mods evidently found it to their liking. It looked like this was to be 'the one'. Beryl's visit to Germany, however, was ill timed. The record had not been scheduled for release there (typical Decca cheapskates) and by late August had started to stall in the UK because of no available public appearances from Ms Marsden. I had thought that we might be able to reactivate the record when we returned (this was not common, but I was so sure that Beryl had cut a hit that I was determined to try anything). Now, however, with Beryl moving into the final trimester of her pregnancy, I knew that the record was effectively dead in the water and I was powerless to do anything about it. Even to this day, I am amazed that *I Know* wasn't a smash hit single, propelling Beryl Marsden into the fame she so richly deserved.

The 'dirty deed' had been done on the previous trip. Evidently the curfews and my attempts at being her guardian and chaperone hadn't worked. Beryl had formed a brief liaison with a London-based guitarist who was on the verge of international success and, to this day, she refuses to discuss the father. 'I know', as the song went, who he is and I'm sure he would be stunned to discover that he has a son. At the time I was more than a little downhearted. I felt that I had failed Beryl from both a personal and professional point of view. I kept thinking to myself that if only I had been a little more circumspect she might not be pregnant; if only I had been a little less eager to take them all back to Hamburg Beryl would have had a hit record on her hands. I could never regret the birth of any child – after all, it's God's gift to us all – but I did feel a little distressed at the wretched circumstances and my own rather woeful timing.

During 1964, following the birth of her son, her somewhat antisocial behaviour increased and her antipathy towards me and mainstream show business grew exponentially. Via London agent George Cooper, I had managed to get her on a tour with Craig Douglas and Millie Small. I had thought that this would be a good platform for her but, in truth, Craig Douglas' days were already numbered and Millie, although a cute ska singer from Jamaica with a number one record (*My Boy Lollipop*), wasn't really a top-drawer vocalist, at least at this stage. So the theatres played were rather second division and the tour was a little dismal for her, especially now that she was a young mother. I'd made a mistake but reckoned that we might as well make the best of it. Beryl, however, had sussed the venue problem right from the start and, together with her almost innate

THE DECCA RECORD COMPANY LIMITED

DECCA HOUSE · 9 ALBERT EMBANKMENT · LONDON · S·E·I

TELEPHONE: RELIANCE 8111 (34 LINES)   TELEGRAMS, DECCORD, LONDON, S.E.1   CABLES: DECCORD, LONDON   TELEX: 28588, LONDON

JZ

Ken Flannery, Esq.,
10, Gardner Road,
Tuebrook,
LIVERPOOL.13.   December 12th, 1963.

Dear Mr. Flannery,

I have pleasure in confirming BERYL MARSDEN'S recording
session at our Studio 1, 165, Broadhurst Gardens, West
Hampstead, N.W.6. on the following date:-

FRIDAY, DECEMBER 20th - 2.30 p.m./5.30 p.m.
                         7 p.m./10 p.m.

Kindest regards.

Yours sincerely,
THE DECCA RECORD COMPANY LIMITED.

Jean Zimmermann,
ARTISTS DEPARTMENT-POP SINGLES.

DIRECTORS
SIR EDWARD LEWIS (CHAIRMAN)   J. GRAY, M.C.,C.A.,M.I.EX.   A. C. W. HADDY   H. C. LAMBERT, F.C.A   M. A. ROSENGARTEN (SWISS)   H. F. SCHWARZ (U.S.A.)   W. W. TOWNSLEY

A letter from Decca Records confirming Beryl Marsden's recording session in
December 1963. (Author's collection)

aversion to any stage presentation suggested by myself, proceeded to make everybody's life including her own an utter misery. On one occasion, at the Chester Royalty Theatre, she became so frustrated with her locale that, right in the middle of her act, she stamped her foot like a spoiled school-girl, shouted to the musicians, 'that wasn't the way we rehearsed it', and promptly stormed off the stage. Despite my apologies to Mr Critchley, the owner of the Royalty, and my pleas to the George Cooper Organisation, Beryl was immediately sacked from the tour. All this after being voted into the *NME* Top Ten of female vocalists that same month.

Beryl's waywardness notwithstanding, I must admit that it was around this time that I became convinced that such agencies themselves were enormous impediments to the careers of this new breed of female singer. They were incredibly snotty and considered the likes of Beryl Marsden lucky to be singing for a living. Cooper told me this in no uncertain terms and had no compunction about throwing Beryl off the tour. He felt no responsibility to sustain her career and was utterly indifferent to popular music generally. He told me he didn't know the music and didn't like the acts. After our little contretemps, I was subsequently always on the lookout for George Cooper; throughout the entire decade of the 1960s I never once saw him in a theatre auditorium, which speaks volumes for his so-called enthusiasm for popular music.

Beryl's excellent score on the *NME* poll prompted Ray Coleman (then just a staff writer for the *Record Mirror*) to phone me with a request to interview the young Ms Marsden about the exciting news. I was ill at the time (this would be very late 1963) but, from my hospital bed, arranged for Beryl to be put on a train to London for the paper to conduct an in-depth interview. However, typically, Beryl never reached London, alighting before Euston because she was 'bored'. Coleman was decid-edly miffed, frantically phoning Kenny at the Carlton Brooke offices in Slater Street asking where she had got to, but Kenny didn't have a clue. However, I determined to find out where my wayward starlet had got to. The Ayland Hotel was famous for its rock clientele. Anybody who was anybody would frequent the hotel in the early to mid-1960s. It was as much a place to be seen at as to stay in, so to speak. I signed myself out of hospital in Liverpool and went down to London, booking myself in at the Ayland, in the hope of catching gossip about Beryl's whereabouts. As soon as I arrived I discovered that Beryl had been spotted at the hotel that very afternoon and had been last seen cruising around the West End of London in a Rolls-Royce.

Sure enough, after a couple of hours and what seemed like hundreds of cups of tea, Beryl emerged from an unnamed star's Rolls-Royce; I was not amused. Not only had she let an important music journalist down by her actions, but she had worried me almost to distraction. Upon spotting the Rolls I immediately walked out of the hotel lobby towards the limousine and, without her seeing me, tapped Beryl's shoulder, asking her curtly but civilly, 'Where the fucking hell do you think you have been?' Beryl physically froze at the sound of my voice. She slowly turned around, her eyes were welling up with tears and her mouth had dropped open; she could barely stutter, 'J-J-J-Joe, how? What? What are you doin' …' She trailed off dumbfounded and embarrassed. The star also became very agitated: 'Beryl, you told me you were a free agent this afternoon … how could you, of all people, do this to me? Your career is at an important stage, you can't just let people down like this — by the way, how old are you?'

She agreed that she had indeed led him to believe that she was a free agent that day and was over the age of consent. 'But I was so bored in the train, I just had to do something,' she cried in her defence. Our Rolls driver was less than impressed: 'So you decided to see if good old ★★★★★ was around, eh?' He was old enough to have been her father and his reply was ironic in the extreme. Furthermore, he claimed not to have any prior knowledge of the arranged interview with Ray Coleman who by this time had also contacted the desk at the Ayland. He exclaimed with all honesty, 'Joe, if I'd have known about it, I would have driven her to see young Ray myself!' Beryl was speechless. A pregnant silence came over our little group as we all paused for breath; I heaved a massive sigh of relief. Beryl, with her tail placed firmly between her legs, immediately returned with me to Liverpool. We did not speak to each other for the duration of the homeward journey. I couldn't criticise her without appearing like an overbearing parent and criticism without value is a waste of everybody's time.

Beryl's last visit to Germany under my management was during the winter of 1964/65. By this time I was pretty much a full-time resident in Hamburg, working with Manfred and the Star Club chain as a freelance agent. This, together with my 'party frocks' approach to management had further alienated Beryl, who was becoming more and more interested in the growing underground scene in London at that time. She was still in her teens and, despite having a young child who was often with the grandparents, was deeply attracted by soul music, Bob Dylan, the growing counter-culture and the alternative music scene that had begun to evolve down there — I think both Liverpool and Hamburg had started to bore her.

Prior to this, another single had followed *I Know* entitled *When the Lovelight Starts Shining Through His Eyes*. A pretty good ditty, it had been the Supremes' first moderately successful tilt at the US charts, but with such an unwieldy title that was of little use to British record announcers and DJs used to short, snappy epithets, it made little impact. Peter Sullivan at Decca had selected the song and hadn't really consulted any of us about it. I made it clear that I was angered by this. I was, after all, Beryl's personal manager and decisions such as follow-up singles to near-chart successes were of interest to us all. In any case neither Beryl nor I liked Sullivan's rather lacklustre arrangement and, in response, her performance on the final take was deliberately laconic for she never threw herself into anything she didn't believe in. Despite our best efforts at promotion, the song probably got what it deserved and sold considerably less than *I Know*. We were all somewhat dejected by this: Beryl's antithesis to the mainstream was amplified by Peter Sullivan's despotism and I felt that I was being overlooked in the consultation process. When, a little later, Sullivan began working with Lulu, dumping her excellent band in the process, and then Tom Jones, the penny dropped and Kenny and I realised that both Beryl and Lee Curtis had probably been used by Peter Sullivan as templates. Beryl's recording contract came up for renewal with Decca with an option for a further couple of singles but, although they were interested, we did not pursue the matter with any real enthusiasm; I could see that Beryl was restless and although she recorded a few demo tracks that were placed in the can, we began looking elsewhere, and during 1965 she was ever so quietly dumped by Decca – what a pity.

In the meantime, although now a mother, Beryl was still an anarchic teenager and as susceptible as anyone her age would be to new musical movements, and the London R&B and mod scene interested her enormously. After returning from her third visit to Germany at the beginning of 1965, she wrote to me (I was living in Hamburg for most of that year) to inform me that she thought it was time for the parting of the ways. She basically stated that staying with my management would mean spending more and more time in Germany, which wasn't what she wanted. Although she appreciated that she could earn good money with Carlton Brooke and the Star Club franchises, she really wanted to try her hand in London and felt that the gigs I could offer her in Germany were rather too old fashioned for her tastes. She thought that the London R&B scene was where her future lay and her interests in such music certainly bore this out. My attempts at making her into a cross between Billie Davis and

Susan Maughan had ultimately amounted to very little and I could detect that she wanted a new, more alternative, challenge. Being a mum, too, was a problem for her, exasperated by those lengthy stays in Germany.

She stayed in Liverpool for the majority of 1965, singing on the by now declining Merseyside circuit and then, as I expected, removed to London towards the end of the year. It was during late 1965 that she first met Tony Stratton-Smith and, along with another Liverpool band the Koobas, became one of his first signings. I did phone Stratton-Smith about this, for Beryl was still officially signed to me, but I was actually genuinely pleased and not a little relieved, to tell the truth, that a London manager had signed her. Stratton-Smith quickly arranged a two-record solo deal with EMI's Columbia label, one of which was the first ever UK cover of a Stevie Wonder song (*Music Talk*), whose B side was an equally great Jackie DeShannon number *Breakaway* (later a hit for Tracy Ullman in the 1980s). However, Tony was also to experience severe difficulties with Ms Marsden. For example, at one stage Beryl even unhyped her own single recording (*Who You Gonna Hurt*) out of the charts by stating to the *NME* that she hated it! This was after Tony had paid a London song-plugger £150 to hype it into the lower reaches of the charts. Nevertheless, it was 'Strat', and not me who managed to give Beryl her fleeting moment of real fame by getting her on to the Beatles tour of December 1965 – their last ever British tour. Also on the bill were the Moody Blues, the Paramounts (later Procol Harum) and, of course, Tony's other Liverpool protégés, the Koobas (or Kubas as they were later renamed). The tour lasted from 3–12 December and from what I can gather was quite unremarkable. As was usually the case by this time, nobody wanted to hear the support acts and the audience simply screamed their way through the entire Beatles set. By all accounts, Beryl also continued to scream and cry her way through the tour, but for different reasons than the adoring Beatlemaniacs: tantrums again, it seems.

Strat and I met one evening in a club in London much later, towards the very end of that tumultuous decade. He had just launched his Charisma label via B&C records, a small independent which had previously handled a lot of reggae and ska. I was effectively out of the music business and about to embark upon my new retail and wholesale furniture operation. We had been introduced by a mutual friend with the ironic declaration, 'meet the other Marsden mug'. We enjoyed a laugh that evening as our mutual memories of Beryl's inflexibilities rang all too familiar in each other's ears. For instance, he told me of the time when Beryl refused to fly to Germany, even though he knew that she had flown with me previously without any problem; he also stated that on more than one occasion, when a gig didn't suit her she just locked herself away in her apartment. He finally employed a minder in an attempt to get her to improve her discipline, but this met with little success for she wouldn't answer the door to him either. I informed him of her countless Hamburg escapades. We both, however, declared the utmost respect for her relatively untapped talent and expressed our regret that she had been unable or unwilling to exploit it fully. I do believe that if Beryl had managed to stay the course with Tony Stratton-Smith she might have been one of the first signings to his Charisma label. Surely this would have helped her considerably, for just like those other relatively unsuccessful 1960s British female vocalists who made a great impact the following decade, Elkie Brooks and Kiki Dee, Beryl needed a well-produced album to show off her talents, rather than the odd overproduced single every six months or so to get lost amongst the deluge of 45s being released in the UK up until the turn of the decade.

Eventually Strat helped to co-opt Beryl into a group project led by keyboards man Peter Bardens. In 1965 Bardens spent a brief spell as the keyboard player with Them after leaving the Cheynes. I think in the long run it was Bardens who had perhaps the most positive effect on her. He was a well-respected musician in and around London, a consummate professional. Beryl joined Bardens' short-lived but highly influential Shotgun Express during 1966 and it was as joint vocalist in the band with that other rather 'difficult' individual, Rod Stewart, that she made a name for herself in and around the London night club scene. Other members of the band at various times included Mick Fleetwood and Peter Green, believe it or not. Shotgun Express were all the rage on the London mod-psychedelic scene during late 1966, but sadly only produced two singles; one was a glorious albeit overproduced effort for Columbia that year: *I Could Feel the Whole World Turn Round*. Perhaps the sum of the collective egos (including Beryl's) was all rather too much for Bardens and he probably willingly extinguished the group in 1967.

Funnily enough, some years later, when Fleetwood Mac were going through their transitional stage prior to the advent of Stevie Nicks and Lindsey Buckingham, Mick Fleetwood invited Beryl to the group's rehearsal mansion for talks and a few sessions. Beryl, to my knowledge, turned him down – again, what a pity! She would have been the ideal seventies female rock singer. She was into these blues-inspired heavier forms of rock as early as 1964 and would have been extremely successful on a label such as Island or Charisma, backed by a band such as say Spooky Tooth. In fact, my dream pairing would have been Beryl Marsden with Spooky Tooth: what a combination that might have been. Beryl and I kept in touch and, during the 1970s, we linked up once again. She had returned to Liverpool at the end of the 1960s and had married a local guy. She also flirted with the local rock and soul music scenes throughout that time, firstly with Sinbad, then with Gambler and finally the Beryl Marsden Band. The latter made quite a splash locally and, by 1976, she had attracted the attention of the national media once again when the *Melody Maker* ran a centre-page spread on the blossoming Liverpool sound of the mid-1970s, citing the Beryl Marsden Band as one of the city's most exciting prospects. The timing of the article was a little off, to say the least, for within a few months the Sex Pistols were to sweep away a great deal of those leftovers from the 1960s. Still, I was delighted to see that Beryl was working regularly again and receiving good reviews in the process.

After some years out of the music business I was persuaded by Clive Epstein to reactivate Carlton Brooke and toward the end of the 1970s Beryl and her band had progressed sufficiently to be signed. We persuaded our old friend Wayne Bickerton, who was by that time managing director of his own label State Records (the Rubettes, Kandidate etc.), to visit Merseyside to take a look at Beryl and the band. We organised a gig at a pub in Birkenhead and Wayne was so impressed that halfway through the set he split a beermat and wrote: 'They're fantastic … I'll sign them.' I was delighted. For the first time, I could see real possibilities of achieving something befitting her obvious talents. I knew that Wayne would not behave like the unprincipled record executives of the 1960s, but what about Beryl? We went into negotiations right away. Speed was of the essence, for, just like ten years previously, I could detect that the market was about to change. A few days later a draft contract from State Records arrived at my house in Aigburth, Liverpool. We were all ready to sign the document when I received a phone call from Wayne. Apparently Beryl had decided to phone him up personally and request cash from him as a form of tax-free personal advance. Beryl was always in some form of financial calamity and probably saw Wayne as a way out: wrong decision. In hindsight, it was probably not an altogether unreasonable request, but it certainly seemed to be ill timed. Wayne was mightily displeased and promptly dropped the band. He candidly informed me that he was not interested in providing cash advances to artists on demand, and that he found Beryl's request excessive and distasteful. What actually took place during that phone call between them I will never know; however, it led to a bad moment for all concerned.

Actually, I also believe that Wayne Bickerton missed a great opportunity to bring State Records out of their own doldrums. I don't think that State was exactly in a position of financial potency by that stage (1977–78) and they certainly needed an injection of new talent. The Rubettes, who had previously been their main provider of income, were a spent force and the catchy pop tunes for which Wayne and Tony Waddington were renowned were also, by the late 1970s, rather old hat. I really don't know for sure, but I do feel that, while Beryl had obviously spoken out of turn, perhaps State's decision to stop negotiations with the Beryl Marsden Band might have been motivated by other more pressing financial considerations; perhaps Beryl's forthright tongue was used as an excuse. Whatever, Beryl not only ruined her own chances once again but those of the four guys in her excellent band. This wasn't entirely the end of Beryl's recording career, but almost. By 1979 she was earning a reasonable living as a session singer and recorded a demo for the somewhat mature producer Ivor Raymonde. It was a splendid version of *Sad Songs*, an equally excellent number by Billy and Bobby Alessi. The Alessi Brothers had enjoyed a hit in the UK with a nice little song entitled *Oh Lori* a year or two previously and their album, which hadn't sold well in the UK, contained a few overlooked crackers, *Sad Songs* being one of them. Beryl's demo was so good that it was immediately released on the MAM label (MAM 188) but, oddly, not under her own name. Instead the moniker on the label read 'Lynn Jackson': a very ordinary title to assume, but perhaps there were contractual difficulties. Also, the recording cites one 'Tab Martin' as the producer when it was clearly Ivor Raymonde. The record sank after a couple of plays by Terry Wogan on Radio 2.

A little later Beryl was auditioned by Willy Russell for a role in *Blood Brothers*. Willy had spent some time at my house while composing the score for the musical and had noticed Beryl's photograph on the wall. He contacted me via Bill Kenwright, who wanted to take the show into the West End, and organised an audition for Beryl in Liverpool at the Playhouse Theatre. The barman at the Playhouse, however, who apparently knew Beryl well, informed Kenwright that she was rather difficult and Beryl was promptly thrown over in favour of Barbara Dickson and then Kiki Dee. Beryl's erstwhile idiosyncratic temperament had finally come home to roost. The part in *Blood Brothers* was absolutely perfect for her, and the songs simply magnificent. It seems so unfair that so much talent was left to lie dormant, but perhaps we all get what we deserve, not what we want. Club singing in Tenerife followed by further regular session work ensured that she would always earn a living. In fact, by singing on an advertisement for shampoo in Germany in the mid-1990s, Beryl found herself vocalising on a hit ambient album in Europe, selling over 20,000 copies (a project with producer Phil Sawyer, I think), but that elusive British hit single eluded her. I think in many ways it was unfortunate for Beryl that she was part of the Merseybeat era. Her career was dogged by not only my own misguided musical ideas but also the Beatles and Cilla connections. Had she been born in a nondescript town in the UK the accident of her birth would not have demanded such close attention, and she might just have been able to record and release material more representative of her as an individual without any of the typecasting associated with the city of her birth.

10

THE VERY ROOT OF MEANING

THE INFAMOUS LOST weekend of Brian and John was still some years away when Brian Epstein and I boarded the plane from Speke Airport to fly out to Hamburg during the early summer of 1962. We wanted to see for ourselves precisely what was going on in this German seaport in the British zone of West Germany. Nobody knew of our visit, few are aware of it to this very day, yet it proved to be a galvanising experience for both of us, personally and professionally. It was on my suggestion that we visited the Reeperbahn. I'm not really sure whether Brian had been before – certainly he'd already arranged for the Beatles to open the Star Club in April – but he was very keen to go, remarking that he wanted to see the venues that the Beatles had already played prior to his management takeover, although I do believe it was essentially because the news coming back from visiting groups was that anything went sexually. Brian Epstein had become the Beatles' manager in between the group's two trips to the Top Ten Club and had done a third deal, not with Peter Eckhorn of the Top Ten Club where the band had made a real name for themselves, but with the owner of the new club on the Grosse Freiheit: the Star Club, owned by Manfred Weissleder. The growth of new clubs and new faces on the Hamburg scene interested both of us. Weissleder had poached artists, minders and punters from Eckhorn (precisely what Eckhorn had done to Bruno Koschmider) and all of the activity, complicity and, in Brian's case, erotica were exciting to say the least.

It was prior to the Parlophone auditions of June 1962 that he and I travelled to Hamburg. My memory of this is confirmed by the fact that it was while on the plane (my first ever flight) that Brian informed me that Pete Best's mother Mona was proving to be something of a nuisance. He said that Mona's very presence was jeopardising the whole operation. I also recall this period well because of Brian's paranoia over the prospective record deal. By this time the Beatles were still unsigned and Brian had promised faithfully that he would find them a record agreement at speed. He had thought that, being a provincial record retailer, he would be able to open doors, but he hadn't reckoned with the aforementioned cartel-like machinations of the UK record industry. While on the plane to Germany he was in a state of perplexity over the meeting he had endured with EMI after transferring the failed Decca audition tapes on to acetate at the HMV shop in Oxford Street, London. He confirmed to me that he was very hopeful that the Beatles would be signed to Parlophone, not necessarily because the Decca material was any good (he told me he thought that it was poor stuff and unrepresentative of their real sound) but quite simply because, at least according to my arrogant young friend George Martin, the A&R executive and producer at Parlophone 'knew sod all about pop'. In more ways than one our weekend proved to be a success. We established a connection with our German counterparts and Brian experienced a couple of delightful young men to satiate his secret desires. We both returned full of plans and renewed hope and energy. I had more work to do than Brian, however. The Beatles were already very popular in Hamburg and they could demand as much as 500 marks. I, on the other hand, had to convince the Germans that Lee Curtis and the All Stars were worth having at all.

That summer of 1962 still 'looms large in my lunchtime', as the Beatles might have said. Boys aspired to be men, and when the early morning light dawned over Gardner Road and a Beatle or two had, yet again, stayed overnight, it was up to me – 'the Colonel' as John and George often called me – to get them home and make sure they were safe in the arms of their families once again. I didn't simply have to do this, I felt committed to doing it. Brian and I had standards and Liverpool has always been a city in which one had to keep one's wits about oneself. It's difficult to remember those four lads as lads, after all this time. But that's exactly what they were; and being somewhat responsible for their welfare and fully aware of where one wrong turn could lead, I felt obliged to keep them and their families (not that John had much of a family life, to be honest) regularly in touch with each other. Running them home at the required hour in the morning was one such ploy. Of course, it was doubly convenient for me. The Liverpool wholesale markets used to open at an ungodly hour in the morning. I had to be up and about to get the bargains; thus it seemed logical to make sure that the lads were chauffeured home safe and sound at the same time.

Dawn in Liverpool, at least in the summer months when it isn't raining, can be spectacular. A big sky full of promise, streaked and blotched with clouds of red and amber fire, can be a rude awakening to a young, bleary-eyed musician who had come off stage at 2 in the morning and slept perhaps an hour or so on an overstuffed chair in front of the fire. No sooner had that fresh, moist, salty air and dramatic half-light hit George or John or Paul than they were immediately awake, talking thirteen to the dozen about the previous night. No sooner, however, had they piled into my lovely Vauxhall Cresta than the fresh air coupled with the heat from the interior of the car had sent them into a sleep-induced trance once again – except for George, that is. The Speke district of Liverpool, where George's family lived, was usually last on my list of drops. It was a council estate on the outskirts of the south end of the city, built alongside the river on the road towards Widnes and Runcorn. It was quite a drive from the Stoneycroft area which housed my flat and, shortly before reaching Harrison's home, George would eagerly persuade me to allow him to have a little drive of the Cresta. It was a big car, but George was fascinated by vehicles and speed, and was determined to learn to drive as soon as possible.

The Vauxhall, with its column change, was state-of-the-art family motoring at the time. It couldn't have been less British and had a distinctly American feel in its design, with rear fly-away wings and masses of internal space. George had admired it almost from the moment I had purchased it: my first new car. In fact, within a couple of months of his first test drives down Speke Boulevard and Western Avenue at 4 in the morning, he had even offered to buy it from me. He'd begun to make a little real cash, I think, after Brian had consulted me about pay rises and equitable wages for the band. Refusing his offer, I distinctly remember telling George something like, 'People who will be working for you will be driving the Vauxhall Crestas of this world, George. Leave it for a little while yet.' Naturally, he laughed in disbelief. Yet, shortly after passing his test, he ended up with a Zodiac convertible, the Ford equivalent of the Cresta.

George's dad, Harry, was a truly lovely, natural-born enthusiast. On every occasion I dropped George off, Harry would be up and ready for work.

His hours were rather like mine. As a bus inspector for Liverpool Corporation's bus fleet, he carried a great deal of responsibility and in those days, because the buses had to begin as early as 4 a.m., so did he. Harry would often prepare a full breakfast for me, in thanks for looking after his son, which I would zealously devour before heading off to the fruit and veg market. As George approached his middle life, he began to remind me very much of his quiet, capable father. Harry was never a man to let anybody down, a great socialist and an important official with the local Transport and General Trade Union. He loved people, always saw their best side and, together with his lovely wife Louise, he became a wonderful contact for Beatles fans. On a return visit to Liverpool from Germany during the autumn of 1964 in order to look for some new bands for the Star Club, I went to visit Harry just to say hello. It was raining heavily as usual as I arrived at his home only to discover at least half a dozen or so Beatles fans in his front room. He had invited them in for tea and biscuits 'because they looked like drowned rats'. I attempted to enlighten him: 'Harry, if you do this once then you'll be doing it all the time.' But he wouldn't have any of it: 'Joe, they're interesting people. They love my son and his mates and they've all got a story to tell. I think they're great.'

After arriving at the Harrisons' residence in my Vauxhall, with George invariably and probably illegally at the wheel – I can't even recall whether I'd asked if he had a driving licence – Harry would have his high-priority, high-fat breakfast ready. I was always in a hurry to get on but George might say 'just listen to this …' and around would go a record from his Chet Atkins collection as we tucked into bacon, eggs and fried bread. George was fascinated by Chet Atkins' style. It reminded me of the music I had heard in the Duck House pub years before, but to George it was a musical world to which he aspired: it was at the root of meaning, the nexus of his being. Atkins, of course, was a great musician to model one's self upon. His technical discipline remained second to none and I do believe that George turned himself into a great rockabilly and country-style guitarist because of these discs. Yes, Albert Lee is truly a great British country picker, but so too was George Harrison. I have always thought that George should have made a country-cum-acoustic album in Nashville.

At that time I just thought that George was another one of those typical Liverpudlians with a fascination for all things American. It was almost a city-wide affliction in those days and I include myself in that statement. But in his case, of course, the ties were far closer, for his elder sister Louise had married an American and moved to St Louis. Nevertheless, I could see that his affection for American guitar greats was not a passing fad. George often appeared to play with an almost mathematical precision for the Beatles: he would open a song by playing the riff, then chug along with a barre chord until a middle eight arrived and then proceed to play a standard pentatonic-style run. However, he was much better than this suggests. Playing Chuck Berry material alone in Liverpool during the late 1950s and early 1960s was not as common as one might imagine, for Berry's riffs were difficult, particularly on those German reproduction guitars that everyone had to put up with until Fender were allowed their licence to retail in this country at the end of the 1950s. So not every Liverpool band actually played Chuck Berry numbers, and those that did often didn't play them at all well. The Beatles, on the other hand, could play as many as twelve Chuck Berry songs and they were known as the Chuck Berry specialists by many promoters on Merseyside. In fact, Sam Leach once informed me that he thought that an indication of a good band was the amount and quality of Berry covers included in an act. A good benchmark, Sam!

George's style also owed a good deal to Carl Perkins, and the Beatles performed at least eleven Perkins songs in their live repertoire. When the Silver Beetles were backing Johnny Gentle in Scotland during 1960, George even used the first name Carl as a small tribute to his hero. He was like that: quiet, unassuming, occasionally moody and certainly introverted – an odd combination for a rock and roller! At Gardner Road you wouldn't even notice him sitting in a room most of the time. He sat, listened, laughed, drank tea, ate buttered toast, just the same as everybody else, but you would find it difficult to remember whether he had been there moments after he had gone. Place a guitar in his hands, however, and he would grow in confidence immediately. It almost seemed as if he had also grown in stature, the change was so remarkable. Whatever, he remained an agreeable young man. Occasionally he appeared a little depressed and at these moments he would converse with Kenny and find Kenny's view of world history quite uplifting. I have often thought that George was waiting for something from quite an early age. He seemed interested in dwelling upon spiritual and metaphysical matters with Kenny, which was right up Kenny's street of course, and the two would then chat into the wee small hours. I was always surprised that reports stated that George wasn't regarded as much of a scholar. Like many of us, he was probably a late developer but he was certainly a deep thinker. He would spend time in your company and enjoy it, but might be thinking a layer or two beneath the superficial level of conversation.

All of the Beatles, in their own ways, were highly intelligent young individuals. To me, no one Beatle was more cerebral than the other. Their intricate communal web held together well and while they might have played psychological games with each other's egos by occasionally running the other down, these rituals were part of the clandestine affiliation process so integral to their internal power. From my, albeit limited, perspective, George only rarely appeared on the outside of all this. There might have been a few rare occasions when a certain chemistry between John and Paul would undercut anything that was going on around them, but it was at times like these that something musical would usually emanate. No, for me, George was part of the triad, no doubt about it. Only Pete appeared more obviously alienated from the rest, for reasons I have given in a previous chapter. George always had the capacity to remain somewhat anonymous, however, whereas John and Paul utterly rejected that concept. A good example of this occurred some years later, I believe, when he was visiting Liverpool and staying at the Adelphi Hotel with Eric Clapton. They had a bet to see whether George would be recognised if he walked from the Adelphi to Lime Street station, a few hundred yards further down the road. As one might imagine, it was Eric and not George who was instantly recognised. George quite easily won his bet. Our paths seldom crossed subsequent to those early days. Even in 1993, when I was returning from Los Angeles after an abortive visit with the Liverpool group the Pies, I discovered George had been on the preceding flight. We missed each other so many times over the years it seemed that fate was playing its part. I still have a pair of his Beatles boots that he left behind at the ABC studios in Birmingham in 1963 from one of the two All Liverpool Thank Your Lucky Stars programmes broadcast that year. I rang him about them the following week but George just casually replied, 'Joe, you'll be able to give them to me sometime.' It was sadly never to happen.

I remember Frank Allen of the Searchers stating on one occasion that, to him, the memories of hit records are directly associated with cars. For example, he stated that *Don't Throw Your Love Away* always reminded him of an E-Type Jag sports car purchased on the strength of that successful hit record. I wonder whether any memories of a certain Vauxhall Cresta ever occasionally flashed through George's mind. If they did, I'm sure he remembered it, and its white wall tyres, with great affection. Speaking of the Searchers, I met John McNally recently and we swapped a few reminiscences. Thinking back, although I was devoted to the All Stars and the Beatles, I have to admit that, of all of the Liverpool groups that I thought people would be analysing in years to come, I was convinced that it would be the Searchers. Their musicianship, stage presence, professionalism, etc. was par excellence. The one thing that they didn't really have going for them, of course, was an innate confidence in their own song-writing abilities. They could write, but they tended to prefer the safe bet of covering material. Tony Hatch probably had a lot to do with this. I met him on a couple of occasions and he struck me as a very arrogant, self-centred man with a rather myopic vision of the pop world (not unlike those two useless articles Dick Rowe and Peter Sullivan) and completely the opposite of George Martin who would clearly allow himself to run with not only his instincts but also ideas emanating from his artistes; Martin never inflicted his own sense of musical authority upon young artistes – I only wish we'd have signed to EMI rather than Decca.

During the time that we worked together, Brian was absolutely desperate to sign the Searchers. He gave them work, tried to butter them up, genuinely loved their sound, but all to no avail. I do believe that the Searchers also wished to sign with NEMS, but were already committed elsewhere. He also thought that the idea of their signing with Pye Records was a bad move. Not only had Pye rejected the Beatles completely out of hand, but his own dealings with them, firstly through his NEMS outlets and then with Tommy Quickly, left him with the distinct impression that they couldn't sell snow to Eskimos. He bitterly complained to me one evening about the Searchers deal. He felt that 'Pye would lose interest in the group' and that 'Tony Hatch had little interest in them to begin with'. It became highly frustrating to me, watching from Germany during 1965 and 1966, to see that Brian's prophecies appeared to be coming true. But what a marvellous group; wouldn't it have been superb to have heard an album of the Searchers produced by George Martin? I think so.

As you can probably gather, I have very little time for the Pyes and Deccas of this world together with their smash-and-grab raids on Liverpool. In my view, for example, Peter Sullivan and Dick Rowe at Decca were both rather aimlessly looking for the musical middle of the road by ironically placing musical extremes on singers. Without any prior knowledge of precisely what or whom they were dealing with, Sullivan wanted Lee Curtis to be an out-and-out rocker whereas Rowe took exactly the opposite tack and wanted to turn my brother into a balladeer. Yes, the appeal of Lee Curtis was actually in his versatility but this was too much too soon. Taking him from a small combo sound with *Let's Stomp* to a fully orchestrated piece with Dick Rowe (*No Other Love* was, I believe, his last recording for Decca) in the space of twelve months was a case of dealing in musical extremis. Rowe is rightly presented in popular musical history as the man who did not sign the Beatles, even after Brian had paid Decca to provide that one-hour audition. What was it he said? 'Guitar groups are on their way out, Mr Epstein.' He learnt fast and signed the Rolling Stones after their audition, but only thanks to an introduction and encouragement from George. Ironic, one might say, that his son, Richard Rowe, made the deal to create a joint partnership with Michael Jackson to publish the Beatles' catalogue as Sony/ATV when he ran the publishing division of Sony Music.

For me, Decca were pissing in the wind for most of the 1960s. EMI, on the other hand, seemed to be able to delegate to individual labels with individual identities, meaning that these satellites of EMI performed rather like American independent labels. Each company, such as Parlophone, Columbia, HMV, had a maverick or two at the helm. If only we'd had one or two genuine independents, together with a couple of regional labels, the problems of recording with these out of touch giants would have been so much easier to avoid, and the process of breaking records into the big league so much more straightforward. The majors would simply have done as they did Stateside: scrutinise regional record-buying activity, look for the best-selling indie record and network it. As it was, majors openly conspired to put independent record companies out of business rather than support them, and even EMI lost artists in their mad rush to capitalise on anything and everything between 1962 and 1970; their motto? Well, according to that great jazz writer Donald Clarke: 'if enough shit hits the fan some of it is bound to stick.' To be honest, despite our collective desires for success, I think all of us managers and fans alike expressed a great deal of irony about actually making it in a southern-based and south-eastern-dominated music business. We all knew what we were up against right from the start, even though the very processes at work in Liverpool, Manchester, Birmingham and Newcastle, together with the great connections made in West Germany, were challenging this stultifying south-eastern-dominated entertainments hegemony.

It was when Granada Television first came on to the air in the mid-1950s and when films such as *A Kind of Loving*, *A Taste of Honey* and *Saturday Night and Sunday Morning* first started appearing on the cinema that I became aware of the public's attention being drawn towards the regions rather than away from them. Brian and I went together to see all of these gritty kitchen-sink films of the day, and we frequently discussed this interesting phenomenon with each other. I recollect Brian stating to me once in Manchester, after he had signed the Beatles, that the London-based industry simply had to take notice of us sooner or later. After all, he remarked, rock 'n' roll and R&B were evidently meaning something to young people in the regions. Had not John Lennon stated to both of us that, for him, prior to Elvis there was nothing and that Elvis was his father figure? In truth I was rather stunned and not a little saddened when John first said this, but I came to understand just how important all of this Americana really was to a group of teenagers being commercially patronised by this south-eastern-managed authority: the very root of meaning.

I do believe that it was precisely because of statements such as John's that the Beatles and the rest of the groups performing in the regions were able to become appropriate spokespersons and symbols for the society that evolved in the 1960s. Mainstream music being purveyed from London by the likes of Cliff Richard and Eden Kane was unable to speak to or relate with young people in quite the same way. And this became even more obvious to me when the London companies converged upon Liverpool, signed up myriad bands, and proceeded to ruin them. Company hacks Dick Rowe and Peter Sullivan at Decca, for example, didn't have any idea where the stimulus behind the All Stars sound was actually coming from; they had no earthly idea of what constituted this new sound in the regions; they were blissfully unaware of the fact that Lee was singing his repertoire of cover versions as a real expression of his social situation. I don't think they believed there was a United Kingdom north of Watford.

If, according to John Lennon, before Elvis there was indeed nothing, then to many of these young men and women Elvis, along with the apostles of rock such as Chuck, Carl, Jerry Lee and Buddy, together with those rock 'n' roll choirboys the Everly Brothers, were at the very root of musical expression; the explanation of existence, even. While Sullivan, Rowe, Hatch and the like simply saw Merseybeat as an attempt to plug the gap left by the ostracised rock singers of the late 1950s and the effective but declining Larry Parnes rockers of the early 1960s, Merseybeat was actually a visible and aural testament to the power and determination of selecting and representing otherness. Merseybeat was a covenant with the initial impact and impetus of rock in this country. It was a gesture of bravado, together with a desperate call for solidarity amongst those who understood it best of all: the young. To play Chuck Berry covers in a dance hall in Liverpool in 1962 was an open act of defiance to an out-of-touch industry that wished to interminably foist the next Gary Miller, Al Saxon or Darryl Quist upon them. These young people were having none of it and remained firmly entrenched in the rock of old (for old it most certainly was: to a 16-year-old in the early 1960s, 1955 seemed aeons ago). I admired these youngsters so much.

The 1950s had appeared to begin with a rather placid silent generation of young people: there were few illustrations of otherness. By the next decade, however, they had emerged as a loud, vociferous singing generation who refused to be coerced by the political economy of the country, even though some of them had derived benefit from it. Early rock stars like Elvis and Little Richard didn't aspire to create serious art: they were showmen and proud of it, but this commercial entertainment was momentous. It was able to express the needs and desires of ordinary people just as much as the intellectualised folk revival it sat alongside. Sadly, of course, our groups also became a testimony to the subsequent insensitivity of that very British recording industry of which I speak. The industry took not only the Beatles, but also groups like the Big Three, and tried to smarten them up musically and personally. The Beatles saw it coming, but as for the rest?

However, when the recording industry tapped into this marvellous resource, they placed new restrictions upon that sound. The Big Three on record, for example, never really sounded like the Big Three live. Lee Curtis and the All Stars never got a chance to sound like their former selves either and the Undertakers – another 'dodgy' deal with Pye – were shadows of their live selves. Perhaps this was all inevitable; perhaps it had to happen so that they were able to learn by this homogenisation process. However, I must admit that, after Brian had decided to leave Liverpool and throw in his lot with the faceless few surrounding Sir Joseph Lockwood and I had been mortified by the actions of Decca's house producers, my own brother and some of the musicians and singers signed to Carlton Brooke, the challenge of London and all that surrounded it began to look rather less than attractive. The root of my own personal meaning began to shift as I took a look around me and began to dislike what I saw, both in others and in myself. In early 1962, after the small matter of a run in with the Liverpool constabulary, I decided to burn my boats and leave for West Germany, Hamburg and the Star Club.

The police matter was something of a damp squib, to be honest, but nonetheless was rather alarming, and certainly a watershed at the time. The retail businesses in Kirkby were very good for me during the winter of 1962. I was spending vast amounts of cash at the Liverpool wholesale markets and seeing a very quick and profitable return as a consequence.

There seemed to be no holding the businesses back as Kirkby continued to expand without any semblance of proper retail facilities for the residents, other than my own. Kenny was also covering a great deal of ground in the mobile shop and was trading up almost as much as the fixed units. So I began to attract a lot of attention from wholesalers, merchandisers and the like looking for a good retail outlet to buy in bulk. Prices became very competitive as I was able to almost 'hold court' with the various wholesale traders around Liverpool and beyond. But my retail successes coupled with a wallet full of money (I always dealt in cash) began to attract the attentions of various characters from that other side of Liverpool: the dodgy traders, the fences and thieves.

Liverpool has always had a thriving black economy. There is nothing new about those who deal in stolen videos, drugs and illegally imported alcohol and tobacco. The items for sale might have changed somewhat over the years but, to me, there is a depressing familiarity about those involved in that kind of trade. Throughout the latter third of 1962 I was increasingly being approached by a variety of these shady customers. I could have purchased any amount of stolen cigarettes, liquor, furniture, even vehicles, at a fraction of the proper asking price and with no questions asked. I refused temptation on all counts. It might seem rather sanctimonious, but I never even considered dealing in stolen goods. Not only was it against my principles, but it was also uncalled for. I was doing very nicely trading via the proper channels, thank you very much. However, a word taken the wrong way at the Liverpool wholesale fruit and vegetable market one morning approaching Christmas 1962 almost placed me in unyielding difficulties. The potato harvest that year had not been good and prices for spuds were at an all-time high. In general conversation one morning at the market I was asked whether I would like to pay a little less for a hundred-sack consignment. Without asking further, and taking the comment as one would a speculative pipedream, I remarked, 'Well, of course, who wouldn't?' and then went about my business in the normal way, thinking no more of it.

Upon arriving home to Gardner Road that lunch time, I was met by a distressed Anne and an entire lorry load of potatoes placed up against my front and back doors. I was horrified. I quizzed Anne about the delivery, but she was utterly oblivious. Where had they come from? Who had sent them? I felt a sickly feeling in the pit of my stomach as, at that very moment, a black Wolsley police car turned swiftly into Gardner Road. My neighbours had rightly become suspicious and had contacted the police. Within minutes I had been asked to accompany the officers to the main

Bridewell to assist them with their enquiries concerning a lorry load of potatoes that had been stolen from the Liverpool fruit and veg market that very morning. Fortunately, Kenny had not yet returned to the flat, otherwise he would have accompanied me as well. When he did return a little later that afternoon he was immediately informed by Anne as to my whereabouts and approached our family solicitor (the man with whom I had shared a love-hate relationship for some years), Rex Makin.

I was questioned at length by the force but, after hours of solicitude, I was not formally charged. As the story unfolded, it became quite obvious to the police that I really had nothing to do with the criminal act itself, and they realised, I think, that although they could have charged me with receiving stolen goods, it would have been a rather pointless exercise with Makin behind me. I had obviously been duped. I left in a terrible state. I had to admit to myself that the whole episode alarmed and dejected me. It was not only the reverberant tone of the police investigators that made the experience so alien to me, nor the lack of self-confidence I must have expressed during the grilling, but more the thought that I was considered to be something of a low-life by the police themselves.

Through their investigations, they discovered that I was also involved in the nightlife of Liverpool and, jumping to conclusions, had decided to brand me something of a petty gangster. Even when I was allowed to go, they treated me with a deep level of suspicion. 'We shall be keeping an eye on your movements, in future, Mr Flannery,' one smart arse remarked as Rex and Kenny conveyed me out of the station towards the waiting taxi. 'How bloody dare they?' I retorted. 'Hold it, Joe, just leave them to their games,' pronounced Rex Makin. But I was very troubled indeed. In fact, the whole incident was a catalyst, a formidable occurrence, and one which galvanised me into action over the forthcoming few days. I contacted my greatest competitors for the sites in Kirkby, the well-respected fruit and veg merchants Waterworths, and duly informed them that the businesses were up for sale. They were, naturally, immediately interested and within a few short days a contract for the sale of all my business interests had been drawn up. I had decided to effectively end my business relationship with Liverpool. Lee Curtis and the All Stars were booked to play Hamburg's Reeperbahn in the New Year of 1963 and I was determined to make a go of this side of my life.

Typical of all things Joe Flannery, I suppose, the booking of Lee into the Star Club was far from straightforward. Following my return to Liverpool with Brian after our own 'lost weekend' I was determined to make the pieces fit and get Lee Curtis on to the Reeperbahn. But how was I to do it? Brian and I had been to a number of clubs: the Top Ten, the Colibri and other less salubrious knocking shops around the Grosse Freiheit. However, I was most impressed by that new club opened by Manfred Weissleder, namely the Star Club. This venture had a far greater capacity than any other club, easily seating as many as 1,500 punters. Weissleder confidently professed to us that his club was going to be one of the most fashionable music centres in Europe. He was determined to capitalise on this rise in German profile. I got the feeling that Manfred was determined to get Germany on the musical map, so to speak. So much so, in fact, that he had engaged American artists for 1962 and 1963 without even having a finished club to show to their agents. The likes of Fats Domino, the Everly Brothers, Brenda Lee, Jerry Lee Lewis, Little Richard and Gene Vincent had all been contracted. A few of these US rock 'n' rollers were considered a little over the hill back in the US (and in the UK, for that matter), but in Europe their lights still shone brightly.

The position of the club on the Grosse Freiheit was a good one, too, but what really struck Brian and I was the idea that it was to be a venue specifically for beat music. Bill Harry later described the Star Club, quite correctly in my opinion, as an early rock venue. He was making a distinction here, I think, between previous night clubs and jive hives of the late 1950s and early 1960s and the future of rock as a meritocratic state. Manfred recognised that beat music was in the ascendancy. Most other club owners and promoters merely saw it as another passing but profitable phase. Brian, of course, had already been persuaded by copious amounts of cash to let the Beatles perform at the club and Weissleder had already sent Horst Fascher and British rock band leader Roy Young (Young, like Tony Sheridan, was one of those early British musical exports to Hamburg) to Liverpool in January 1962 to book as many Liverpool groups as possible. Neither Kenny nor I had been available to speak to either of them during this visit, owing to my business commitments, and I received the sharp end of my brother's tongue for missing a golden opportunity.

So, after returning from Hamburg that spring, I made a direct call to Horst Fascher to suggest Lee Curtis and the All Stars for the Star Club. The phone call, however, did not go to plan. Horst was very charming but was not going to commit to an unseen band. I foolishly tried to convince him that he had already seen my brother playing in Liverpool on a previous visit, but he wouldn't be duped. Horst later told me that although he regarded himself quite rightly as a great champion of Merseybeat, he was also becoming worried about a glut of average Liverpool groups demanding disproportionate fees. A familiar story, such apprehension later proved to be correct, of course. I was very disappointed after the phone discussion, but not put off. I simply dared not go back to my brother and tell him I had failed. I rang the Star Club again later that day. This time I was able to convince Horst via my own enthusiasm that Lee Curtis was at least worth looking at. He concurred but remained unconvinced about parting with any money. I decided to throw in a challenge.

'What if I brought the group over at my own expense for one week's work?'

There was a pregnant silence at the other end of the line: 'You mean you will pay?'

'Yes, Herr Fascher, I will pay, but if you decide the group are good, and want to rebook them, you must then pay them for any future engagements.'

'Well Joe, if you are so convinced that your boys are that good, how can I refuse? We cannot lose … I will arrange a week for the All Stars and will send you the contracts. I will be in touch soon. Of course I will have to confirm our conversation with Herr Weissleder; however, I do not think there will be any complications. I will write to you very soon.'

I sat back in my favourite armchair at Gardner Road, relieved that I'd done it – but exactly what had I done? This was going to be an expensive exercise. Obviously the band were very excited when I told them later that day: even though Anne's daughter Girda was present that day as eye candy, the lads didn't hang around for long and shot around to the ABC Bowling Alley for an impromptu celebration. However, when I discussed the deal with Kenny he was rather less than enthusiastic. He supported me in principle but challenged my acumen somewhat. After all, he argued, it would cost a great deal of money and there was no guarantee that the band would be deemed good enough or even suitable for a venue such as the Star Club. It all seemed rather iffy to him but he gave me his blessing while stating that he would stay at home to keep things going on that front. The contracts duly arrived from Germany within a week or so, stating that Lee Curtis and the All Stars were to play the Star Club the following March 1963 (I flew out on the 19th); I must admit that I was a little frustrated for March seemed so far away. But, as things turned out, my brush with the law during the winter of 1962/63, together with the moderate success of the Beatles' *Love Me Do*, focused my attention on Hamburg. How does it go? 'The Lord giveth and the Lord taketh away.'

11

GERMANY CALLING

IN THE LATE nineteenth century the Grosse Freiheit was not policed at all. There were drinking houses a-plenty and St Pauli was a kind of no-go area. Harbour workers and local civil servants used to meet on the Grosse Freiheit at weekends. In Hause 39 (later the premises which housed the Star Club) dancing and political meetings took place. During the 1920s the local communist party used to meet there (but not for long, I suspect). It was after the war, when St Pauli was only loosely governed as part of the British sector of occupied Germany, that it became a black spot, from necessity, probably, for the locals were often starving and without adequate food or shelter. Things had improved somewhat by 1949, however, and Hause 39 became a cinema. It was this cinema (Stern Kino) that Manfred Weissleder purchased and, making only a few alterations and improvements, he turned it into the Star Club. As luck would have it, by the time we embarked upon our first visit to Hamburg, Merseybeat had been recognised as the British new wave of popular music (and not simply a cheap supply of Liverpool rock bands for Hamburg), and had quickly spread to the continent via good old Radio Luxembourg. Following the success of *Love Me Do, Please Please Me* really opened things up in January 1963 and by March Gerry and the Pacemakers (another Hamburg favourite) were also on their way to the top of the charts with *How Do You Do It?*

Lee Curtis and the All Stars were in the throes of recording their first single for Decca, having been signed by Dick Rowe and Peter Sullivan in the wake of national interest in all things Liverpudlian. This was all great news, of course, to pre-empt our first visit to what was now the hottest venue in Europe, but I was unable to capitalise on it all. In fact, you may remember that it was costing me money. The previous summer of 1962, when I had informed Horst Fascher that we would be performing essentially for free, seemed light years ago. I had signed the agreement, however, and it was all sewn up. Now we were expected in West Germany as a main attraction, all courtesy of yours truly. Still, I couldn't really complain. Nobody was to know just how quickly the music business was to change over Christmas 1962. We knew something ought to happen, that the London cartel had to be challenged, but little did we think that practically all the young people in the country thought the same.

Kenny duly stayed at home to look after the sale of the shops in Kirkby as Lee Curtis and the All Stars arrived in Hamburg on 19 March 1963, together, of course, with Pete Best as percussionist – a draw in himself – and we were booked to play one week at the Star Club. The band was scheduled to play four one-hour sets per evening for which they would receive all payments and expenses from me. I had kept it from them that I would be footing the bill. It didn't seem appropriate to tell them that they were ostensibly giving their services free of charge. After all, they were becoming a name group which had inflated both their fees and egos back home. To tell them that they were effectively 'on approval' would have been cruel, and would probably have had an adverse effect on their performances. That was the last thing we needed, for the band was buzzing.

It was truly fascinating watching the group at work and play that week. Pete Best played the experienced old hand role to the full, whereas Lee, Wayne, Frank and Tony were like immature boys let loose into the real world. That world included sexual deviation of every conceivable nature, a few drugs and copious amounts of alcohol, the chief intoxicant at that time. Despite Pete's so-called experience, however, he fell foul of the Reeperbahn in no uncertain manner. I became aware halfway through the week that he was besotted with a local girl. She was a regular at the club, a real stunner and totally worth the effort. However, towards the end of the week things must have got a little serious in the trouser department for, to Mr Best's surprise (and anguish no doubt), he discovered that she was a transvestite. So much for the worldly ex-Beatle!

Groupies, of course, had a large role to play in the Star Club, male and female; in fact the management encouraged them. Pretty girls didn't have to pay to get in. The girls who were rather less fortunate paid and sat at the back of the club. It was only 50 pfennigs to begin with but, as the club's popularity grew, so did the entrance fee, which by the time I left for Liverpool in 1967 was 10 marks – but of course band fees had risen extraordinarily by this time, which contributed to the venue's decline. Many of the girls were prostitutes but didn't charge groups for their services. So, the band certainly earned their spurs that week. As for my brother, what more needs to be said other than he was a randy sod who worried me greatly. In that one week he was rampant, despite being by this time a family man back in Liverpool. Astrid Kirchherr, that pale-skinned, blonde beauty who became engaged to Stuart Sutcliffe, loved the band and she, Lee and I became good friends. Indeed the 'Exies' (Existentialists), which included Klaus Voorman and Frank Dostal, attended most of the late evening performances of the All Stars that week. Interestingly enough as I look back on these days, the Exies were clearly significant in the popularity of Liverpool bands in Hamburg. However, it is always amusing when I think of how young German popular music fans would have reacted to a group called the Beatles in Germany, for most Germans use a very soft 'b' which sounds rather like a 'p'. In German the group appeared to be called The Peatles, and this is German vernacular for a penis. Therefore, it could be argued, music aside, that the Beatles were popular amongst the Exies because they were pricks – just a thought!

On stage the band were really cooking on gas. For the entire week Lee and the All Stars showed what all the fuss had been about back in Liverpool. Playing high energy rock 'n' roll mixed with a fair smattering of ballads, they grew in stature every night and by the final performance that weekend they were not allowed to leave the stage until 4 in the morning. To be honest, they didn't want to come off the stage either. The thought of returning to their grotty rooms and then back to Liverpool was beginning to fill them with dread. Towards the end of the last set, the call came from Manfred Weissleder to meet in his office. I was standing in the wings of the stage, across from the massive backdrop of the Manhattan skyline, when I was informed politely but very firmly that he wished to see me right away. I followed my escort to the rear of the Star Club balcony, past a door which led to the Erotica Film Club, where Herr Weissleder apparently indulged his pornographic movie fetish, and then continued up the staircase to another floor which, at that time, housed Manfred's office and apartment. I had only spoken briefly to him before for he had previously left all negotiations and small talk to his lieutenant Horst Fascher. The great man began to speak in perfect Germanic English: 'Well Herr Flannery, your combo has been a great success.'

'Yes, Herr Weissleder,' I replied. 'I told Horst that I wouldn't let you down.' I remembered my words to Joe Loss from almost a decade previously and was aware that I was stuttering rather nervously. It was all more than a little intimidating.

'In that case, Herr Flannery,' came the reply, 'what would you say if I was to offer the group an extension to their stay with us? We can make sure that the authorities are kept fully informed; I can guarantee that there would be no problems with visas.'

I was stunned, but overjoyed and replied, 'I would be delighted, of course, Herr Weissleder, but I simply have to go back to Liverpool tomorrow – business, you know. Who would look after them, make sure they behaved themselves? They are young men after all!'

A third voice joined in from the area of the still-open door; I hadn't noticed Horst enter the room: 'Joe, that is what I'm here for: I look after all our English groups. They are good, let us keep them a little longer.'

'How much longer?' I enquired.

Herr Weissleder directly replied, 'We do not usually do this Joe, but your group and the Liverpool sounds are the hottest thing to hit Germany in a long time. I would say that they could even rival Tony Sheridan here. We want to keep that boiling as long as we can. I think that we have lost the Beatles now. Herr Epstein does not think that they will be visiting us this year at any price. If we cannot get the Beatles, we must have a Beatle group from Liverpool. Horst tells me that the All Stars are the best group that he has seen at the Star Club. I am prepared to offer them a whole month here.'

'Immediately?' I gasped.

'Yes, immediately,' came the reply.

'Well I shall have to talk to the group. Lee is expected home in a day or two–' I dared not tell Manfred that Lee was married '–But if they are agreeable, then I am also. And thank you very much for trusting my word … they could have been a load of rubbish.' I added this last stupid comment in a thunderstruck state, biting my lip.

'No, I don't think so, Joe,' replied Horst. 'We made a few discreet enquiries about you after your visit to Hamburg with Herr Epstein – we also found your starting offer last summer very equitable. We knew that you would not let us down. Brian Epstein speaks very highly of you.'

'Well, thanks, that is good to know,' I replied, rather flushed with embarrassment by his openness.

'Herr Epstein also told us that he would very much like to manage Lee Curtis,' Horst laughed.

'Is that so?' I was rather taken aback.

'Yes, he told us that little piece of information some months ago, but he also said that he would not dream of disrupting anything at Carlton Brooke, at least for the moment,' stated Manfred Weissleder.

'Well, how gracious of him,' I rejoined. 'Thanks again gentlemen for your trust and information. I shall speak to the group as soon as they come off stage.'

'One more thing, Joe … I can call you Joe, yes?' Manfred called me back as I was about to exit down the stairs to the Star Club. 'How much has this little excursion cost you?'

'Well, all in all, exactly £98 17s 3d,' I replied.

They were convulsed with laughter. 'You will be fully reimbursed … see the bookkeeper first thing in the morning,' was Manfred's parting shot.

I left. My heart was pounding. It had worked; it had worked. And I wasn't even going to be a pfennig out of pocket. They liked the group and they liked me. They were reasonable men: now to let the lads know of the good news.

I really didn't want to leave them all and return to Liverpool. The week had been such a roaring success that I was loath to leave it behind. Not only that, but the new deal Manfred had spoken of was more akin to Beatles money: in the region of 500 marks. There was evidently great potential for the band in Germany and it was this part of the equation that occupied my thoughts as I slipped away next morning (after a visit to Manfred's cashier) to catch the train and then boat back to England – I hadn't booked a return flight, realising that there might be one or two twists and turns before returning home. The band would now follow me in a month's time in the second-hand Commer van that I had purchased for them prior to the trip. There were no farewells: they were sleeping (or something!), becoming acclimatised to the nocturnal work practices of the Reeperbahn. On the return journey my thoughts turned to that 15 year old who had been so disappointed after we'd left her behind to go to Germany a week previously: Beryl Marsden.

The band returned home in late April, with all parts of their respective anatomies enlarged, no doubt; not only their heads but probably their 'Peatles' too. They were not allowed to rest, however, for their exploits (at least those on the stage of the Star Club) had been duly noted by the Liverpool music press, ensuring plenty of bookings. In addition, they had a record to promote. Both Lee and Pete Best were ecstatic about this: my brother, naturally, because it was his voice on the record; Pete because it was effectively two fingers to the Beatles. There was a serious problem over that first recording, however. Decca had decided to release two tracks from the February recording session (*Little Girl* and *Just One More Dance*) as a single while the band were away in Germany. Some bright spark at Decca had decided that the best way to capitalise on the Mersey sound was to release something as soon as possible. They never consulted me at all about the whereabouts of the group. So the single *Little Girl* was released in March 1963 minus a group to promote it until the following month: far too late, especially that year when the musical tide was changing by the week. I was badly shaken by this fiasco.

Furthermore, our working relationship with Rowe at Decca was never good and, as previously stated, steadily deteriorated throughout the summer of 1963. To his credit, Lee knew what numbers would serve him best and which songs were not effective from a recording point of view, and he and I constantly made suggestions to Rowe and Peter Sullivan about potential Lee Curtis singles for that year. With a voice like Lee's it should have been obvious that some of the great R&B floor shakers would have been best suited. But we were apparently just ignorant northerners – what did we know? For example, we suggested *Twist and Shout*, but Rowe said no, stating that the Beatles had made it their own. Yet by May Decca (no less) had released an inferior version by Brian Poole and the Tremeloes, and it eventually spent fourteen weeks in the charts, finally peaking at number 4. I then suggested that Lee's superb version of *Money* ought to be considered. Even though the Beatles did that one too, the song was a Merseybeat classic by 1963. Rowe and Sullivan derided this idea, stating that it was already too well known; yet by November 1963 Bern Elliot and the Fenmen were also enjoying time on the charts with that very song, courtesy of Decca Records. Lee then suggested one of the band's best live tracks, *Shout*, the old Isley Brothers number. The Beatles had also used this song but had stopped performing it the previous year. We argued that it was only a matter of time before it would be a hit for somebody. Decca once again refused our pleas, and then released the song the following May by the Glaswegians Lulu and the Luvvers. Even when Lee changed tack and suggested the ballad *It's Only Make Believe* they refused (laughed as I recall) and then promptly gave it to Billy Fury (also on Decca, of course). It was a litany of non-compliance, but they must have loved our tastes in music.

Little Girl was only a very average song. Lee and I thought it was pleasant, but little more than a ditty. Yet with the right release together with a little promotion it probably would have reached the lower rungs of the charts (which would have been quite acceptable for a debut single). However, with Decca falling over themselves attempting to capitalise on Mersey-anything that year, they foolishly neglected the one thing that could have helped them: a personal appearance by the 'fab-gear' Lee Curtis. The single now remains a limpid example of the artist, technically a failure, while the live power of the group at their peak that year is lost forever in the mists of time.

One incident which occurred during that spring to lift my spirits somewhat was an article from Judith Symons in the 'Go Go Go' column of the *Daily Express*, which was entitled: 'Why that Scouse sound has knocked the others for six'. Judith was kind enough to interview me and then discuss in print how I had sold my greengrocery chain to become a full-time promoter on Merseyside, and how I was helping to take the 'Liverpool Sound' to Germany. The article had its degree of invention, suggesting that I had once been on the dole (I have never drawn dole in my life); however, the general tenor was accurate in that Hamburg club promoters far preferred Liverpool groups to those from London, and that back in Liverpool what was once friendly rivalry had turned to serious competition. There was a photograph of me adjacent to that week's top twenty listing, at the top of which was the Beatles' *From Me to You*, which was nice.

Just how I ended up being 'employed' by Manfred Weissleder is a complicated affair. The basic logistics of the situation, however, were as follows. Shortly after I had gone to Germany with Brian in 1962 as manager of Lee Curtis and the All Stars, Horst Fascher had been poached by Weissleder for his Star Club enterprise. The Star Club, opened in 1962, was deliberately designed to wipe out any competition from the rest of the Reeperbahn and effectively make Manfred top dog in St Pauli. This had largely been achieved by 1963 and the Star Club was the rage of Europe, attracting not only the Beatles and the best of British R&B bands, but also any visiting American performers too. Previously, however, the one thorn in Manfred's side was Horst. He was the heavyweight on the Reeperbahn and, although nominally employed as a bouncer by Bruno Koschmider and then Peter Eckhorn, he threw his weight around in more ways than one. He had a fearsome reputation in the area, not simply for violence but also for attracting female clientele into the clubs, dealing in a variety of contraband items, and having a thriving protection racket. Indeed, his gang Der Hoddles, made up of former boxers, was notorious.

THE DECCA RECORD COMPANY LIMITED

DECCA HOUSE · 9 ALBERT EMBANKMENT · LONDON · S·E·1

TELEPHONE: RELIANCE 8111 (34 LINES)   TELEGRAMS: DECCORD, LONDON, S.E.1.   CABLES: DECCORD, LONDON   TELEX 28588, LONDON

Please reply to
ARTISTS DEPARTMENT

EPX
VK/
JM

30th July, 1963.

The Manager,
CARLTON-BROOKE AGENCY,
26 Slater Street,
Liverpool, 1.

Dear Sir,

We have pleasure in attaching hereto cheque value £48.-.-d.
in payment of your account rendered in respect of
~~the~~ the following:-

  All Star Rhythm Group @ £7. each per session
           ....£28.-.-d.
   Expenses @ £5. per person ....£20.-.-d.

recorded by LEE CURTIS on the 7th June, 1963.

Kind regards,

Yours sincerely,
THE DECCA RECORD CO. LTD.

Irene King

Artists Department.

DIRECTORS
SIR EDWARD LEWIS (Chairman) J. GRAY, M.C., C.A., M.I.Ex. A. C. W. HADDY H. C. LAMBERT, F.C.A.
M. A. ROSENGARTEN (Swiss) H. F. SCHWARZ (U.S.A.) W. W. TOWNSLEY

A letter from Decca Records with payment for Lee Curtis and the All Stars'
recording session in June 1963. (Author's collection)

Horst, however, had proven to be very popular with the visiting British groups and, level headed and dependable, had given them his protection ostensibly free of charge. Now, this was a very astute move on his behalf. Whomsoever could look after the British bands, ensure their safety and make sure they appeared on time and in good condition every night was in great demand from the few influential club owners the length of the Reeperbahn. Horst's efficiency in controlling both bands and trouble in the clubs had led to Peter Eckhorn poaching him from Bruno Koschmider in the first place. The Top Ten Club was opened by Eckhorn in 1960 and, along with Horst, various club personnel, together with Tony Sheridan and the Jets, were poached by Peter. Bruno was not a happy bunny, but Horst's power in the area dictated that Bruno could not get his own back in the way considered honourable – i.e. through violence – for one was bound to lose such an argument with Horst. In truth, the club owners themselves were more than a little frightened of the man. I detected from an early stage that it was advisable as a manager from Liverpool to follow Horst's progress along the Reeperbahn very closely indeed. One needed to know who had become his enemy and why, and who he was working for. He was stubby, rather confident and yet curiously self-effacing and genial. He certainly didn't look like a man who was organising a protection racket in one of the most dangerous cities in Europe.

I got to know Horst well. Fortunately, he loved seeing Lee Curtis perform and considered him to be one of the top attractions on the Reeperbahn. He treated us all very well and during that trip in 1963 we wanted for very little. But Horst was only ever a short distance away from danger. During our residency at the Star Club in 1963, he was convicted of manslaughter and placed behind bars for five years. Manfred Weissleder was bereft. Not only had he lost a very useful lieutenant in Horst, but also the direct influence of the most important enforcer in St Pauli. He was afraid that Horst's enemies, of whom there were many, might muscle in on his territory. It soon became obvious that this could never be possible as Horst showed Manfred that he was still an effective enforcer from prison, whatever the inconvenience. The day-to-day running of affairs was, however, another matter altogether. Of all the people with whom one might suggest Manfred replace Horst, positively the very last person would be me! But sure enough, and on Horst's recommendation no less, Manfred approached me to take over the direct running of the Star Club and also to assist him in his growing franchise of the Star Club name across West Germany. In truth, he was not intending that I should replace Horst at all. No, Manfred wanted me to act as his PA, talent spotter back in England and as stage manager at the club. Having burned my bridges back in Liverpool, I readily accepted the offer over expensive German coffee and cake in the patisserie opposite the Hotel Europa. My working title was 'Artist Booking Manager'. A new era had evidently dawned, but what had I let myself in for?

My first experience acting for Manfred as his club manager was almost my last. Manfred had booked Brenda Lee but, for reasons known only to him, was not taken with the artiste. Manfred might have previously been a member of the Hitler Youth and now owned half of the Grosse Freiheit, but he had come up against quite an adversary in Brenda Lee: she was not called Little Miss Dynamite for nothing. The disharmony was exasperated by the fact that Brenda's shows had been running too short, which displeased Manfred and on the evening of her last show for the Star Club he was waiting for her to come off stage five minutes early in order to repudiate her contract and, thus, her fee. I heartily disapproved of such tactics and so, as stage manager that night I passed a hastily written note to Brenda as I heard her announce her last song. The billet-doux informed her that she had to keep going for at least another ten minutes, otherwise she would invalidate her contract with the Star Club. Brenda understood the problem and eventually went three minutes over her allotted time. Manfred was furious.

Brenda was very grateful but, as she was leaving for her Pan Am flight later that day, I did tell her that she was the lucky one. She could leave whereas I had to stay and face the music with Herr Weissleder. The subsequent post-mortem was a potent reminder of the man's latent power. He told me coldly and effectively that my first responsibility was now with the Star Club. 'Money doesn't talk, Joe,' he stated. 'It shouts.' And despite a good-natured comment that he actually respected my morals, he left me in no doubt that he didn't buy my perspective at all: 'Joe, you think you are right; I know I am right. Next time around I expect you to match the resolution with the artiste. For the Star Club, Brenda Lee had been what Americans call a pain in the ass – you cannot indulge yourself in such value-free judgements.'

Manfred was far happier with Lee Curtis, however. Indeed, for many years a large picture of Lee Curtis looked down upon the performers and punters from the balcony of the Star Club, such was his appeal. And how he earned it! A typical performing day for Lee would begin at 4 in the afternoon with an hour's slot followed by a three-hour break, while another three groups would perform. He would then be back on stage between 7 p.m. and 8 p.m., followed by another break until 11 p.m. He would then be back on stage until it was deemed time to come off. This could be after an hour; it could be until the early hours of the morning – it just depended upon the bill and/or the punters. He would get through five shirts every night.

Once I commenced my booking trips back to London and Liverpool in search of bands to play the Star Club during the summer of 1963, it soon became apparent to me that the pop scene that I had known back in Liverpool (or at least the one I thought I had known) was already changing. Being ensconced in West Germany, I was always aware that recent developments might be passing me by. The year 1963 belonged to our Liverpool groups, as we had predicted, but when I came to work for Manfred in my capacity as freelance booking manager I realised immediately that even the apparently revolutionary Merseybeat movement was to be short-lived. British popular music fashions had started to move at an incredibly fast pace. No sooner had Merseybeat peaked than it was deemed horribly unfashionable by the music inkies. Indeed, it was already being replaced back in England by another, raunchier sound.

While I had previously thought that the likes of the Roadrunners and the Rolling Stones had just been noisier versions of the Beatles, I soon came to realise that this harder R&B sound was the tip of an enormous iceberg of dedicated talent interested in using the blues to extend their musical abilities; the beginnings, indeed, of a future British rock meritocracy. As I previously intimated, Beryl Marsden had certainly seen it coming. She informed me that the blues scene was creating an entirely new hierarchy of musicians and she thought that the possibilities of Lee now making it back in Britain were minimal. After a very salutary visit to London in the autumn of 1963, on the lookout for talent for the Star Club, I could only agree. I witnessed a storming set from the Yardbirds at the Marquee in Soho, which convinced me that there was no turning back. I knew that any failure to recognise this watershed on my behalf would result in financial disaster for the Star Club. The Yardbirds were also followed around by a small but rabidly anti-commercial crowd. Students, beatniks and mods, and I had to recognise that there was a clear generational and cultural gap widening by the day. One year previously the mainstream had been prepared to accept the Beatles as the new hope; now this lot were making the music that was coming out of Liverpool old hat. There was also a clear affinity between the old folk intellectualism and new pop music. This group, and their fans, were taking themselves very seriously indeed.

By the time Brian Epstein had contacted me during September 1963, suggesting that I should join him in NEMS at his new offices in London, I already realised that despite the growing popularity of all things Beatles, the city of Liverpool was receding back into provincial obscurity via, oddly, overexposure. I hadn't heard from Brian for a few months and was delighted to meet him again. He had an immense joie de vivre at this stage and was looking forward to a New Year's trip to the US with his boys. His style as a businessman had developed exquisitely. He had become an extremely careful man in word and deed. He now measured his sentences very carefully, never saying or doing anything that wasn't pre-thought. Totally preoccupied with the Beatles, he was also now unbelievably ambitious and I got the impression from him, as we sat in his Moorfields offices prior to his move to London, that he was attempting to take himself very seriously indeed. It seemed light years since we had been driving around Liverpool in his little car, eating pies at the Pier Head, waiting to hear *Love Me Do* on Radio Luxembourg, and yet it was barely twelve months ago.

He repeated his interest in bringing Beryl and Lee into the NEMS stable, with he and I joining forces once and for all. I was very flattered and tempted, particularly after the previous six months in Germany, but I knew that Lee would have none of it. He remained convinced that Brian had a sexual interest in him and his homophobia at the time, like his ego and libido, had increased during his time in Germany; there was no point in even discussing the matter with him. Sadly, without Lee Curtis and the All Stars my roster looked pretty paltry to say the least and so I knew that Brian was indeed still interested in Lee as much as me. During our conversation Brian continued to affirm that, despite the move, he was still firmly committed to Liverpool; but I detected from his tone that he had been well and truly romanced by London. He had also gone way beyond considering the music from the standpoint of the fans and bands he claimed to represent. His approach was already obviously more focused upon professional decisions rather than aesthetic judgements. I was amazed to discover just how much he had picked up about recording methods, producers, arrangers and other industrial minutiae. I suppose that I shouldn't have been so amazed; after all, he was the perfect example of a musical magpie. Brian was able to learn by listening and watching: that's all he had ever done, really, and once he had moved beyond anything I could show him he just kept picking up more and more shiny bits and pieces in London.

Listening to Brian in his soon to be abandoned Moorfields office that autumn was a pure experience. At times previously he had been vague to the point of irritation, but now he was very systematic. He had finally developed that critical faculty for which he had searched all his young life. The Beatles had liberated him in a way that nothing else could. I was so pleased for him. Yet, while acknowledging its inevitability, I also deeply regretted his forthcoming move to London. I couldn't blame him, of course; after all, how on earth was one to perpetuate a flourishing music scene in a provincial backwater once the initial impact had died down and the London A&R men had had their pickings? Nevertheless, I felt, as did a good many Liverpudlians at the time, that elevating Merseybeat by placing it into a broader social context was also an act of defalcation.

Brian also told me that day that he felt the Liverpudlian attitude was proving Merseybeat's undoing. The bands' parochial chauvinism towards the south-eastern-dominated industry was already legend by 1963 and, of course, whenever the time arose to do business, they proved intransigent negotiators. I agreed. In fact, from my vantage point in Germany the whole Merseybeat phenomenon did have its downside. For many Liverpool bands coming over to the Star Club by 1963 it was a case of 'we are right, you are wrong; we saved rock 'n' roll, you didn't'. Eventually, by the mid-1960s, there would be interminable arguments about the most ridiculous of things, and Manfred grew so tired of Liverpool groups to the extent that with a few notable exceptions, he would prefer me not to book them. Yet again I was reminded of those words of Russ Conway concerning egos.

So, as long as Lee Curtis remained popular as a live performer in Germany with the impending probability of a recoding deal via Manfred's own Star Club moniker with Philips, I was happy to see him prosper there, and I graciously declined Brian's final entreaty for NEMS and Carlton Brooke to combine, while also accepting a lucrative booking for the Remo Four to come to the Star Club. It would be some months again before our paths crossed. My decision seemed a good one when it was reported to me that in my absence Manfred had allowed a pennant to be flown right across the Grosse Freiheit advertising Lee Curtis and the All Stars. This was something that he would normally restrict to visiting American stars like Fats Domino or Brenda Lee. I felt vindicated. The problem with placing the Curtis eggs firmly in the German basket was that, as his appearances in Germany increased, so his absence from Britain also extended, placing him further and further back in the minds of potential record purchasers.

Together with the aforementioned problems of production and A&R at Decca, Lee was becoming increasingly frustrated by his decreasing visibility in the UK. We could both see that the potential market for his style of singing lay in Europe. I could also see that the likes of the Yardbirds and John Mayall were narrowing the field at home, and yet we both also agonised about that elusive hit single in Britain.

It was never to come. We had a further release on Decca in between our visits to Germany. *Little Girl* was followed during the early summer by a cover of Bobby Comstock's *Let's Stomp*, which Lee hated. As previously stated, neither could capture the magic of an All Stars live performance and neither was suitably promoted. It seemed to me that by the latter months of 1963 his future lay securely in Europe. This was confirmed to me when the *Mersey Beat* poll of December 1963 contained no sign of Lee Curtis and the All Stars. The fact remains, of course, that being in Hamburg played havoc with Kenny and I filling in all of the poll cards, as we had done the previous year.

In any case, by the end of 1963, I was physically and emotionally exhausted, and after returning to Liverpool once again that November, I was rushed to hospital with suspected pneumonia. I spent a very frustrating couple of months in a hospital in south Liverpool. They say one always remembers where one was when Kennedy was assassinated: in my case, it was flat on my back in the male ward of Mossley Hill Hospital next to Sir Douglas Crawford's palatial abode. I was back on my feet by the time Lee's third Decca single, *What About Me*, was finally released in February 1964. Despite my intervention wherever possible, the disc raised very little interest among the British record-buying public, although demand for the single from Germany was so intense that copies were imported into the country (yet still Decca didn't officially release the damn thing in Germany). I was offered the services of a record hyper and seriously considered his offer over dinner. However, he wanted £500 and it was simply too much, and the record too weak and misrepresentative of Lee's work; by the end of the meal, I thanked him but respectfully declined. British sales being disappointing, Decca's option on further Lee Curtis releases was not picked up during 1964, and via the Manfred Weissleder Star Club label, we immediately signed to Philips, thereupon somewhat reluctantly concentrating only on the German market.

Not that we had an enormous amount of success, record-wise, in Germany, to be honest. The deal that Manfred agreed with Philips was rather flimsy and promotion was firmly placed at our door. I certainly had no idea at that time about promoting records. Indeed, occasionally I wondered why I had landed myself in such an uncharted area. Nevertheless, Lee enjoyed some small success with *Ecstasy* towards the end of 1964. This song was specifically recorded for the German market and oddly became a 'Record of the Week' on Radio Caroline, the pirate radio station broadcasting into Britain. Philips, however, didn't realise that the disc had potential in Britain and delayed its release until the Christmas holidays, whereupon it was lost in the deluge of novelty releases one normally associates with that period. There was also a Lee Curtis album released in Germany by Philips on the Star Club label which actually sold well over a long period of time without ever troubling the German album charts, as such. It's a testament to his popularity, and Decca's blunder, that all of his German recordings have been reformatted on to CD and continue to be rereleased and updated on the continent. And he continues to prove a popular attraction over there, despite British success eluding him.

Although the winter trip back to Merseyside in 1963 resulted in my incapacitation, Lee Curtis and the All Stars were not left wanting. They too returned home after their successful stint at the Star Club and, although rumour had it that I had let them go to another agency because of my own ill health, the truth was that I was organising their gigs from the ward of Mossley Hill Hospital. Kenny was a real brick at this time, covering the ground of two men. This odd lacuna also brought me together with another act that was to prove popular in Germany without making so much as a ripple over in Britain, namely the Liverbirds.

12

LIVERBIRDS IN LOVE: THE DECLINE AND FALL OF CARLTON BROOKE

WHILE BECOMING VERY excited about bringing one act (the Liverbirds) to the Star Club for the beginning of the New Year 1964, I was fully expecting to lose another of my acts. I had heard on the grapevine that all was not well with the All Stars. They had also returned home and Kenny and I had found them plenty of bookings over the Christmas break. Lee and the boys didn't want to stay in Germany for the festive season. Although the money was fantastic, it was terribly lonely, very cold and incredibly depressing in and around the St Pauli district at that time of year. Christmas in Germany has always been a family affair. Lee was also married to a Liverpool girl and was expecting a child.

There was dissent in the ranks, however, and Brian Epstein rang to inform me that the All Stars had approached NEMS for a management deal without Lee Curtis. Their approach was, of course, rebuffed and I was pleased that NEMS snubbed them. Immediately I realised that the end was nigh for the band. Not only did it seem a preposterous act of contrition for Pete Best to approach the man that had sacked him from the Beatles, but it was doubly tiresome for them to do it without Lee Curtis, the only Carlton Brooke artist that Brian Epstein actually wanted to sign. It became quite clear to me over the Christmas period that the All Stars had finally run dry on being a backing band to an egomaniac such as my brother and that they also saw Best as the focal point for a higher profile. On the surface, the All Stars deal had looked very sound. There was plenty of money for all, but the discord to which I previously alluded had carried on for months during

1963. I had even managed to get Lee on the George Cooper-promoted Ronettes, Rolling Stones and Dee Dee Sharpe tour for 1964, but the band was evidently not happy. Tony Waddington, Wayne Bickerton, Frank Bowen and Pete Best had experienced enough with Lee Curtis.

One morning in our new Slater Street offices in Liverpool, where the bands would meet in the morning to be allocated their gigs (no longer at Gardner Road), Kenny and I expected the All Stars, but they failed to show up. Within days we learnt that the Pete Best All Stars were now available for bookings, care of Mona Best. Upon hearing this news it all made perfect sense to me: Brian's worries about interference, Pete's removal, Mona's phone calls. The All Stars were now a vehicle for Pete and Mona was now manager. She was back in the frame once again and instead of destroying the Beatles for the sake of her son she had destroyed Lee Curtis and the All Stars. We had to re-form the All Stars immediately for there were gigs to be played over Christmas, the Ronettes et al. tour in the New Year and then back to Germany by February. Predictably Decca were in for the Pete Best All Stars like a shot and a singles deal was signed in January 1964. Equally predictably, nothing came of the deal. A pathetic cover of *I'm Gonna Knock on Your Door*, if my memory serves me correctly, followed by a change of name to the Pete Best Four in April and a disastrous excursion to the United States only served to galvanise Wayne and Tony into moving into song writing and production, which they duly did with some success. By March the following year the Pete Best Combo, as it was now called, became extinct. I wasn't bitter. Most importantly Wayne and Tony had discovered their professional salvation in pop music. Both were driven not only by the music but also by the thought of becoming moguls. They expanded their roles and carved out unique and powerful positions in the years that followed; Wayne eventually headed up the immensely powerful Performing Rights Society for some years. Pete's experiences in the pop boot camp were of a more salutary nature but he was eventually able to live within the shadow of the Beatles quite comfortably and much later was able to reap the rewards of the Fab Four's unending popularity when a track on the best-selling *Anthology* series included him on drums. The royalties ensured a peaceful and contented second childhood. We remain friends to this day.

Meanwhile, the new All Stars consisted of Paul Pilnick, who later went on to great success with Stealers Wheel; Piggie the acetate and vinyl presser, who would sign his pressings with the moniker 'Porkie's'; John Puddifer; and Mushy. This line-up lasted about twelve months and was later augmented at various times by Joe Walsh, Mike Cummings, Mike Banks and a guy by the name of Simon, who later became a DJ on the Reeperbahn for the Revolution Club. In truth, the later All Stars became the backing band that Kenny, Lee and I always wanted. They were professional but unremarkable: very unlike the original All Stars who were individually greater than the sum total of the All Stars name. They were perhaps a degree or two less talented but a little easier to handle. Incidentally, the Ronettes tour was rather less than a success for Lee. This time he attempted to tap off with Dee Dee Sharp; Dee Dee's mother accompanied her daughter as her chaperone and was horrified to find my randy brother trying his hand once again. Lee was immediately reported to the tour manager who in turn sent a telegram to George Cooper; for the second time in twelve months I had to suffer the indignity of a Carlton Brooke artist being removed from a UK tour. The resultant telephone conversation with George Cooper ended with Cooper's statement: 'Peter's brains are in his balls.' 'I couldn't agree more,' I replied as I gently lowered the telephone receiver for what I presumed (at least at that stage) to be my very last business discussion with George Cooper.

The Liverbirds were getting ready to travel to Hamburg courtesy of Carlton Brooke. Visually, they were probably years ahead of their time for they were a female four-piece R&B group, not, as one might expect in those days, a vocal group. They wore their hair in a cross between a Beatles cut and a 'mod bob', and wore leather jerkins and tight-fitting slacks with winkle pickers on their feet: quite a shock for the male-orientated scene in Liverpool. Actually, they had found things very chauvinistic in Liverpool and it had taken a successful support gig with the German band the Rattles to bring them to our attention. We already knew the Rattles, and it was they who convinced Kenny and me that there might be a future for the Liverbirds in Germany. The Rattles, incidentally, had spent most of December 1963 in Liverpool and had become quite a draw at the Cavern. They returned to Germany just before Christmas in order to promote their recording *The Stomp*, which was a massive hit on the continent.

There were simply no female group role models and few precedents back in the UK. Instrument-playing female groups have always been rare but back in the 1960s they were like proverbial hen's teeth. America's Goldie and the Gingerbreads were knocking us out with their musical ability in early 1965, but the Liverbirds were a full twelve months before this. There were plenty of girl pop acts of the successful and unsuccessful variety; many made good records, too, usually for the scurrilous Decca:

my own Beryl Marsden, for example, Julie Grant, the Orchids, the McKinleys, the Chantelles, Vashti, Jan Panter et al. But the business was biased towards male performers and many such girls fell on the stony ground of the 'male gaze'. I had attempted to explain to Beryl that there were limited chart openings, but these were quickly occupied by Dusty and Co. or else by the likes of the Supremes. To compete, any new local girl group not only had to contend with these well-established rivals but also with the seemingly unassailable brigade of boys. No wonder so few of them cracked it. Kenny and I discussed this at length and decided at an early stage, if the Liverbirds were agreeable, that we should target Germany exclusively. We knew that the group would by association be described by the West German music press as 'female Beatles' for the word 'Beatles' by 1964 was an encryption: a genre directly associated with any group to come out of Liverpool with the appropriate sound and hairstyle. Tapping into this relationship would be superb publicity for the girls before they even played a note. So we duly contacted the German music press prior to the Liverbirds leaving the UK in order to hype up the arrival of the girls in Hamburg.

Between the New Year and our departure for Hamburg in mid-February the girls were heavily booked. Carlton Brooke placed them in as many venues as possible in order to expand their skills and repertoire. With the help of Bob Wooler we were able to get them regular gigs at the Cavern alongside such luminaries as Chick Graham, the Koobas, the Riot Squad and the Remo Four. Their most successful gig, however, and one in which they seemed to physically grow on stage, was supporting Alexis Korner's Blues Incorporated one Sunday in January (the 26th to be precise). They were up against a very knowledgeable blues crowd that evening, all students in duffle coats and sandals, but the girls handled the gig well and were commended by Alexis, which was praise indeed. The hype certainly worked for there was a large posse of press and male pop fans at the airport when we arrived with Lee Curtis and the All Stars Mk 2 during late February of 1964.

The band consisted of Pam Birch, effectively the leader of the group, who was not an easy client to keep happy and was something of an eccentric, but she was totally her own person and I admired her for that. I'd brought Pam into the group myself at a late stage after Mary McGlory's sister had decided that the beat group life was not for her. Pam had been attempting to make a name for herself on the folk scene in Liverpool during 1963 but had found it equally misogynistic and intransigent.

She was at times rather unpredictable but was always willing to take musical risks and never followed trends. She was fully aware of trends, however, for she had worked in the NEMS Record Department buying imports from the USA. She was a mine of useful information concerning the band's new R&B repertoire. Mary McGlory was the bass guitarist. She was a very quiet individual and I always thought that she would have made the perfect nun; instead she married songwriter Frank Dostal in Germany. I shall never forget Mary's first sight of the Reeperbahn. Our taxi dropped us off near the Catholic church around the corner and Mary remarked that her parents would be really pleased. We then walked around the corner to view all of the strip clubs and prostitutes. Val Gell played rhythm and I always thought that she was quite butch but she was as straight as they come. She eventually married a young fan by the name of Stefan who, having met the band at the Big Apple Club in Munich, had attempted to drive to Hamburg to see the group again, but was involved in a car accident which sadly left him paralysed. Sylvia Saunders played drums. Syl was the mothering type and quite bossy and independent. She ultimately met and married a drummer from the Bobby Patrick Big Six, came back to Britain but then subsequently spent some time in Benidorm, Spain. I believe she is now back in the UK.

Of course, having a girl band in tow meant that both my self-perceptions about being a father figure and my paranoia about their welfare increased to an extreme level. I regarded myself as their 'angel overseer' and frequently rang home to their respective parents to convince them that all was well. I was constantly sending telegrams and making expensive phone calls, on one occasion even sending back a little money to Pam Birch's family to convince them that she was earning enough. She was, of course, but she was spending as soon as she had earned it; as usual the money that went back to Liverpool was from my own pocket.

This period with the Liverbirds was very promising, even though I realised that the UK would be a tough nut to crack for the group. It was potentially the beginning of what should have been the perfect mentor-protégé relationship that can occasionally spring from the lower rungs of show business. I was fired up by the Liverbirds, particularly Pam who had even begun writing her own material, and I could see only good things ahead for them. If Manfred liked them my plan was to stay in Germany for as long as it took to attract the British press – perhaps six months or so – and then to move them back to the UK. I had already metaphorically 'bitten my lip' and contacted the ubiquitous George Cooper, who initially demurred because of his previous experiences with Carlton Brooke's finest, but then warmed to the idea and was even prepared to put a little money behind them despite never having seen them perform live – as appeared to be his wont.

Once in Hamburg, in the first instance the Liverbirds were given a support slot on the Lee Curtis bill without being officially booked as such, which was a similar arrangement to the one that had given Lee his opportunity back in March 1963. Lee and the boys were not especially pleased, thinking that they were playing with a bunch of amateurs. I must admit that although I knew the Liverbirds could play a little, I did have some reservations about their musical abilities, mostly to do with their lack of volume. They could play but Pam, who was ostensibly the band leader, had been the aforesaid folky before entering the beat world and, despite the exhaustive pre-Hamburg gig schedule, she was still not used to playing with the drive and volume demanded in Germany. But I felt that their novelty value was enough to fill the Star Club for at least a week and the musical ability stuff could take care of itself. Sure enough, despite a few rocky moments during that first week, they tightened up as a band immeasurably, turning the amps up to full blast along the way. The prospect of an all-female band did indeed fill the Star Club for the whole week. Placing them on the bill with Lee (a kind of Lee Curtis revue) was a guarantee for a full house in any case. We were all bowled over by their energy and enthusiasm, and no one less than Manfred. Sitting in the Hotel Pacific the morning after their first week's engagements Herr Weissleder began to critique the show in between slices of cake and coffee, pointing out the Liverbirds' strengths and weaknesses. From experience, I knew this to be a good sign that usually meant Manfred was very interested; I knew the group would be officially booked.

So the pieces were falling into place quite quickly. Manfred Weissleder liked to operate in this way. If the girls did well for a week or so an official contract would follow. They weren't even paid a wage at this juncture but received an allowance from Carlton Brooke and, of course, it was left to yours truly to make up any shortfall when they had visited the shops on the Herberstrasse. But I was perfectly prepared to do this, for I had plenty of money coming in from the retainer I earned from my Star Club work, the percentage I received via the Lee Curtis engagement, together with any gigs that Beryl was obtaining back in the UK, not to mention the sterling work done by Kenny back in Liverpool. Indeed, my bank balance had hardly altered since the Waterworths deal. Carlton Brooke at least seemed to be going from strength to strength in the UK. We were handling bookings for several of the Top Rank Organisation's ballrooms and were placing artists in Blackpool, Crewe and Newcastle, as well as our Birkenhead home at the Majestic Ballroom. Kenny was also helping to launch *Combo*, the music paper for the north Liverpool area which dug into *Mersey Beat*'s sales only a little.

While most of the other agents and managers were trading from home (just take a look at old issues of *Mersey Beat* and you will see myriad adverts with home phone numbers), our offices in Slater Street had been established to provide Carlton Brooke with an upper hand locally, and it was working well. By having office premises like NEMS we were showing that we understood the music business. We were professionals in every sense of the word; at least we thought we were. Kenny deliberately made the environment rather intimidating because he felt that this would deflate egos. He deliberately positioned a dirty, old office desk at the far end of the office on which would be piled contracts next to his ever-present typewriter and telephone. So high was the pile of contracts that one could barely see who was sitting behind the desk. Kenny would observe the groups perform auditions from behind his pile of papers and was, at times, deliberately obtuse. I recall, however, when things started to unravel and Kenny informing me by letter that a few problems had started to develop. This would be during 1965 when the quality control surrounding many Liverpool groups slipped. In Kenny's diary dated 14 May 1965 I much later noted that he had written the following entry:

> There's nothing for Joe and Germany, here. I can't make out which group is which as they all appear to sound the same [and they are just] trying to cover Tamla Motown music. None of them seem to have a personality or front man. [We have] hit the bottom of the barrel. In any case how many decent groups can one Northern city throw up? Will ring tomorrow and tell him the Kirkbys are not available – off to Finland. He will have to ring Betesh.

Although Kenny was somewhat cynical about pop music of any description, he understood the artistic tendencies of the bands well and, in my absence, made a lot of things happen locally, but by 1965 he had detected that matters were drawing inexorably to a close and he informed me during that summer that he was going to look for a job and wanted to close the office. I told him to wait a little while longer but fully understood how the wind of change was moving the Merseybeat saga closer and closer towards its final roll of the dice.

After the Liverbirds had played the Star Club for about three weeks, I sent them home just to let them recharge their batteries and see their folks. They went back to Liverpool full of hope and with a little money in their pockets. Once back in Liverpool, however, they became quite anonymous, although Kenny allowed them a few gigs 'just to keep their hand in', and they quickly wanted to return to Hamburg. After playing in Birkenhead once or twice during March and in the Cavern with the Koobas once again, they were more than ready to return to the Reeperbahn. Absence makes the heart grow fonder and, sure enough, Manfred was keen to see the group's return. He was now downright enthusiastic and wanted the girls to sign a deal with his Star Club record label, which they promptly did. For Manfred, the Liverbirds were obviously bankable and he couldn't wait to have them back in Germany again. By April they had returned to Hamburg and I do not recall them subsequently playing one gig back in Liverpool. The recording sessions would have to wait, for contracts were drawn up and work permits obtained. All artists had to go to the Berlinertour building to sort out such matters and usually these were rather difficult items to obtain. However, I was put in touch with a certain Herr Knopf who made things easier for Star Club artistes. He evidently knew either Manfred or Horst, perhaps owing a favour or two. Having obtained the requisite work permits, the Liverbirds embarked upon an extensive tour of West Germany performing at the Star Club franchises right across the country.

After only a very short time the group had built up a strong following and had developed a great live set which was enhanced by their ability to mach schau. But there was also something about their material that the fans loved. This was in the main based upon the Chicago-based Chess Records catalogue plus a handful of originals. One of the things that initially attracted me to the local Liverpool bands in the first place was their way with obscurities. But by the time Merseybeat had taken off nationally it seemed to me that almost everybody was playing either *Dizzy, Miss Lizzy* or *Long Tall Sally*. What I seemed to miss and misunderstand with Beryl Marsden's tastes for R&B, I came to appreciate with the Liverbirds and their fans. Their repertoire of R&B numbers wouldn't have been out of place in the Marquee or the Crawdaddy clubs in London. I distinctly remember absolutely storming versions of *Got My Mojo Working* (Muddy Waters), *Too Much Monkey Business* (Chuck Berry), *Diddley Daddy* and *Roadrunner* (Bo Diddley) – this was what was happening, and these girls were making it. Finally a Carlton Brooke band was really making it – but nothing is ever quite so simple in the life of Joe Flannery just when you think that something might work out for the best.

The daily ritual in Hamburg would begin at 10 a.m. From my room at the Hotel Pacific in Fiedermarket I would pay the Liverbirds, the All Stars, and any other groups that I had booked into the Star Club via Carlton Brooke, their allowances for the day and sort out their travelling and food requirements. Once Manfred had taken a liking to the Liverbirds it was my job to ensure that if they were booked into a franchised club elsewhere in West Germany, they would also be booked into proper accommodation. If both Lee and the Liverbirds were destined for the road together I would always travel with them for I still loved travelling and I considered my role as a manager to be exclusive and on a personal basis. I believed in the authenticity of my artistes and would share their problems and perils. I came to learn, however, that close personal management had its drawbacks.

Indeed, the weight of caring and planning for these few Carlton Brooke artists began to tell on me. In fact, I began to feel more and more like a wet nurse or a therapist than a pop manager, especially once I had discovered that during one of our many German tours of 1964 my already-married brother had started to enjoy secret liaisons with Pam Birch of the Liverbirds. I was truly dismayed. Being a good Catholic boy further accentuated these feelings of bewilderment and betrayal. What made matters worse was that this wasn't a quick leg-over event, which in some ways might have been understandable, perhaps even forgivable. Rather, this seemed to be an out-and-out clandestine love affair. Each was clearly besotted with the other. The German music scene was akin to a small fraternity, but the emphasis here remains on 'small'. One couldn't move without being noticed and, sure enough, a member of a German band with whom I had dealings, the Rivets, reported Lee's disloyalty to me. I challenged him without delay but was met with a stony silence. However, I knew from his squirming that the affair was a reality: he told me they were 'in love':

> In the first place, Peter [I screamed], either you want a musical career, or you don't. If you do, you must keep your nose clean. What if the music press here in Germany gets wind of it; what if Manfred discovers what you've been doing? You know the way he sees the world. In the second place you simply must tell me everything. If you don't you have to be prepared to take the consequences. Whatever noble motives you have about yourself and Pam you must realise that you have to recruit people

into any conspiracy: in other words, *me, you bloody fool! – and what about your family back in Liverpool?*

He just shrugged his shoulders and smiled ironically: he didn't care. He told me he had found his true love and that they would be forever together. All of this from a married man who had only recently been thrown off a major tour for trying to shag Dee Dee Sharp. I couldn't believe what I was hearing. Furthermore, I couldn't believe what I was hearing myself say. I was going against all my own principles just for the sake of my wayward brother. To add further to this familial turmoil, I knew that if Manfred was to get wind of the matter both Lee and Pam would have their contracts terminated forthwith. Despite attempting to warn Lee that it all had to stop, I left our encounter promising that I would keep this secret while he tried to sort it out. Lee's performances were not affected unduly; in fact, I do believe that the whole thing was a further boost to his ego. I don't think he ever loved her but Pam was evidently smitten and seemed to be losing her enthusiasm for the gigs. I too was deeply troubled. I returned to Liverpool on one of my usual talent-scouting excursions (this time I brought Steve Aldo and David Garrick, amongst others, over to Germany), and it was quite apparent to all at home that I was having a bad time, psychologically. I was, however, able to keep the news from Lee's wife Beryl as well as my own dear mother, at least for the time being.

Upon returning to Germany I discovered that things were becoming even more tempestuous between Lee and Pam. In the meantime, my brother Teddy had hitchhiked to Germany with the news that Beryl's mother, Mrs Eves, who always disliked Lee in any case, had been planting seeds of doubt in Beryl's mind. Word had got back to her that Pam had been heard discussing her affair with Lee when back in Liverpool over Christmas 1964. Hilda Eves had even written to Manfred Weissleder advisedly reminding him of Lee's marital status. Manfred was infuriated and gave me a really bad time over it. I was piggie in the middle but there was little that either Manfred or I could do about it. He later apologised, stating that the whole sordid affair had upset his sensibilities. I think he was just worried that it might upset his bank account.

The Christmas holiday back in Liverpool was a decidedly low-key affair. My thoughts were constantly about my errant brother. By the time I had returned to Hamburg in January 1965, a drastic shift had taken place in our relationship. Because of Pam's influence Lee began to perceive me as an oppressor who had more money, more power and more control than he did, and I think he really hated me for that. Other things were changing: having returned I discovered to my surprise that Beryl Marsden was playing at the Top Ten Club, which was a rueful moment for me, for this was none of my doing. She was joined by the Liverpool group the Harlems, who had previously backed the Chants. I learnt from Ray Deane of the Harlems that Brian Epstein had decided to release the Chants from NEMS and this further saddened me for the Chants were probably the first black British vocal band and should have been a massive success. It further convinced me that Brian was beginning to behave a little Machiavellian, to say the least. Despite caring very deeply about my other clients at the Star Club, especially the Pretty Things, whom Manfred had originally hated because of their unkempt appearance but who packed the club time and time again, and the Hep Stars from Sweden, who became good friends, I soon became less capable of responding to anything other than the Lee and Pam crisis. I pretended everything was all right: I was stoic, I suppose. But to handle the strain I started taking Preludin. I was taking 'prellies' on a regular basis because they prevented me from sleeping and the very last thing I wanted to do was to sleep and allow my anxieties to rush over me. In truth I was being a coward and had run out of gumption: I just couldn't keep things going as they were. There was nothing I could do but go back in my mind and take it all apart again, but even this was becoming desperate, for how many times could I rerun this nightmare?

What made matters worse was that by early 1965 everyone else around me seemed to be using heroin. While I had not been averse to keeping this regular supply of Preludin, I always hated heroin. I had first come into contact with it many years previously when I was aware of a little heroin use in the Ivy Benson Band. Jazzers in the 1950s seemed to like it; they seemed to think it helped with their playing, but all I saw was misery. As for Hamburg, it was controlled by the club owners who were, it would seem, not making enough out of the prostitution and softer drugs and wanted to create an unending demand. I saw someone literally give some away one night in the Star Club and I instantly thought that things were getting far too edgy. It seemed that with the arrival of a harder drug culture on the Reeperbahn in 1965 each band, each singer even, appeared to need an enormous amount of attention and pampering, the Pretty Things being one case in point. Bands were totally unable to self-manage anything when the hard drugs scene took a hold. It wasn't an epidemic as such but everybody, of course, was far too young and untamed. And the drugs were incredibly 'hip' and mysterious. But whereas other drugs could be quite sensational, heroin just seemed to detach people from reality. For me it was all starting to become unutterably depressing and I felt I was drowning in a sea of self-indulgence.

By mid-July 1965, I'd received two letters to further demoralise my now already morose frame of mind. One came from Lee's wife Beryl and was dated 26 May; the other came from my mother dated 11 June. I still have them as gloomy keepsakes for both pieces of correspondence were heart-breaking, discussing in their own way the news that they were fully aware that Lee and Pam were an item. There seemed to be little that I could do other than threaten Lee with termination of his contract. This I did following the letters and Lee, perturbed I would guess by the prospect of a withdrawal of finances, promised to do something about it before going off to Munich for a week's work at the Circus Kroner, where he was appearing with the Animals. At one stage he threw his tie into the audience and it was retrieved by a 'fan'. Mysteriously or not, as the case may be, it ended up being in the possession of Pam Birch. What on earth could be done? I was so frustrated. The ultimate destiny of any personal manager should be to break with an artist, but only at such a time when that artist no longer needs the services of a manager but a bookkeeper. This time had not yet arrived for we hadn't even scratched the surface of potential popularity in Europe. I could see that both Lee and the Liverbirds were heading for real longevity over there. We had just received interest from Italy for a series of Lee Curtis gigs and we were turning down Liverbirds offers. It just didn't seem fair that he and Pam were threatening all of this, especially when the man had a wife and children back at home in Lee Park, Liverpool. The aforementioned letters were followed by a personal visit from my mother, Beryl and Lee's daughter Tracy that summer. He was able to convince them that everything was OK but as soon as they had returned to Liverpool it all started again.

One had to admit to a kind of novelistic or poetic discourse about the whole affair. I had attempted to develop two personae (Lee and Pam) who believed that they were so different from all others and so transcendent in regard to other people's feelings that, as soon as they spoke or sang, others listened. Of course, the truth of the matter was quite the reverse. Being essentially creations, they were at this stage in their lives rather shallow individuals. Perhaps this was no fault of their own for what they thought were their personalities were actually inventions. In a funny kind of way they no longer preceded the images and songs that they presented to their fans, for they were synchronic and believed in the immanence of themselves.

Anything that preceded this charade: mother, wife, children, etc. became unreal for them. They simply believed in what they thought they were, but failed to see that they were ideological compositions. The representation A (male: Lee) had poetically fallen in love with the representation B (female: Pam), an inverse mirror image of itself. I previously mentioned that I found love something of a difficult phenomenon to locate. There is no better example of my bewilderment with such emotions than the disregarding, essentialising 'love' between Lee and Pam.

In the meantime, both Lee and the Liverbirds had recorded their first albums for the Star Club record label. It was also looking very promising on the recording front and *It's Lee and The Liverbirds* LPs were selling quite well in West Germany. Whereas in those days in Europe many bands were given one-off payments for recordings, I had insisted that Lee and the girls were paid on a royalties basis, as was customary in the UK. Manfred and the parent company Philips reluctantly agreed and, as the albums continued to sell during 1965, 1966 and 1967, my artistes were continually rewarded with nice little earners every three months or so. Even to this day, the CD reissues reward the various musicians with the occasional payment from time to time. I was also active in assisting the organisation of perhaps the first pop music show on German TV: *Beat Club*. We had been approached during the summer of 1965 by German TV. They were looking for a *Ready Steady Go!* style of show and were keen to broadcast such an event direct from Germany's premier club, featuring Lee and the Liverbirds. Manfred was delighted and, after the necessary financial arrangements were put in place, the first edition of *Beat Club* went ahead, live from the Star Club in September 1965. By that time there were pop music clubs in every town and Star Club franchises across all of the larger cities. West Germany had embraced popular culture as never before and it was a truly national phenomenon. The East Germans were baffled and bewildered as more and more young people tried to escape from the DDR – and we were at the epicentre of it all – how could it go wrong? We even ran a talent competition via the television for young German bands, for I was always very keen to foster indigenous talent; the first winners of that competition were a group who gained a great deal of success in Germany during the 1960s and 1970s: the Lords.

We visited Berlin a great deal as part of the Star Club franchise, although it was often rather difficult to get into Berlin via normal overland means. When a gig was forthcoming in Berlin I would contact my usual people at Lufthansa and arrange for my artistes and myself to be flown in, which was far easier. The East German bureaucrats seemed far less efficient when dealing with this different level of technology than the interminable road blocks around the city and I found that I could manoeuvre bands quite easily in and out of Berlin Airport. I did become known to the East German officials owing to our frequent visits and this led not to an interrogation, but to a couple of gigs in the DDR. These were strange affairs. The trips through Checkpoint Charlie, for example, proved to be highly charged as invariably one Scouse wit or another would launch into a tirade of ironic abuse during our document checks. Once in this former Russian sector, the expeditions to the gigs were oddly dispiriting: on one occasion we were flanked by motorcycle outriders put-putting along on rather vintage two-stroke motorbikes; on another we were followed by Wartburg police cars to our official (in other words, dingy) hotel. The lack of street advertising hoardings is one of my most enduring memories of these trips, together with burned out carcasses of buildings: war damage was still prevalent everywhere.

There were few sound checks in those days, but at least in the West the bands would get some time to rehearse. Not so in East Berlin, however, for one was expected to turn up, play, come straight off and be escorted back to the West. We presumed that the East Germans were starved of rock and tended to treat the two adventures east rather like pilgrimages; we handed out *Lee and Liverbirds* LPs to some of those present at the gigs. However, I later learnt that many youngsters listened to various European stations such as Radio Luxembourg illegally and were pretty au fait with pop culture – it was just that they couldn't get their hands on much of it. In terms of youth culture and rock music in the East, in 1965, shortly after our second and last visit, they had banned the 'escalation of the beat rhythms'. Erich Honecker, later party leader and head of state, pointed out that rock music and the decadent lifestyle of the beatniks was not in accordance with the goals of his socialist worldview. We learnt that live performances were drastically constrained and young beatniks were forced to cut their hair. The situation escalated when in October 1965 the so-called 'beat riots' took place in Leipzig after a ban of local amateur pop groups. The participants were beaten by police and arrested. I recall reading about such events with horror from my office at the Star Club. I could tell from standing in the wings at both gigs in the East that the audiences wished to let themselves go, but were actually and symbolically restrained. So, the jaunts to East Berlin were paradoxical affairs. Although there was a level of personal satisfaction in bringing our sound to them, the two gigs were soul destroying. I later discovered that our Eastern audiences were largely made up of sons and daughters of influential party members, in any case, and so my altruistic ideas about cultural liberation were pretty far off the mark. However, I still take some comfort from the fact that some of those in the audiences may have commenced in their own individual ways to react against the state via some minor actions. The history of socialism has met with several such moments of ambiguity and discourse over the years. The DDR discovered that such uneven communal activities were democratic, not socialist.

Oddly, however, I also recall news items from across the border concerning a Beatles LP being released in the DDR by the state-owned Amiga label – perhaps this was early 1966. Although the authorities had tried to establish a counter programme against the cultural imperialism of the Star Club and Carlton Brooke, the party could not suppress their young people listening to the aforementioned radio stations or Feindsender (adversary radio stations), as they were called. Neither could they prevent people from watching *Beat Club* on West German TV. Beat and rock music spread all over the DDR and imported records circulated on the black market. The government finally had to accept the fact that rock 'n' roll had become an integral part of youth culture even in the socialist bloc; I must admit I was mightily pleased, but what a bloody farce of utterly vulgar proportions.

By the last few months of 1965 Lee and I were still working together, but without a contract and without speaking a great deal to each other. I was actively avoiding conflicts, but our relationship had deteriorated to a very poor level. Perhaps a stand-up row might have helped, but it's the way one is brought up, I suppose: I hated conflict. What made matters worse was that one weekend, quite out of the blue while I was away in Cologne organising a series of gigs for the Rattles and the Rivets, Brian Epstein turned up. He had already made a few unaccompanied trips to the city, but on this occasion he seemed interested in mixing a little business with his pleasures. I later discovered that he knew I was away on business and was attempting one last time to lure Lee Curtis away from my management and into the NEMS stable. Liverpool singer Steve Aldo had something to do with this, I think. Steve had been very close to Brian and had also been performing under my auspice in Hamburg at this time. Brian wined and dined Steve and Lee, but my brother held firm and spurned any advances either financial or sexual, and Brian returned to London empty-handed. However, he left in his wake a Lee Curtis with an even greater and over-aggrandised opinion of himself: 'Imagine the Beatles' manager still wanting to sign me!' This was the last straw and, coupled with the domestic problems, this made it impossible for us to work together.

At the Star Club, just before Christmas 1965, Lee turned up with Pam to a performance by Little Richard. They were wearing matching jackets and were flaunting their relationship right in front of me. It was as if they were inviting me to have a rant. Well, they got it. I lost my cool and promptly threw a double scotch over Lee, screaming at him: 'Consider yourself fucking launched! Well if this is what you want, go ahead, but why do you have to rub my nose in it? Haven't you done enough damage already?' I petitioned God and wondered aloud about the justice of allowing the faithful – those like myself – to be so brutalised in this way. Lee and Pam just looked at me. They could see my pain but failed to respond. They left as they came in, surrounded by those mid-sixties sycophants who seemed to crawl out of the woodwork all over Europe at one and the same time. I was left wondering what to do next. In that one night I saw the future and it didn't appear to include me, or Carlton Brooke.

It seemed as if, just like my brother, everybody was living life on the edge. Word had got back to me via Pete Brown that Brian, too, was doing this 'edgy' thing. But, for me, I found it steadfastly unattractive. What was 'the edge', in any case? It appeared to me to be a state of mindlessness. Hedonism was certainly ruling the Star Club by the New Year of 1966 and I hated it. But everybody else appeared so cool and 'repelled by bourgeois conventions'. However, life on the edge had its drawbacks and isn't open to everyone. While the sight of Lee making love with Pam in a German night club was for some an artist exploring the boundaries of his sexuality, for me it just appeared to be boring male self-indulgence and posturing. When Mr Drunken Pop Star made a fool of himself in the Star Club he was supposed to be infused with Dionysian spirit. All I perceived was an inebriated idiot. For me, those who wished to live on the precipice were welcome to it. The myth that their excesses in the 1960s offered us poor souls some kind of enlightenment in which inebriation provided us with a special insight into our human condition was bullshit of the worst order. As 1966 moved along I was beginning to think that this great escapade that I had gotten myself, Lee and many of the new groups I had booked for the forthcoming year into was heading towards tragedy, farce or both. Suicide, for me, was never a consideration, given my faith; however, I well remember walking to the bridge in Hamburg that night, looking down into the murky waters of the Elbe and seriously considering that one way or another I needed to remove myself from this hell hole.

Manfred was eager to see my relationship with Lee and Pam repaired, so for his sake I decided to continue with the Star Club as their booking agent and stage manager, but to cease functioning as Carlton Brooke. Kenny approved, for as we have seen, acting as our local agent in Liverpool he had already realised that cracks were beginning to appear in the entire Merseybeat scene. In fact by 1966 it was all over. During February of that year the Cavern had closed. Most people were aware of Ray McFall's precarious financial state after the abortive Cavern Sounds Studio set-up, which proved to be a terrible failure. We were also aware that interest in beat music, which had peaked in late 1964, was now well on the decline. Actually, in June 1965 I first heard Dylan's *Like a Rolling Stone*. This single was an interesting disclosure to me. It became obvious that folk music, with its associated counter-culture and political overtones, was becoming commercial and the scene was set for a showdown between out-and-out pop singers and the more self-conscious artistes. Different texts were coming to the fore as album sales were becoming more important than singles. The words 'rock' and 'folk' were beginning to carry meaning other than merely words describing styles of music. Liverpool's days as part of a flourishing beat centre were numbered once this act of musical self-immolation had begun.

It was all brought even closer to home when Chas Chandler, the ex-Animals bass guitarist, rang me to ask whether I might be able to assist him in promoting his latest find, a guitarist by the name of Jimi Hendrix. It came as no surprise that Chas was beginning to discover the other side of the business: both he and Alan Price had a healthy interest in management. Alan had already persuaded me to book Goldie and the Gingerbreads during 1965 and Chas was also interested in record production. I was pleased to agree and was delighted when Jimi played two spots at the Star Club in March 1967. He was a real gentleman and took his music very earnestly. Throughout his short time in Germany he was eager to learn as much as he could about using his small combo sound as expansively as possible. I found it interesting that he was not only concerned with developing his music, but also finding ways to make it as what he described as a 'rock star'. He told me in no uncertain terms that he wanted 'lots of fame, chicks and money' and further remarked, after hearing about my own interests in the electric Dylan, that he was attracted to combining Dylan with his own musical approaches.

I've since heard many times from black US writers and journalists that Hendrix actually objected to performing rock with white Englishmen

– that somehow he deemed this to be 'inauthentic', a sell-out. Nothing could be further from the truth. In fact, during the brief period that Jimi and I knew each other, he frequently saw the Experience as the strongest possible unit for personal success and he even told me that he was extremely happy to regard himself as a quasi-Englishman because of his high profile on the London underground scene of that year. Jimi soon returned to London with the Star Club under his belt and I was invited personally to see one of his London theatre performances at the Saville Theatre. Chas Chandler rang me and stated that Jimi did not wish to perform unless he knew I was in the audience; because of his experiences in Germany he felt more confident if I was there to witness the event. I was so pleased that he felt this way and was only too delighted to be present. As I sat in the audience and the curtains opened I could instantly see and hear that he was becoming a monumental star. I must admit to feeling a small tinge of self-satisfaction when the opening lick from his guitar burst forth and from Jimi's lips came the eternal words: 'Hey Joe.'

However, the scenes surrounding Hendrix appeared alien, at least to me. The whole thing was increasingly based upon an 'us and them' theme. Hip people versus straight people. There was a perverse cult of personality about these new stars, delineated by a romantic hipness and exclusivity. Somebody as painfully polished as myself found it increasingly difficult to get into this covert world. There was a great deal of rhetoric about liberated society and assuming freedom but there was also another side that angered me a little. It was clandestine and one got the feeling that who was in and who was out was solidifying by the week. Chas Chandler was fully aware, I think, that there was now a new bourgeoisie surrounding these 'authentic' artists and that managers such as myself now had to play catch-up. During my return trips to London in 1966 – there was no longer much of value in my beloved Liverpool, sadly – I had some dealings with Kit Lambert and Chris Stamp. They were young and vibrant, decidedly 'in'; master gamesmen who were learning their lessons very quickly indeed. They made me feel old.

The personal split with Lee was the first indication that my work for the Star Club was drawing to a close. The sea changes indicated above also showed me that I was losing my enthusiasm for management in Germany. There were now no other personal clients to divert my attention from club business and I was by this time solely responsible for booking bands and beer into the Star Club franchises across Germany. Hendrix aside, it became quite a bore, to be honest. There is always something about popular culture that has its relations with lifestyles. I was, by this time, 35 years of age and the new lifestyles seemed to me unfathomable and rather transient. I was, by definition, part of an older generation and I already felt quite comfortable with my own lifestyle choices by that time. I suppose one could say that I was ill equipped to handle the liberation. So, although I was attracted to some of the music of the mid to late 1960s counter-culture, the social mores seemed curiously irrelevant.

I approached the brewery responsible for all of the Star Club beer sales with a view to their sponsorship of a new project. I had decided to purchase my own bar. Kenny was in agreement and he and I discovered a good business just off the Reeperbahn in Hamburg. Kenny immediately closed down Carlton Brooke in Liverpool and joined me in Hamburg. We made an offer, it was accepted and the finances were quite easily put into place. Just prior to Christmas 1966 I informed Lee that I was officially severing all business ties both with him and the Liverbirds, and that I would in due course be leaving the Star Club. His response was somewhat predictable: rather bitter and belligerent. He peppered his response with a flood of profanities but he was philosophical enough to realise that I had never cheated him. I advised both Lee and the Liverbirds to sign to Star Club Management, who also handled the Rattles and the Rivets, as well as a number of other local Hamburg acts, which they duly did.

As I look back with the benefit of these decades of hindsight it seems that the time of the paternally vigilant manager had all but faded. In fact, I well remember that 1960s cry of 'never trust anybody over 30' ringing in my ears as I sat in the patisserie opposite the Hotel Pacific contemplating my management experiences over a cup of Herculean German coffee. 'OK,' I thought. 'There had been a baby boom and the surplus of teenagers like my brother had needed guidance and instruction throughout the late 1950s and early 1960s. Throughout these years I had become an arbiter, a devoted guardian who ensured correct and proper behaviour; my close relationship with my artistes even hinted at a philosophy and morality – but what had happened? The changing times had done me out of a job!'

The problem was that the cult of youth that had grown in the wake of our management had challenged this paternalism. Indeed, that aforementioned crucial age difference had established a distance that could not be overcome in the 1960s. I had learnt a great deal up until my break with Lee, but one thing I hadn't gained knowledge of was how to extend my own sense of taste and go along with the 1960s maxim that pop could be serious. Let me explain. Musically, for example, I came to hate the excesses of extended jams; the hedonistic concept of 'seamless music'; the unfocused elitism of a new musical direction. I also loathed that division between the so-called authenticity of rock and the apparent inauthenticity of pop. I never really held with the philosophy that the 33rpm album offered liberation of the psyche. Mostly it seemed to me that good old-fashioned pop was no longer hip because music was no longer supposed to be fun: it was now deadly serious, po-faced, even. Rock artists seemed unwilling to call themselves entertainers any longer, to please crowds or to be successful. I had a seemingly regressive preference.

This musical transformation had also led to a change in the music business that I also disliked – and I was never much of a fan of the industry in the first place. By the mid-sixties the business was so powerful and such a money-spinning operation that more and more specialists had entered the field. Accountants and solicitors, indeed professional advisors of every description, were assuming positions of prominence and their lists of rock clients were beginning to multiply. By the end of the decade, while I was back home listening to the likes of Neil Diamond and Harry Nilsson, I was also witnessing the outcome of this unproductive generation gap: over-serious artists concentrating their efforts on pleasing or should that be appeasing elitist record buyers with over-long albums full of boring, self-indulgent music. Like their advisors, groups like Yes, Emerson, Lake and Palmer, and Electric Light Orchestra, all of whom passed through my hands via the Star Club in other guises (the Warriors, the Nice, and the Move respectively), had assumed an establishment mentality – it was corporate music for a corporate age where big was apparently beautiful.

Kenny and I had returned home for Christmas 1966 and it was intended to be our last visit back to Liverpool for some considerable time. We were both looking forward to returning to Germany for our new venture as bar owners in the New Year. I was constantly worried, however, that I was becoming something of a dormant species. Something was wrong, very wrong. I also sensed that my estranged friend Brian was in trouble in some way. Was he experiencing similar concerns? Did he also feel a bit useless and bit surplus to requirements? Once home I rang Clive Epstein in Liverpool. He was unaware of any problems, but I was still ill at ease about Brian. I contacted his London office but was informed that he was only infrequently seen there. I learnt from Pete Brown, however, that he was spending more time at the Saville Theatre in Shaftesbury Avenue and I decided to call him there. After a few abortive attempts, I reached him on the phone in early November 1966; Brian was very eager to see me and invited me to the Saville as his personal guest. In truth, I had already made mental plans to go to London in any case. I had business dealings with Tony Stratton-Smith over the Koobas/Kubas and had learnt that the Four Tops were due to appear at the Saville in Brian's NEMS promotion on the 13th; I simply couldn't miss the dulcet tones of Levi Stubbs.

Brian was waiting in his Rolls-Royce at Euston on the afternoon of the 13th. We dined together and I informed him that my latterly sagging venture into management was heaving its last gasp. I was to continue with Manfred for another six months or so and then move into my own bar later that summer. Brian was genuinely delighted at the news. He immediately apologised, too, about his last bid for Lee Curtis. He admitted to me that it was misplaced and, perhaps hinting for the only time that he did indeed fancy my brother, stated that he thought Lee's image was 'beautiful but rather dated'. We had a wonderful evening, but I was rather worried overall about both his business acumen and his state of health. To my way of thinking, the Saville Theatre appeared to be at the wrong end of Shaftesbury Avenue and I was rather worried that he had taken a pig in a poke. More importantly, his health seemed rather fragile; when we went to dinner he ate very little. Playing with his food, he reminded me of the young boy I used to serve at the Adelphi all those years ago. More evidence, I thought, that the Dionysian lifestyle was a trickster, a fraud and a phony: it only appeared exciting. Brian was even to remark later that year in an interview with *Queen* magazine that he was on the side of hallucinatory drugs but looking at him that night in November 1966 I felt that I would never underestimate just how incautious it all really was. I learnt something very valuable that night. The road of excess does not lead to the palace of wisdom, but to illness, despair and decay. Despite the joy at being with my old friend, my sorrow was never very far from the surface that evening.

Brian came clean before we entered the theatre. He told me that, notwithstanding everything that had happened over the past four years, he still felt like a novice; that he was worried about a deal with 'the Australian', as he put it, namely Robert Stigwood; that he was beginning protracted negotiations with EMI that he felt would surely wear him out (this, I believe, was the revamped Beatles recording deal); that he felt superfluous now that the Beatles had come off the road. All of this was probably true but, in all honesty, I didn't altogether believe him. I felt that Brian was hopelessly addicted not only to a kind of masochistic self-effacement, but also to a chemical something or other. He was rather exquisite that evening, but also morbid, nervous and rather depressed. I knew that, unlike myself, he had decided to embrace this new era of 'self-fulfilment' and reckless mind expansion. It seemed as if he too was attempting to play an interminable game of catch-up with culture's own pleasure principle. But it wasn't working. After the gig, Brian walked me to my hotel. We embraced. 'Joe, I'm so lonely,' he said and then turned and walked away. That was the very last time we spoke.

13

THIS IS THE END, BEAUTIFUL FRIEND

FOLLOWING THE CHRISTMAS and New Year festivities, Kenny and I returned to the Star Club in the first week of February 1967; it was very cold and wet in Hamburg that year. We were now staying in Manfred's sumptuous apartment by the river. I had won keys to the apartment the previous year after proving to Manfred just how popular the Pretty Things were (he had doubted them and my ability to book gems until he saw the queues around the block) and life was looking promising. Eric Burdon and the Animals, Cream and Jimi Hendrix were due to play at the Star Club in the following months, together with the myriad British and European groups still making a beeline for the venue. We had already informed Manfred Weissleder about our forthcoming departure and he had taken it all very well, appreciating that it was time for us to move on. Immediately following our arrival in Hamburg, however, Manfred requested my presence at the ubiquitous morning coffee session in the patisserie. This time it was not to be one of those run-of-the-mill meetings.

I suggested previously that ageism had become the perennial bugbear of the pop industry, that somehow during the course of the 1960s popular music assumed some kind of fatuous nodding acquaintance with youth and rebelliousness. I'd heard Mick Jagger sing 'what a drag it is getting old' the previous year, with him never dreaming that it was to be his turn next, trapping himself into some kind of middle-aged groundhog day for the rest of his life. It appeared to me that metaphorically speaking the age of 30 was spelling 'the end' in bright neon lights across the Grosse Freiheit.

Manfred, too, following my notice of resignation, had got the message: 'Joe, I'm also getting out.' These were his first words to me as we sat staring at our steaming coffee and waist-expanding gateaux across the filigreed design on the table; he was in point of fact very emotional, which was a very unusual demeanour for this hard man of Hamburg:

> I've made plenty of money out of this venture, Joe – even the *Star Club News* [Manfred's German version of *Mersey Beat*] has performed well financially. But after you informed me about your own misgivings before Christmas, I've also come to a similar conclusion. I understand why bands come into the business, because they see it as cool and hip. In the old days they just wanted to have sex, be cool, you know. But now it's about art and poetry and privilege. I don't get it any more. If you get it you can carry on, if you don't get it – like myself – I honestly think it's time to go.

I was astounded, but I couldn't agree more. How were those of us who suddenly found themselves 'well over 30' supposed to comfort ourselves in this post-45rpm age? The problem with the aesthetic theories abounding during the forthcoming Summer of Love was that theories of creativity and transcendence don't take into account the kind of social and historical beings we really are. There is always a good deal more at stake, I thought. I remember a year or so later meeting up with Beatle publicist Derek Taylor during the great Apple Records fiasco. Derek and I had never really got on: he'd realised at an early stage that I had been closer to Brian than he had ever been and he rather resented me for it, I think. I had asked Derek what Apple was all about and he curtly informed me that the Beatles were trying to 'eliminate business lies', that business was 'obscuring the truth' and that truth 'hung somewhere in the generation gap ... at least before Youth took over'. I couldn't believe his acid-soaked naivety. While he was speaking, the heads around Apple were fleecing the company of a million quid, but it must have been OK to Derek because 'they' were cool. As John Lennon informed Jann Wenner in 1971, it was rather like *Satyricon*; Petronius' novel might have been written for the 1960s. Encolpius and his lover, a handsome 16-year-old boy named Giton, travel through a variety of vignettes. Throughout the novel, Encolpius has a hard time keeping his lover faithful to him as he is constantly being enticed away by others.

You see, for me, business had been a salvation. My little shop, for example, was all I had after so many disappointments and so many tribulations.

I was devoted to people and business brought me into direct contact with people. Yes, I was able to make money, but I saw nothing wrong with that as long I was able to help people get what they wanted. You might argue that they were only deceiving themselves, that they didn't really want what they thought they wanted, but I think comments such as those that were abounding from the counter-culture and the left during the 1960s were fatuous and condescending in the extreme. How patronising to inform a person who had worked hard in order to earn money that they were essentially fooling themselves; that they didn't really want that little piece of something special; that they were being mass manipulated by moguls such as myself. No sooner had Manfred announced his imminent departure than *The People* Sunday newspaper back in the UK released a sex and drugs story about the Star Club. To imagine anywhere on the Reeperbahn without sex and drugs is like trying to imagine a hotdog in New York without mustard and sauerkraut. Nevertheless, this adverse publicity from the UK tabloid press laid Manfred even lower, coming, as it did, from the country in which he had placed his musical faith for over five years. The engine of his imminently departing pantechnicon had been well and truly fired up by the British tabloid press.

A new management team came in at the Star Club almost immediately with Henry Henroid, another Englishman, supposedly at its helm. I state 'supposedly' because Henry had previously been little more than a ligger in and around the Star Club for about eighteen months. It was reputed that he was an agent with direct connections to Mickie Most and that he had boasted that he could bring over those artists signed to Most's production company, RAK. His connections were not as concrete as he had alluded, however, and we seldom saw any end results. The Animals had been one of his first captures for the club, which was mightily impressive. Nevertheless, from memory I don't believe we saw anything of Donovan or Lulu, which was a pity. Terry Reid, however, did come over and he was marvellous. As a consequence of these 'connections' Henry was kept on by the new management team as they attempted one last time to lure me back into the fold, but for me the writing was on the wall.

Live music immediately went into decline after the new team decided, rightly or wrongly, that star guests were now beyond their means. They were probably right: together with inflated artistic tendencies came inflated fees and that heinous word 'disco' also started to creep into the vocabulary along the Reeperbahn, as well as back at the Cavern in Liverpool via Billy Butler's 'platters that matter' sessions – I guess that said it all, really. Indeed, by mid-1967 it had all become rather tacky, which is saying something for the Reeperbahn. I was serving out my time with the new management but finding that, rather like my soldiering days in Abergavenny, I knew I was merely killing time. It was another of those periods that we so often go through, a sort of cusp between what you are and where you want to be. But for me that new era was not really presenting any set of values I could fully understand. The future appeared strange and this little interval was like a sort of last gasp, a long goodbye.

A psychedelic disco opened a couple of doors away from the club which instantly made the Star Club look rather old hat. My brother, still plough-ing his way around the German circuit, had no need of me at all. Without Manfred, the Star Club record imprint was placed into suspended anima-tion and no further releases were scheduled for Lee or the Liverbirds. The girls were playing constantly, but, Pam Birch notwithstanding, were also preparing to settle down with their respective boyfriends. The Rattles, the Rivets and the Lords all obtained major recording deals away from the Star Club (Decca, Philips and Columbia respectively). The latter's album, *Ulleogamaxbe* for Columbia, was one of the best German albums of the entire decade, in my humble opinion, but I had nothing to do with it.

There are no brute facts that state that either the Cavern or the Star clubs should remain; life moves on, times change, and by 1967 the heyday of live rock 'n' roll, of uncomplicated musical texts, of unpretentious popu-larisers, was well and truly over. Kenny and I discussed our future at length in the wake of Weissleder's decision and the immediate decline in the Star Club's fortunes. Our new venture was also supposed to be a live music venue, but things were not looking very promising. Kenny could see that I was worried, that all of the previous certainties were now suspended; he was philosophical. The gist of our decisive conversation concerning the matter revolved around asking ourselves what conditions had determined Manfred's decision. Whatever had happened to the concept of music as a social practice would give us several clues about which direction night life was heading on the Reeperbahn: technology had moved on so much that bands were more interested in studio work; the expense of booking name bands seemed excessive; PAs were becoming increasingly expensive. Could the books be balanced? If not were we to resort to cabaret trios and discos? Kenny suggested that we needed to enquire into the material conditions involved in the making of music in 1967 and not base our ideas on our previous experiences. Surely if technology was changing things so much, uncomplicated live rock 'n' roll music could well be a thing of the past.

Horror of horrors, perhaps people even preferred to listen to records whilst in a club. We needed to think about how the product was being consumed. We could certainly no longer assume that people listened as we did. What was happening when people were listening? How were they now listening? What role was recorded music actually playing now? We decided that we didn't want a bar full of people listening to records; neither were we going to go against the grain and not book live bands – it just didn't seem right, somehow. But, of course, what if those live bands were uncommercial or 'underground'? If we booked singles-orientated groups would punters interested in club life go to see commercial groups in any case? It didn't seem likely. So ultimately what about our investment? It was all appearing to be rather too risky. We decided that spring to come home and leave the music business once and for all.

We called off all negotiations with the German brewery. They were disappointed and not a little angry but were very gracious about the matter; after all, it was their money they were keeping in the bank. I contacted mother and the rest of the Flannery clan and informed them that Kenny and I would be returning home during May. Mother was mightily relieved. After the Lee difficulties, she felt vindicated, I think, about her opinions of the music business. I never told her that the decision actually had nothing to do with her pressure, although that is what she believed until her death. However, Lee's wife Beryl was disturbed at the prospect of me returning home without him. She already knew that he was no longer under my guiding hand, and my return without him made matters worse for her. As for the rest of the family, well, they were very understanding. I simply told my brother Teddy that my work was done, that the era in which I moved to Germany was now at an end; that I had gone from a lost age of innocence to an age of lost innocence. Teddy understood and helped me get a job back in Liverpool – I told him I'd take anything going.

Things were beginning to get tight back on Merseyside. Although the economically devastating era of the 1970s was still a few years in advance, good jobs were not as prevalent as they had been in the early part of the decade. However, with a few words placed here and there, he was able to get me into the electronics group Lucas. It was factory work and I merely regarded it as a stopgap until I was able to afford to move back into retail, which I did the following year. Kenny resumed his ambulance driving. How commonplace the visage; I had returned to an unfinished canvas and nobody had noticed I'd even been away. The composition of Liverpool had faded considerably and that so-called psychedelic Summer of Love also appeared washed out, discoloured. I just got on with the job. Working in Lucas' was like looking at the remains of a late lover's body, decaying and disappearing before one's eyes.

So, as you can see, the era of peace, love and harmony was no cake walk for some of us. My own doors of perception stayed firmly closed. The likes of the aforementioned Derek Taylor were openly recommending that reality was somehow a fiction and that excess led to enlightenment, but for me Derek was living his life in inverted commas. There was certainly no avoiding the evidence that a youth consciousness existed and that things required challenging: this is a central theme of the 1960s and I applauded all of that, for it was in contrast to the elitism that we had all endured. But we weren't all there in the 1960s – wherever 'there' might have been, 'Pepperland' perhaps? (It was more like the 'Sea of Green' to me.) Hippie consciousness was actually an immense network of discontinuities, determined by miscellaneous visions of the world stretching from, say, one person parading a psychedelic tie at work to somebody else buying a copy of *IT* in the London Underground. Myriad circumstances, and for many people it was all happening in the next street, figuratively speaking. An old friend of mine, the distinguished organist Michael Delfonte, once remarked to me that as he played across the country during the 1960s whatever was supposed to be happening always appeared to have happened before he arrived in a particular city, town or venue. Often he recalled to me someone saying to him: 'You should have been here last week!' In truth 'the sixties' was part myth. So, these histories of the 1960s do tend to stick in my craw somewhat. They are strategic and essentialist. My actual summer of love (1967) involved piecework at Lucas', the unnecessary death of my boyhood friend Brian, followed by the inescapable disintegration of his greatest dream. The Star Club, incidentally, closed its doors in 1969 – probably two years too late. Nothing dates faster than yesterday's view of the future.

Brian's death in August just about put the top hat on everything. I was sitting with Yankel Feather at his beautiful home having dinner when the news came through on the television. The Epstein family, who knew I was back in Liverpool, contacted me immediately, asking me to go to the funeral, but I just couldn't. The word was out that Brian had committed suicide and I just knew that, despite the problems he related to me the previous winter, he could never have taken his own life. It was the drugs that killed him, surely; an error of judgement. The pusher, once again, was to blame. Whosoever provided Brian with his ameliorators – legal or illegal –

was undoubtedly responsible for his death. As far as I was aware he had been on prescription drugs since the late 1950s. Those doctors and later sycophants who provided him with the wherewithal to make such a tragic mistake were the culprits, of that I had no doubt. And there they would be at the funeral, standing beside the grave.

Clive Epstein pleaded with me that I would be expected by everybody in the family, but I just said that I was with Brian more than anybody when he lived, and that I didn't have to appear in public to let Brian know about my love for him. Clive was hurt, but understood. He didn't pass on my comments to Queenie, who had also lost her husband Harry in Bournemouth only a few weeks earlier. Much later, when Clive also passed away, the Epstein family entrusted me with the responsibility of contacting everybody. I felt that I failed miserably in this task but this was now the 1980s – the age of *Brookside* and the Liverpool 'scally' – and out of all those 'beautiful people' from NEMS of the 1960s, only Gerry Marsden bothered to turn up. This was another world, apparently. Ever the thoughtful one, Gerry even took the trouble to wear a yarmulke.

So I went to work the day they buried Brian. I was on the factory floor working amid the dismal void which lies at the heart of most factory buildings. I felt at home in one of those dark and friendless buildings upon which our welfare once depended. It was that sense of reality that I now craved in this retreat from the madness of the music business; it was like a penance, too, like an act of soul searching; like a re-evaluation of my life; like a healing process. The absurdity and meaningless confusions of contemporary existence could be dealt with by a kind of indifference, a self-conscious attachment to the lack of depth of factory life. The production lines of consumerist capitalism are not all moral vacuity. They can focus the mind, relieve the tension and express an exhaustion that other forms cannot. I can't say that I enjoyed it, but for me the mundane in a factory encouraged habit, and it was habit I craved – this I thought permitted me to reflect on the immediate past, while at the same time economise on the present and to focus on the unforeseen.

Brian was only 32 years old when he passed away. I visit the Jewish cemetery in Long Lane, Aintree, only occasionally now. I feel that he is not really in the appropriate place. There, in Section A, Grave H12 is my friend. What a long, strange trip it had been. From children playing and arguing over a coronation coach, to great associates, perhaps even lovers of sorts, to forever absent friends. Brian was a hero of modern times. He may not have been the working-class hero so beautifully satirised by

John Lennon a few years later but, challenged by a set of circumstances that nobody could have predicted, he was, in the process, a massively expressive and influential individual. But it was hard earned and extremely costly. By describing Brian as a hero, I do not wish to add glamour to him; but his real sorrow, his real misery, his care and his hardships concerning his sexuality, all include, at least from my perspective, elemental qualities of the hero.

'EXCUSE ME, MR LENNON, A MR FLANNERY'S ON THE PHONE'

ONE MIGHT INITIALLY presume that after all of the devilment, all of the excitement and all of the heartache of the 1960s the following decade for me was either a blur or excruciatingly boring, but neither evaluation is at all accurate. After a year or so working at Lucas', taking on as much overtime as I could possibly work to fill my beleaguered bank account, I began looking once again for a retail unit in order to resume my self-employment. I was not alone in attempting to return to normality as the 1960s were turning into the 1970s. The 'yeah yeah yeahs' of the early years of the decade were now well and truly behind us all and those groups and artists who had stayed together as professionals were now finding things very difficult in the new rock, soul and pop environment of the high sixties and early 1970s. The Merseyside groups had all but dissipated and those that had not broken up were mostly plying their trade around the developing cabaret circuits.

Without Brian Epstein I thought that the Beatles were struggling somewhat – not exactly floundering but musically searching for a new identity and not always succeeding, with their quality control sometimes highly questionable. All this while other forms of British popular music were becoming either heavier, more countrified in the wake of the Band or, at least by 1970, wearing more make-up. Rejects from the 1960s such as David Bowie, T. Rex, Slade, the Sweet et al. were appealing to a younger generation who had little to no recollection of the Beatles in their pomp, while the likes of Neil Diamond, Andy Williams and Gilbert O'Sullivan held the copyright to the twenty-somethings market. No longer did verse after verse of *Got My Mojo Working* ring around the Star Club in Hamburg; no longer did Bobby Parker's *Watch Your Step* blast out of Billy Butler's record deck at the Cavern. It was all over and, despite some really good music, I thought it all a tad depressing. The best place for Joe Flannery was back in the real world, suggested both by my mother and Kenny. Kenny, after finally closing down the Slater Street office prior to Brian's death and joining me in Hamburg for our abortive bar scheme, also had gainful employment. He was a proctor at Riversdale College on the banks of the River Mersey – a job he kept until his untimely death. I had mostly enjoyed myself in my dalliances with the music industry but along the way had lost a best friend, the affection of a brother and as a consequence had erected barriers in my private life that were never to be removed: 'something gained but something lost', as they say.

One thing that made me want to return to retail was the evident growing upward mobility of British society. I watched while all around me Liverpool started to empty: young couples; middle-aged, white-collar workers; factory hands at Fords and Vauxhall Motors were all able to improve their lives by leaving the by this time decaying city. They removed to fringe developments, such as those on the Wirral, in Maghull or St Helens, Ince, Ashton-in-Makerfield or Walkden. In the main they were purchasing new housing or even empty plots and needed such properties kitted out with the latest furnishings. I took an empty unit on Park Road in Liverpool 8 in 1970 – not what one might call an affluent or upwardly mobile area by this time (quite the reverse, in fact) – but by placing such a business on a busy working-class high street such as Park Road, passing trade was high and rents were low, not to mention Liverpudlians were always interested in bargains. An advert or two in the *Liverpool Echo* of a Friday night would ensure people beating a path to our doors for either cash business or sales via the Provident Cheque Company, Paybonds or any other such hire purchase one could lay one's hands on. This was well before the lights started going out all over the country in 1973, before the Miners' Strike and before a sense of reality dawned across the country that we were once again spiralling into debt.

During the first half of the 1970s I made plenty of money and, as a consequence, in 1971 I purchased a house at 8 Mayfield Road, Aigburth, just before UK housing prices went through the roof. It was a great investment and was paid for in a very short space of time; meanwhile, business kept on getting better and better. I expanded the Park Road shop into three units by the early 1970s, one of which became a book-shop for Kenny on a part-time basis at weekends. At one stage I took over nine shop units along Park Road. This was after furniture manufacturer Rosenblats of Kirkby went into liquidation and I was able to make a successful bid for their stock. By 1975 I had also made a tentative step back into the local music business by running three mobile discos across the Merseyside area. Of course, by this time it did not really seem to be a part of the music industry to me, for I could never really come to terms with recorded music being preferred over live music – but preferred it was, and we covered many weddings, 21st birthday parties and even the odd bar mitzvah (such as Henry Epstein's). Kenny and I moved again in 1976 to a larger property in Mayfield Road, which is my present address. We had seen the auction board go up and we made a sealed bid, which was accepted. We moved in right away and sold number 8 in a very short space of time at a profit. It was something of a rash move but it all worked out for the best in the long run.

By the late 1970s, however, business matters began to complicate as Liverpool City Council decided to demolish the properties on Park Road. I didn't mind this because I only went into them in 1970 owing to their semi-derelict state. They had been severely neglected and this led to their low rentals. I knew that it was only a matter of time before the demolition orders were posted and I certainly had no interest in buying them. Compensation was eventually forthcoming and the business closed on a financially happy note in 1979. I had been ready to come out of it all as VAT rates had risen and further complicated bookkeeping while cash stock-in-trade was being replaced bit by bit with credit and late payments. Nevertheless, I had enjoyed a very good run of almost ten years, had plenty of money in the bank and a good business reputation. I thought I would take a month or so out to re-evaluate things and it was during this phase that I was approached by Clive Epstein, brother of Brian, to consider re-joining the music business as an agent. After experiencing Clive wining and dining me and showing me a lovely suite of offices on Allerton Road, I half-heartedly agreed to give it a go. I insisted that Clive should not try to repeat anything that NEMS had previously done. My thoughts were that the media would murder us if we were to do this. So with overheads being low (the Epsteins owned the offices on Allerton Road) and a blank piece of paper to start with, my curiosity and guarded enthusiasm took me back into management and (this time) concert promotion.

We began by searching out the latest hot band in Liverpool, which by late 1979 I felt were Motion Pictures. This New Romantic post-punk band had a lot to offer and we were able to find a record deal for them with Wayne Bickerton and Tony Waddington's successful State Records. We also placed them into the important New York club scene via contacts with none other than Sid Bernstein. By this time Sid was renowned for his promotions and he was able to help the band. We also signed two young singer-songwriters, Phil Boardman and Peter Wynne, and I re-signed Beryl Marsden. By this time the Beryl Marsden Band was performing all over Liverpool and enjoyed a good residency at the Star and Garter pub in the city centre. We made a bid to manage Liverpool Express but our financial offer to the ever-difficult Hal Carter was rejected. Nonetheless, we were able to book the group into some very interesting venues as agents. Clive and I also promoted several important concerts at the Royal Court Theatre in Liverpool; indeed, I was responsible for removing the seating from the stalls of the theatre, a move I have subsequently had mixed feelings about but which improved the atmosphere and expanded the capacity of the venue. We promoted Roy Orbison, Mary Wells, Tom O'Connor and Tommy Cooper. All of these promotions were commercially successful.

However, it was not a working partnership for I was literally doing everything. Clive was basking in a once-removed glow of the music industry while at the same time both his wife Barbara and his mother Queenie were horrified that he was even involved in the business that, as they saw it, helped to destroy Brian. I later learnt that Barbara had tried everything to discourage Clive but she was unsuccessful; his decision irrevocably harmed their relationship. I felt terrible about it but by this time I had agreed to the partnership: officially Carlton Brooke Enterprises (with the 'Enterprises' being a tribute to NEMS). I was Carlton Brooke once again and I was not really comfortable with this. Although we had made money from the promotions, we also needed to invest in our artists. I was perfectly prepared to do this, and did so, but Clive was reluctant – somnambulant in fact – and meetings could be endlessly delayed or, when they happened, they were fractious. His mantra was always 'it doesn't stack up', which if truth be told was a way of saying that his enthusiasm did not run to capital investment in something that was about intellectual rather than physical property. Clive was a furniture man, not a music entrepreneur, and he could never really get his head around copyright, studio times or costs pertaining to song creation and production – I don't suppose any of it was tangible enough for him.

Mayfield Records, my independent label, was mooted as early as 1980 as an adjunct to Carlton Brooke: a way of copyrighting songs via actual releases. But the label stalled in this respect and although I carried it through and it still exists to this very day (see appendix), the first few releases were literally charitable affairs – at least until Tom O'Connor's recording for the International Garden Festival sold thousands and thousands of copies as a point-of-sale item at the Festival Gardens. So despite the early gains, I came to watch some of my well-earned retail money dissipate, and all thanks to Clive's reticence. I was sorry we formed the partnership at all but soldiered on regardless. By the autumn of 1980, and largely thanks to Clive's inactivity, I effectively was Carlton Brooke once again (it felt at times like I was already trampling all over my popular music grave). Motion Pictures were playing New York and seemingly doing well, but I was later to find that internal disagreements were to lead to their implosion the following year; concerts had done well, but my partner had decided to become a sleeper and wasn't interested in throwing any more money at the Royal Court. I spent most of the autumn in the Allerton Road offices reading the music press, and it was here that I came across the news that John Lennon was back in the studio. I had been defending him for at least three years, letting people know that when the time was right he would return to his muse. I had read that John's musical ambition was to 'do something as good as *Heroes*', the 1977 album by David Bowie, which I also happened to like a great deal.

Yoko Ono had approached producer Jack Douglas and gave him John's demos to listen to: there were dozens of songs. By the time I came to read about this activity they were already being re-recorded with the studio musicians from the Hit Factory in New York. I thought, what the hell, I'll see if I can ring him from my office and try to catch him at the studio to tell him how pleased I was, and how much I had supported him. I rang about tea time to make sure that it would have been around lunch time in New York and told the receptionist who I was and that I was a good friend of John's and asked to speak to Mr Lennon. She dismissively replied, 'Mr Flannery, you'd be surprised how many friends Mr Lennon has.' My immediate retort was to suggest to her that before she put down the phone she should do herself a small favour: pass in a small note to John stating that Joe Flannery was trying to contact him from Liverpool. She agreed and I put the receiver down. Twenty minutes later my office phone rang and the receptionist asked, 'Mr Flannery, just who are you?' I asked why she was enquiring, and she said, 'Well, Mr Lennon is currently dancing all over the studio and wants me to put you through right away.'

EMPLOYMENT AGENCIES ACT 1973

LICENCE NUMBER NW 714

The Secretary of State for Employment, under the provisions of the above Act, HEREBY AUTHORISES

CLIVE JOHN EPSTEIN , JOSEPH MICHAEL FLANNERY

trading as CARLTON-BROOKE MANAGEMENT

to carry on an employment agency and employment

business at 2ND FLOOR

81-83 ALLERTON ROAD, MOSSLEY HILL, LIVERPOOL

from 1 OCTOBER 1980

up to and including 30 SEPTEMBER 1981

signed

on behalf of the Secretary of State for Employment

Date 2 9 SEP 1980

Issuing office DEPARTMENT OF EMPLOYMENT, NORTH WESTERN REGIONAL OFFICE

SUNLEY BUILDING, PICCADILLY PLAZA, MANCHESTER M60 7JS

Notes

1   Section 2(7) of the above-mentioned Act requires the holder of a licence within one month of any change in the particulars accompanying the application for that licence to give to the Secretary of State notice in writing of the change. (Any such notice should be forwarded to the Department of Employment at the address given above.) Any person who fails to comply with the above provisions will be guilty of an offence and liable on summary conviction to a fine not exceeding £100.

2   Nothing in the above provisions shall be taken as authorising the holder of a licence to carry on any business otherwise than in accordance with the provisions of the licence.

3   Subject to the provisions of Section 2(6) of the said Act, THIS LICENCE IS NOT TRANSFERABLE.

DE Department of Employment
EA1   MCR 20487/1/8030152 11m 6/79 TL

A certificate from the Department of Employment for Joe Flannery's and Clive Epstein's Carlton Brooke Management. (Author's collection)

John and I then enjoyed a lengthy conversation. We talked a lot of rubbish, of course – he called me 'Flo' after one of his aforementioned wordplays: 'Flo Jannery'. He was very well and happy, but he missed Liverpool, he missed 'the others' and he missed London 'after a fashion', but he told me at one stage that he regretted 'getting too political'. He said that he had made a bit of a 'tit of himself'. I told him not to worry: I had been defending him locally at least. We came to reminisce about our times sitting at the Pier Head, eating crap pies and him wanting to go 'over there', meaning the United States. I also informed him of my partnership with Clive and he was very interested in this; in fact, he was excited. 'That sounds good,' he said. 'We should start talking about me coming home before that bastard Nixon gets me.' I was rather taken aback by this comment and asked him to explain. John launched into a diatribe against the former president. He appeared convinced that even out of office Nixon carried power and wanted him dead; he felt that some kind of curse was hanging over him. It was not any kind of wizardry to which John referred, but his thoughts that the US government was effectively out to get him. It was clear to me that John was not simply expressing his generation's deep concern about Richard Nixon and his presidency, but all of the machinations of the political establishment of the US. His tone bothered me a little, expressing as it did what sounded like a touch of paranoia. 'It would be good to come home for a bit,' he finally stated. That Richard Nixon tried to deport John Lennon in the 1970s is not beyond any reasonable doubt. John was convinced that his peace activism and lyrical barbs had made him a government target.

My surprise at his comments came about because it seemed to me that the press were always at pains to suggest how happy he was in the United States. John, however, told me wanted to return to the UK at least with a tour in mind. He even suggested that Clive and I should book the QE2 for his return to the city and that I should fly out to New York when the time came to return with him on the liner. I was flattered but mentioned to him that I wondered whether the QE2 could actually get down the Mersey. 'Look into it,' John shouted. 'I want to come home in a blaze of glory; when you've done it you and Clive can join me on the liner.' In retrospect, I suppose I would have discovered that the QE2 could indeed have weighed anchor in the Mersey, but of course we were never to find out. We exchanged many pleasantries and his enthusiasm was palpable. I recall after his death Andy Peebles, the famous UK DJ, also suggesting that off air John did discuss returning to the UK; Andy even thought that it might have been for good, I think. I later learnt too that the musicians from the Hit Factory were all informed that they should not take any engagements in the New Year of 1981; one might presume this was with another album in mind, but the tracks for *Milk and Honey* were already in the can. I firmly feel that John wanted them as his touring band, a kind of Elephant's Memory Mk 2. I can only confirm that he definitely wanted to return to the UK for at the very least a tour and that Carlton Brooke Enterprises would have been at least partly responsible for that tour. As one might imagine, I was buzzing after this wonderful conversation with my old friend. Of course, it was not to be and I was soon to lose another friend pointlessly.

Brian had gone, John had gone and my 'right hand' passed away in 1982. Kenny had battled a debilitating brain disease throughout those early years of the 1980s and by 1982 his strength had given out and he died peacefully, without any fuss, the same way he had lived his life. I forcibly threw myself into work and a little later in 1982 I came to be albeit briefly associated with a group by the name of Nova, an American band recording at Electric Lady Studios in New York. At the same time I found myself marginally involved with Hall and Oates' big selling *H2O* album, from which *Maneater* was a massive hit single. This was one of the very first albums – at least as far as I was aware – that had individual sponsors on each track and I had wisely invested some money on that later hit. So there I was, in New York, under considerable duress, kicking my heels and rather frustrated with the usual studio shenanigans and muso egos. At the end of one such exhausting day I was asked to appear on a New York TV telethon. It was something I considered rather novel and allowed me the privilege of spending a little time in a TV studio for the evening; I readily agreed to take part. My first interview took place at about 10 p.m. and I enjoyed relating a few of my stories from the old days. I thought I might be there for perhaps an hour or so. Well, they simply wouldn't let me go and after I had been on air for over three hours, with different parts of the United States being networked into the programme, I was exhausted, running out of stories and opinions, but very happy and most amused that people still appeared to be interested in those early days of Merseybeat. I even learnt around midnight that a showing of a black-and-white film classic had been cancelled so that I could remain on the air. Proceedings finally came to an end at about 1 a.m. and as I set off to leave the building the commissionaire informed me that a sizeable crowd had gathered outside to see this 'Beatle person', as he put it. One or two of these Beatles fans were allowed in to the reception area of the TV studios to say hello and one young man even gave me his graduation ring so that I could throw it into the River Mersey (I couldn't bring myself to do this, so I still have it).

There had also been one or two phone calls, apparently: one from Michael York, a great Beatles fan who wanted me to join him for cocktails at the Waldorf Astoria; the second call, believe it or not, from Katharine Hepburn, who wanted me to join her for breakfast. I visited Michael first: he was very charming and wanted to learn a little more about the early days in Liverpool. As I left him after a cocktail or two to go to see Katharine Hepburn he told me that while he was officially supposed to be a film star, he had never had the opportunity to meet Hepburn: 'You're a lucky man', he told me as I left the bar of that famous hotel. I was driven to a tree-lined road just off Fifth Avenue and entered a lovely town house where I was greeted by the great lady herself. Over a very early breakfast she informed me that she had been watching the telethon throughout the evening and was fascinated by my name. I was asked whether I knew of her relationship with Spencer Tracy. As a great film buff of the post-war era I replied in the affirmative and was able to inform her that I still had a picture of both of them and that I understood why they were never able to marry. Hepburn then told me why she had asked to see me: 'My pet name for Spencer was "Flannel" and I just had to let you know that hearing your name brought back so many lovely memories for me.' With a shaking hand she gave me a photo and said 'don't ask me for an autograph – friends don't do such things', and I left with what is still a highly treasured possession. It's wonderful to think that such a shy boy from Liverpool could meet one of the greatest of movie stars via music and the opportunity to raise a little money. By 6 a.m. I had returned to my rented accommodation in Port Jefferson tired but extremely contented.

A little later, and after another particularly exasperating day in the studios with the band Nova, I treated myself by going to see Lauren Bacall's *Woman of the Year* stage production. Prior to this I had already arranged to visit Yoko Ono at the Dakota Building. Before going up to see Yoko, the doorman at the Dakota introduced himself to me and in the process assured me that John had died on the chair in the corner of the lobby rather than on his way to hospital. I took a photograph of the chair – what an odd thing to do. I suppose this might have comforted me a little, for in my own mind I reflected that he might not have suffered quite so much as I had previously imagined. I was received very well by Yoko and it was all so lovely. Sean was there too – a beautiful little boy; he turned to Yoko and said, 'Mummy, Joe talks just like daddy.'

A MAYFIELD RECORDS DISCOGRAPHY

	Artist	Title	Year	Format	Notes
MA 101	Sr Annunciata	*Known Only to Him*	1981	45 vinyl	
MA 102	Sr Annunciata	*Hey Father Christmas*	1982	45 vinyl	
MA 103	Phil Boardman	*Much Missed Man*	1983	45 vinyl	Reissued 1986
MA 104	Tom O'Connor	*Festival Song*	1984	45 vinyl	
MA 105	Benny Bendorff	*Jog and Rock 'n' Roll*	1986	12in vinyl	
MA 106	Benny Bendorff	*Flowers of Liverpool*	1986	45 vinyl	Also released in Germany
MALP100A	Benny Bendorff	*Flowers of Liverpool: A Tribute to the Beatles*	1987	vinyl LP	
MA 107	Gerry Marsden	*Much Missed Man*	2002		An Ozit release; catalogue number allocated but not released

MA 108	Cirkus	*Song, Women and Wine*	2002	CD single	
MA 109	Next		2002	CD single	Archive recording only
MA 110 & 111	Stephen Pratt, RLPO	*String Trio, Piano Sonata; Uneasy Vespers, Fruits of the Ground, Some of the Number, Dead Leaves*	2002	2 x CDs	Test discs
MA 112	Jukebox Eddies	*Slippin' Around, A Fool Such as I, Mystery Train*	2003	CD single	
MA 113	Stuart Almond	*Empty Chairs at Empty Tables, Bring Him Home, Beyond the Sea, Fly me to the Moon, No Matter What, Buidoi*	2003	CDR	Demo
MA 114X	Chester Gateway Theatre Sound Effects production	*Handful of Songs Selection, Five Guys Named Mo*	2003	CD	
MACD201A	Various	*This Is Merseybeat Volume 3: Folk, Blues and Beatniks Compilation*	2003	CD compilation album	
MACD202A	The Liverpool Rockers	*Red Hot & Rockin'*	2003	CD album	
MAEP001	The Sue	*The Sue EP*	2003	CDR	Demo

MAEP002	Death by Association	*Electronic War*	2004	CD extended single	Also released as Sonica 1002
MAEP003X	Willard and the Poor Boys			CD	Demo for Groovin' Records
MA 115X		*A celebration of 21 years of Radio Advertising*		CD compilation	For educational purposes only
MA 116X				CD compilation	For educational purposes only
MA 117X	Death by Association	*Electronic War*	2004	CD	Reissue with different catalogue number (not a joint release with Sonica)
MA 118X	Oscar Tyrell	*30 Minutes with Oscar Tyrell*	2004	CDR album	
MA119X	Matt Baker	*Groovy Grubs*	2004	CD	Seven tracks of synthesised music for children's theatre production
MA 120X	The Womersley Brothers	*Nicola*		CD	Demo; not released
MACD203A		*Tales from the Vinyl Junkyard Volume 1*	2004	CD compilation album	

MACD204A	Benny Bendorff	*Flowers of Liverpool*		CD	Not released
MACD205A	Neil Campbell	*Through the Looking Glass*	2003	CD album	
MACD206A		*Hope Songwriters 1*	2007	CD album	For educational purposed only
MACD207X	Michael Delfonte	*Autumn Sonata*	2004	CDR	
MACDprojGS					Radio Merseyside Folk Scene Archive; Geoff Speed Archive
MACD208A	Al Willard Peterson	*The Lawnmower Man*	2005	CDR	Joint production with Groovin' Records; released on Groovin' Records
MACD209X	Matt Baker	*Pool of Dreams*	2005	CDR	
MACD210X		*Colonel Bagshot's Incredible Bucket Band*	2005	CD compilation remixed; not for sale	
MACD211–223	BBC Radio Merseyside	*Brock 'n' Roll*	2005–07	Archive CDRs	
MACD212X	29th & Dearborn	*Underhill*	2007		Re-mastering only
MACD213	Not appropriated				
MACD214	Not appropriated				

MACD215A	The Mojave Collective	*Rust and Dust*	2008	CD album	
MACD216A	Alan Richard's Touring Production	*George*	2009	CD album	
MACD216A	Gerry Murphy	*Crescent City Daze*	2011	CD album	

INDEX